THE
WORKING
WOMAN'S
HANDBOOK

THE
WORKING
WOMAN'S
HANDBOOK

___

The essential
reference guide for every
working woman

POLLY BIRD

PIATKUS

First published in Great Britain in 1996
by Judy Piatkus (Publishers) Ltd of
5 Windmill Street, London W1P 1HF

A catalogue record for this book is available from the British Library

ISBN 0-7499-1416-5

Typeset by Action Typesetting Limited, Gloucester
Printed and bound in Great Britain by
Mackays of Chatham PLC

To
REBECCA, NAOMI, SARAH AND SUSIE

the next generation of

working women

Contents

Acknowledgements

I am grateful to the many organisations that helped me with *The Nanny* ... Book ... information. All the ...

Addresses: at the end of ... ... Abbey Life; Deborah Milner ... Jane Ageros of Abbey Nat... Black Horse Financial ... Operative Bank; Conno... Legal Education Depart... ... Jonas; Embassies and High ... ... Opportunities Commission; ... Faux of Wardrobe; Faw... Harvey Nichols; Hyatt ... Institute of Management ... Another Mathias; CBI ... ... Suzanne Moore of the Guard... National & Provincial ... Union; NUPE; Reed Associates ... Lamplight Trust; Table... Companions; UNISON ... Chartered Accountants; WAS... ... Harassment); Wild Rose ... ... Bureau.

Special thanks to ... Hannigan and Jenny Hughes ... three children also have ... patient while this book was ...

Polly Bird
Chester, 1995

Acknowledgements

I am grateful to the many organisations and individuals who have helped me with *The Working Woman's Handbook* by providing information. All the organisations are included in 'Useful Addresses' at the end of the book. Particular mention must go to: Abbey Life; Deborah Ackerley of Women's Enterprise Forum; Jane Ageros of Abbey National; Bank of Scotland; Barclays Bank; Black Horse Financial Services; Canopy Training; The Co-Operative Bank; Commission for Racial Equality; Council of Legal Education; Department of Trade and Industry; Dickins & Jones; Embassies and High Commissions in the UK; Equal Opportunities Commission; The European Commission; Susie Faux of Wardrobe; Fawcett Mill Fields; Forte plc; Harrods; Harvey Nichols; Hyatt; The Institute of Chartered Accountants; Institute of Management; Island Horizons; Legal & General; Annette Mathias of The Open University; Midland Bank; Suzanne Moore of The Association of British Insurers; NALGO; National & Provincial; National Westminster Bank; Norwich Union; NUPE; Pearl Assurance; Fiona Price & Partners; Suzy Lamplugh Trust; Talbontdrain; Tiger Travel; Towry Law; Travel Companions; UNISON; Kate Walker of The Institute of Chartered Accountants; WASH (Women Against Sexual Harassment); Wild Rose; and The Woman's Travel Advisory Bureau.

Special thanks go to my agent, Teresa Chris, and to Sarah Hannigan and Jenny Hiney at Piatkus. My husband Jon and my three children also have my gratitude for being so supportive and patient while this book was being written.

Polly Bird
Chester, 1995

Introduction

This book is for you. You are a woman and you work. You know how difficult it is to juggle your home life with your work life, your children with your business trips, your desire to succeed with the need to be up-to-date with the latest theories and systems. You may be working your way up from the bottom or be forging ahead to the top. Wherever you are in the world of work, this book can help you.

The modern working woman needs a vast amount of information to keep on top of things – not simply about her own area of skills and expertise, but also about general working skills and lifestyle management. She needs answers to questions such as: Where can I get training to help me improve my job prospects? Who will look after the children? What do I need to know for my business trip abroad? Do I need to make any special financial arrangements? Can I be self-employed?

This book tries to make it easy for you. Instead of making you search the library shelves for separate books on each subject, I have drawn together as much information as possible so that you can have one volume on your desk. It will be there to refer to and to use – and to throw on the floor when work gets too much for you!

What will this book tell you? It will start with information on equal opportunities legislation, and also discuss racism and how to combat it. The book looks at the differences in pay and promotion between women and men and how to overcome them; the working woman's lifestyle; where and how to get training; dealing with your finances; how to network effectively; what to do about child-care; how to improve your image at work; how to be healthy and safe in an acceptable work environment; travelling for work in the UK and abroad; how to deal with sexual harassment; what happens if you lose your job; and becoming self-employed. Finally it tells you where and how to relax.

Obviously this book cannot go into every point in detail, but I have included as many addresses of useful organisations and helpful books as possible so that you will know where to go for help and advice. See 'Useful Addresses' and 'Further Reading' for this information.

No working woman is an island. We can stumble on alone refusing help and gritting our teeth against adversity, or we can call on other people to help us, to give us the knowledge and clout that seems to come more easily to men. In return we can encourage and help other women to get the best out of their working life.

I would like to keep this book as up-to-date and accurate as possible. So use it thoroughly. Thumb through it, mark pages, scribble comments – and then write to me with your views via Piatkus Books so that I can incorporate changes and additions into the next edition.

WARNING

I have tried to be as accurate and up-to-date as possible with the information included in *The Working Woman's Handbook*. But there is no substitute for contacting organisations mentioned and making your own enquiries. This is particularly important in areas involving the law and finance; when embarking on any financial or legal action, always consult an expert.

CHAPTER 1

Equal Opportunities

WOMEN should have the same opportunities in the workplace that men do – natural justice and common sense tell us that anything else is wrong and unfair. Discrimination because of a person's sex is unacceptable in a civilised society. But in spite of this and the efforts of the past twenty years, men and women still get different rates of pay, and many people still regard some jobs as 'women's work' or 'men's work'. More women than men live in poverty in old age because it is they who have had to combine family care and paid work. There are also some groups of men who still put up a great deal of opposition to women trying to get or getting good jobs.

Another problem is that the recent recession has meant the restructuring and contracting of many firms. As companies try to rationalise their working practices, employees are dismissed. The most vulnerable employees are women, who are often employed in the less favourable jobs or who do not qualify for employment protection.

Several things could improve this situation. Firstly, ensuring that boys and girls get an equal start, and making equal opportunities a reality. Secondly, it should be made possible for women and men to reconcile work and family life, which means that good quality, affordable childcare must be made available. Britain's tax and Social Security system needs to be modernised to reflect the change in the labour markets, changed social structures such as the increase in single-parent families, and the different effects these changes have on men and women.

This chapter will tell you about the British and European equal opportunities legislation, with later chapters discussing some problems of inequality in more detail. It will also cover racism at work, and what you can do about it.

WOMEN AND EQUALITY AT WORK

Lack of childcare facilities means that many working mothers have to work shorter hours than they wish, so they earn less pay; the catch is that they then cannot afford the childcare necessary to work longer hours. Some employers therefore make the assumption that women are likely to take too much time out of work for family commitments to make it worthwhile employing or promoting them.

Women take less time out of the workplace for childcare than is generally supposed, with on average a working woman taking out only five years in total. But during that time she will have lost her place in the promotion queue, and often has to start again in a new job from the bottom. Skills gained before having children are therefore lost to the market-place. Childcare problems also mean that women are more likely than men to be part-time workers – there are 6 million part-time workers in the UK, and 87 per cent of them are women. Information about childcare choices is given in Chapter Seven.

Many women also have to cope with an unfair family system. Equal opportunities problems at work seem to be built into their whole lifestyle. Problems juggling family life and lack of training in appropriate skills all contribute. Even though working women's earnings are often vital to family finances, they usually take on the domestic role at home in addition to paid work. Single women and women with children who do not have a male partner may also be the sole or most important breadwinner of the family.

Most women in full-time work tend to be in clerical or unskilled, insecure work with few promotion prospects and poor pay because they do not have the training or length of service to climb the promotion ladders as men do. Those who do often have to sacrifice home life, children or partners, although this is changing for the better. Even when they do not make these sacrifices women have to take on a heavier workload than men. Pay and promotion are discussed in Chapter Three and training in Chapter Four.

There are a number of things that women can do to gain equality in the work place:

- seek promotion and learn skills such as interview techniques, and the confidence to be more forthright and express their own ideas;
- seek as much training as men and in similar areas;
- organise more together to support each other in the workplace;
- seek to be more integrated with men in the workplace;

- demand equal pay for work of equal value;
- demand fair procedures and equality in terms of redundancy or dismissal;
- make the most of opportunities for self-employment;
- refuse to accept that they are more dispensable then men.

EUROPEAN LEGISLATION

As we are part of the European Union the UK has to take note of directives from the EU. The Commission of European Communities takes very seriously the question of equal opportunities for women in its member states.

The bulk of the European Equal Opportunities legislation is based on Article 119 of the EU, and the Equality Directives. Directives are laws which have to be integrated into the legislation of member states.

The Directives enshrine the following concepts:

- equal pay for men and women;
- access for women to employment;
- vocational training, promotion and working conditions equal to those of men;
- the progressive implementation of the principle of equal treatment for men and women on matters of social security;
- the importance of the principle of equal treatment for men and women in occupational pension schemes;
- equal treatment for men and women engaged in an activity, including agriculture, or as self-employed workers;
- protection of self-employed women in pregnancy and motherhood.

More protection for working mothers is needed, and a proposal still before the European Court is for protection at work for women having recently given birth.

Ongoing European proposals

There is still more to do, and the European Commission has further proposals which it expects to go forward soon. These include the broad aims of defining the scope and concept of equal pay for work of a similar nature; clarifying the scope of individual discrimination; communicating on the occupational or benefit schemes which fall within the scope of Article 119; reporting on the application of the principle of equal treatment between men and women in a particular activity; and raising awareness of the issue of equal opportunities.

The Commission requires that member states shall ensure:

- that all new legislation is free of unlawful discrimination;
- that sufficient resources are made available;
- that pay legislation should apply equally to men and women;
- that there should be improved standards of information concerning legal standards for equal opportunities by training people in Community Law.

Equal opportunities will not happen overnight, in spite of these well-meaning directives. The Commission recognises that women are discriminated against in education by poor access to training and by childcare difficulties. The combination of inadequate training, and the difficulty in getting that training because of their children's needs, is a major factor in keeping women in the lower paid sector.

The Community Initiative programme aims to remedy that by research into the position of women in the labour market; by exchanging information and promoting best practice in equal opportunities; by helping the creation of businesses by women; and by promoting workers as entrepreneurs in business.

This coincides with an overall trend in the UK for men and women to become self-employed and to start their own businesses. Women often find this particularly attractive because it means they can fit their work around childcare as well as have control over their work environment and earnings. Chapter Fourteen provides more information about women and self-employment.

Committee on Women's Rights

The European Commission also has a Committee on Women's Rights, which provides information for the Women's Unit of the European Commission and the European Women's Lobby.

One of this Committee's research functions has resulted in an international address file of women's organisations, which is available for hire either in the form of a list of addresses or as self-addressed labels. This is divided into *Women in Europe* and *International Women*. New associations wishing to be included or anyone wanting information can contact the Research Institute for the Development of the European Cultural Area (see 'Useful Addresses' p. 203).

The present

The European Commission has enshrined the idea that women who wish to return to work, the long-term temporary employed and the unemployed under 25 are entitled to help; that unemployed women or women under threat of redundancy or those employed in small or medium-sized enterprises in certain regions should be helped; and that all women of working age in certain regions should get help.

Individual member states need to prove that women, who make up over half the European Community – approximately 190 million in fifteen member states – are being treated fairly.

BRITISH LEGISLATION

In 1975 Britain introduced a law against inequality in the form of the Sex Discrimination Act. This outlawed the practice of discriminating against potential employees on the grounds of their sex. It also assisted the concept of equal pay for equal work or work of a similar nature.

Women are a vital and increasing part of the workforce; in 1984 they constituted only 41 per cent of it, but now make up 45 per cent of workers (including the self-employed). Of those working for others they make up 47 per cent of employees. Yet they also make up seven out of ten unpaid family workers – that is women who help in a family business without receiving wages.

Equal Opportunities Commission (EOC)

The battle for equality in Britain is the responsibility of the EOC. Its remit is to promote equality between men and women in the areas of employment, pay, education, training, provision of housing, goods, facilities and recruitment advertising. It was not set up solely to deal with discrimination against women, although a large part of its work is concerned with this. It has to deal equally with discrimination against men by women. Its aim is to obtain equality of opportunity, equal pay and equal status for men and women in all parts of the United Kingdom.

The EOC has identified five key areas in the battle for equality:

- equal opportunities in education and training;
- equal pay and non-discriminatory pay systems;
- better rights for part-time workers;

- fair pensions;
- proper access to justice through simpler and better legal processes.

The aims of the EOC are to empower people through knowledge of their rights, and to make the law accessible to all. These aims would be best served by an Equal Treatment Act to clarify the laws, simpler tribunal and court procedures and clearer law and simpler procedures on equal work for equal value. Equal value cases are heard by an Employment Appeal Tribunal.

The present laws are complex and unwieldy. Most women do not pursue claims for discrimination because these are costly and very lengthy procedures. Women who do bring a case find it highly stressful and sometimes permanently damaging. On average an equal value case takes two and a half years. The longest time through the process so far is ten years for a case which, at the time of writing, is still running. The time leading up to a case produces its own stress, and women may be harassed and out of work during that time.

Unfortunately, women still face discrimination at work in spite of the 1975 Sex Discrimination Act and the efforts of the EOC since then – and in spite of European legislation against discrimination.

Justice

Under the Sex Discrimination Act the EOC must consider requests for assistance from individuals who believe they have been a victim of unlawful sex discrimination. In 1992 there was a distinct rise in enquiries and complaints.

The EOC has achieved some well-publicised successes in recent years. It has managed to bring certain groups of people habitually outside the justice system into it, and to gain payment and recognition of discrimination. Notable was the successful challenge to the Ministry of Defence against its policy of dismissing servicewomen who become pregnant. About 5,000 women were dismissed and the Armed Forces admitted discrimination. Some women failed to claim but by October 1995 as many as 4,865 offers of compensation had been made, of which 4,314 were settled, leaving 551 cases outstanding. The average settlement was £10,717.64. A few service women lost their cases on appeal.

The EOC is continuing to work to increase equality awareness in male-dominated sectors such as the police, prison and fire services.

Scotland and Wales

The EOC is active through its national offices in Wales and Scotland. In Scotland women's economic activity rate is lower than that in England but higher than in Wales, and women's earnings are lower than men's in Great Britain as a whole. Women in Scotland are also concentrated in a narrow band of industries.

In Wales many of the male-dominated industries such as mining have closed, and this has created a great change in the nature of the workforce. Women have started to move into the workplace in large numbers.

RACISM: THE DOUBLE JEOPARDY

Many women are exposed to racism as well as sexism in the workplace. Racism is treating anyone unfavourably because of their race, colour, nationality, ethnic or national origins. Racism is not only perpetrated by white people against non-white but can and does include black against white, black against Asian and vice versa, and any other combination of inter-race discrimination. Even within the white community racism exists – the anti-Semitic and anti-Irish bias of some employers and employees has led to successful cases against them.

Religious groups are not covered by the Act, but if you are Sikh or Jewish you are protected because you also belong to an ethnic group. Other religions are not protected by the Act, but may be covered by the ban on indirect discrimination.

Racism can be direct or indirect. Direct racism occurs when you are treated worse than others because of your race, colour or origins. This includes segregation, being called names and employers refusing to accept certain racial groups of applicants. Racism can also be indirect, such as arranging job conditions so that certain groups cannot apply, or requiring uniforms to be worn which some people find unacceptable because of their race. Indirect racism is more insidious because everyone *seems* to be treated the same way but discrimination is still taking place. If an employer only asks for applicants from a certain area and most of the residents are white, then that indirectly discriminates against other ethnic groups.

WOMEN AND RACISM

Women can be discriminated against in the job market because of their sex and race, origins or colour. More white women are economically active than non-white women, and of the latter women from Pakistan or Bangladesh are the least likely to be in paid employment. In 1994 only 52 per cent of women of minority ethnic origins were economically active, compared to 72 per cent of white women.

These figures need to be considered carefully, because in some communities women are expected not to work outside the home. But the figures still expose a huge gap in the labour market between white and ethnic minority women. Also, non-white women get herded into the lower range of jobs and into certain sections of the job market. The health sector has a high proportion of women employees and of these a high proportion are non-white.

Where ethnic minority women *are* employed the majority are in the lower paid and more insecure jobs; few are in the professions or at the top of the business sector. Nowadays, many more women who are Asian or black are going into business, however. Many go into self-employment.

Racism at work

Racism can confront women before they even get a job. In the job application and interview the range of questions and the attitude of the questioners can involve racism. When you go for an interview, see if any of the other candidates or interviewers are non-white. If you are shown around the workplace beforehand take note of how many employees are non-white and whether any are in high positions in the firm.

The job application form should not ask your place of origin (except for such government jobs as the civil service), nor should a photograph be required.

The problem many women have to face at work is the question of whether discrimination is the result of sexism or racism or both. Racism was the obvious cause of distress to an Irishman who was the butt of Irish jokes at work from his male colleagues. There was no question of sexism here. A woman in the same situation might have found it difficult to decide whether her sex or race was the reason for the offence.

What can you do?

It may be better to ignore racist remarks if they are slight and infrequent or the result of ignorance. A quiet correction will embarrass many well-meaning but ignorant people if this is the case. If it goes on or becomes unbearable, not only causing you misery but endangering your job or chances of promotion, then there are steps you can take.

First tell your line manager or supervisor and see if the problem can be dealt with informally. Keep a note of all the times you have suffered discrimination and write to the perpetrator telling them that you do not want this kind of abuse.

You have redress under the Race Relations Act 1976, which makes it illegal to discriminate against anyone because of their race, colour, nationality (including citizenship), ethnic or national origins. You can go to the Commission for Racial Equality (CRE) which was set up as the main agency for enforcing the Race Relations Act (see 'Useful Addresses', p. 202). It can give you advice about your case, help you find a lawyer and help settle your case in or out of court. It can also investigate companies and other organisations suspected of racial discrimination.

Other places to go for help include Racial Equality Councils (of which there are approximately 100 in Wales, Scotland and England), Law Centres, your union and solicitors' firms. Your first port of call will be your union, if there is one where you work. Otherwise contact the CRE for help.

You can take your case to an Industrial Tribunal, where it will be heard by a panel of three people. You need to get your application in within three months of the date of the incident. If you miss the deadline you can be refused a hearing. A copy of your application will go to the defendant's team.

If you want to be legally represented at the tribunal you have to pay for it yourself. In some cases the CRE may help you prepare your case and represent you at the tribunal. If you want them to do this you must contact them as soon as possible.

There is no maximum to the amount of money you could be awarded; compensatory award limits were removed by the 1994 Race Relations (Remedies) Act. If your case is about promotion or dismissal the tribunal can ask your company to give you your job back, but it cannot force them to. You can appeal against a decision within 42 days, but very few cases go beyond the tribunal so you must get legal advice about this.

Other cases of race discrimination are heard at the county courts, or Scottish Sheriff courts, within six months of application.

The disadvantages of taking a case

As in sex discrimination cases the victims of racism are often the ones who suffer even after a successful outcome. Either they are not reinstated in their jobs because the firm considers them trouble makers, or if they are reinstated they have to work alongside the perpetrator of the discrimination.

Exceptions

The law applies to all employers, whatever the size of their firm. It also applies to subcontractors, employment agencies, job centres and training organisations.

There are some exceptions, where the law does not apply because of the particular nature of the job. In these cases it is lawful to discriminate. These exceptions include:

- jobs in private households e.g., cooks, gardeners;
- jobs which need someone from a particular background e.g., a Bosnian psychologist to work with Bosnian refugees;
- jobs which have to be done in a certain setting e.g., ethnic waiters for ethnic restaurants;
- jobs involving national security.

Racial harassment

Discrimination is one thing, but abuse and harassment is another. It is one thing to be refused promotion because you are not the 'right' nationality; it is another to be physically attacked or orally abused because of your origins.

Persistent racial abuse is harassment. Many non-white women and men suffer name-calling and threats every day of their lives.

Racial attacks are crimes and are covered by several laws. In England and Wales the relevant laws are the common law of assault and battery; the Offences Against the Person Act 1861; and breach of the peace under the Public Order Act. The Football (Offences) Act 1991 makes racial chanting or abuse from the terraces illegal and inciting racial hatred is a crime. Councils also have duties under the Race Relations Act. Scottish law is different but gives the same basic rights.

If you have a concern about racial discrimination at work then you can go to an Industrial Tribunal. If you are attacked then you can go to the police. Some victims think that the police do not respond quickly enough or take racial abuse seriously. The police say that it can be difficult to find out who the suspects are. If you suffer from racial attacks or abuse then you should take these steps:

- tell your manager or personnel officer;
- tell your union;
- tell the police;
- keep details of all incidents;
- contact all witnesses;
- tell the council and get them involved;
- if the authorities don't act contact the local media;
- you can also bring a private prosecution in a magistrates' court.

Helping other working women

Help combat racism in your place of work by educating other workers. You can:

- ask for an in-service course for all employees, including managers and bosses, so that everyone has a clear understanding of the issues;

- talk to your colleagues and employees and try to help them understand the issues.

Find out what your company's and union's policy statement is on racial discrimination – if they don't have one, ask them to get one worked out – and make sure it is promoted.

The Working Woman's Lifestyle

THERE can be no doubt that a working woman's lifestyle differs immensely from that of a man. We all know that women have to juggle home life, work and personal time. Attitudes are changing in society and within individual families, and some men do take on this kind of load. It is still mainly women who shoulder these responsibilities, however.

Inside the workplace the difference is again marked. Not only are women inadequately represented in positions of power, but they have to work harder to get there.

Because they rise higher up the work ladder and at a faster speed, it is men who have the support services that work offers – secretaries, PR assistants, subordinates to take care of their workload and comfort. Even when women do achieve this status, it is they who go home and take on the larger part of childcare, housework and food preparation.

So while men may get stressed because of work, women's stress doubles by being in subordinate positions at work and by having to run the home. Women without a partner may also have sole responsibility for children or elderly relatives.

Women in managerial positions get just as stressed as women further down the work ladder. In order to get and keep positions of power, they have to put more effort into keeping up with the workload and proving their ability than their male colleagues. Although they can alleviate the burden of work in the home by their greater purchasing power for childcare, dependant care and domestic help, this also eats into their pay.

THE LIFESTYLE BACKLASH

There is a recent sign that women in managerial positions are opting out of the high performance, high workload rat race and are opting for less pay and responsibility and an improved, more stress-free lifestyle. Quality of life is becoming more important to them.

This may not be an option for lower paid women, for whom the level of pay can mean the difference between necessities and survival only.

The superwoman trap

Women often try to do too much. Even where paid help, willing partners and domestic appliances are available, many women do not delegate. They may fear that their family will not consider them 'real women' if they do not show their commitment and love by doing the physical chores. Many also believe in the idea that we should all be a superwoman, who can fit home life, work and leisure into an easily planned and coped-with day.

Don't try to be the mythical superwoman. If you attempt to do everything, not only will you be too exhausted to enjoy any leisure time but your work will suffer. You will not be able to concentrate and may become uptight. You may also find that this fear of letting go intrudes into your work life. If you cannot delegate for fear of losing control then you will overwork, and may antagonise your subordinates. You will not be considered good promotion material if you cannot distribute your workload sensibly.

This overworking at home and at work means that your leisure time will suffer. Leisure is vital for your physical and mental health. It will also affect your work prospects if you cannot spare the time to socialise after work at dinners, conferences, meetings or a drink at the pub. Without the time and opportunity for vital networking your job prospects will suffer for lack of contacts.

Attitudes

Some of your attitudes have probably become ingrained, and you may not feel capable of changing them. Take a positive look at your life, and appreciate that planned change in the right direction is exciting.

Organising your partner

Ask your partner to share the domestic tasks equally, but make sure you discuss it with them – don't demand. If necessary, simply don't do half the work. Remember the joke about the husband who comes home to a chaotic house to be told by his wife 'I thought the best way to show you what I do all day is not to do it'? For working women too this principle can apply for time they are at home.

HOW TO IMPROVE YOUR LIFESTYLE

The main components in an improved lifestyle are the alleviation of stress and time to enjoy life apart from work and home responsibilities.

Most people accept stress and limitations on their spare time as part of life, without considering whether it could be changed for the better. Often illness and anxiety are the result of stress, but people do not look to stress as a cause.

COPING WITH STRESS

Stress eats into your work and home life. Some stress is good for you but too much is debilitating and can affect your health. You can be over-stressed for a long time without realising it. Consider using relaxation techniques regularly – Yoga, meditation or massage can all help.

Free time

An important part of reducing stress is the availability of some free time of your own, which can be as little as 20 minutes once a day. But it must be a time when you can consider yourself alone, undisturbed. You may choose to use that time to do nothing or something constructive but unrelated to work or home.

It does not matter how you spend your free time – with a book, a bath, exercise, doing a crossword, TV, or sleep. The important thing is that you have some time on your own which you control. Plan it into your day even if it means getting up half-an-hour earlier or leaving the house on a Saturday morning. Ask your family not to interrupt you.

Make the most of your moods

Every woman feels better at some times rather than others. Instead of trying to compete with your moods, use them to your advantage. When you are feeling down do tasks that do not require you to be on top form, such as dictating letters or reading routine papers. When you are feeling energetic and enthusiastic tackle major tasks that require your full concentration.

Sometimes you will have to work hard through bad moods, but it is possible to anticipate when you will feel low – for many women this is just before a period or after they have visitors for a weekend. In that case you may be able to plan by arranging meetings at other times, for example.

EFFICIENT – DON'T MAKE ME LAUGH!

Inside many women is the fear that being good at organisation is somehow 'unfeminine'. Never mind that they have had to juggle family life and work for years. Any woman who keeps a house running smoothly (more or less!) and also works is a model of organisational efficiency.

But efficiency is an unappreciated skill in many quarters. It can engender feelings of guilt and inadequacy in others, causing them to try to undermine the confidence of an efficient person.

Don't respond to this. Read those reports, keep your desk clear, organise your timetable and turn up to committees with the relevant paperwork. You will be getting things done while your colleagues are foundering.

Planning does not eliminate surprise. If you have planned a life and career path and a golden opportunity presents itself you have a solid foundation for taking a chance. High achievers take calculated risks, but on the basis of a forward plan and adequate information. Women who don't take charge of their lives get stuck at middle-manager level. Often companies want to promote more women to higher grades but are unable to find enough who articulate their ambition. Women need to understand that not only should they make their aims known, but it is up to them to plan their progress and learn the skills needed for promotion.

Planning

It is important that working women take charge of their lives and plan their lifestyle. It is otherwise too easy to get sucked into other people's lives in an unstructured way and find that you are living your life entirely around their needs. If you want to succeed at work without collapsing under the strain then you must carve out your own lifestyle and career game-plan. Although having a plan won't guarantee you can carry it through, you will at least have something to aim at.

It is easy to end up in a supporting role at home or work because society still expects women to be carers rather than doers. This is changing, but many women still have an instinctive feeling that their needs are secondary.

Take time to evaluate your future. Decide an alternative course of action for possibilities such as marriage, children, the offer of a job in another city or country, or dependent relatives.

Outline your life and work goals – do you have a particular career path in mind, or a broad area you would like to aim at? Then work out what objectives you need to achieve along the way to reach your goals. For example, if you want to work abroad, learning a relevant foreign language is an obvious intermediate objective.

When you have a good idea of your ultimate aims, then you will begin to look out for opportunities to fulfil them in a more focused way.

How to plan

Decide your overall aims and then work out the steps you need to take to achieve them. Use these guidelines:

- write down your aims and objectives;
- be as specific as possible;
- write down the steps needed to achieve your aims;
- the steps should be positive actions;
- set yourself realistic goals;
- decide whether you can achieve your goals alone or need others to help you;
- set realistic time limits for achieving each step and each final goal;
- don't be afraid of changing your goals as your priorities change.

If you discover that your plan conflicts with other people important to you, such as your partner, work out a compromise.

Decide your priorities in life and list them in order of importance. By writing down your priorities you may find that an important one is missing from your present lifestyle. If you do then you can take steps to compensate. List your tasks in order of importance each morning or the night before and tackle them one by one. You won't manage them all but it will make you more productive. The most successful managers get through their day with a list and a notebook and keep their desk clear.

Keep a notebook to record useful information, or your ideas during the day. *One* diary/notebook is quite sufficient, and more efficient than several. Write *everything* in it – notes, dates, appointments, ideas and so on. Check your diary at the start of each day and the beginning of each week. Ask your secretary to tell you about any important appointments so that you can note them in your diary immediately, and each morning compare diaries with your secretary so that you both have all the dates noted down.

Keep to one item when it comes to handbag and briefcase too. It is more practical and efficient to use a bag that doubles as handbag and briefcase than struggle with two items.

Digesting information

Whether planning your life or managing your career, you can be overloaded with information. Be selective. Read and watch only up-to-date, relevant material. Skim contents lists and indexes for relevant chapters or articles in books and magazines.

Saying 'No'

The simple word 'no' can improve your lifestyle 100 per cent. Women often take on tasks in the community and home that they don't want to do or more work than they can cope with because they feel guilty for refusing.

Be clear about what you want to do and say so. Always refuse by saying 'no' first. You can then soften it with a reason, if you want to. Keep saying 'No. I can't do that' until the listener gets the message. By saying 'no' more often you free your life of irrelevant activities and clear the way for your life-plan. Don't feel guilty – leave that to somebody else.

Learn to delegate

At work and at home it doesn't always have to be *you* who does a particular task. If other people have more time or relevant expertise

let them do it. Some women cling to work because they equate it
with power. The more successful and powerful people, however,
have learnt to delegate early on. At work it frees them for more
important tasks and time to make useful contacts. It also means
they are training a successor so they can move on up knowing there
is somebody to replace them.

You won't help yourself by keeping your colleagues down
because you are scared they are after your job. A good manager
picks first-rate people for his or her team; a second-rate manager
picks third-rate people. Your team reflects on you, so it pays to
pick the best people you can. If they can take over your job then
you are doing your job well, and this shows you are ready for
promotion.

At home delegating frees you to live more of your own life,
creates a sense of responsibility in your family, makes you less
tired and frees you from guilt about being unable to cope.

Using the phone

Both at work and at home the phone is a great time-waster. If you
can keep incoming and outgoing calls to a minimum you will have
more time to yourself and your work will be more efficient.

When making outgoing calls:

- make a note of what you want to say;
- have all relevant paperwork to hand;
- keep to the point when talking;
- make most of your calls on one or two mornings or afternoons a week only;
- list all the calls you want to make and go through the list one
  by one;
- if you don't really need to make the call, write a note or fax.

Surprisingly, you will know when most incoming calls are likely to
occur and who will be phoning. If you do not believe this, keep a
phone log for a few weeks. To deal with incoming calls try these
tips:

1. Get your secretary to deal with as many calls as he or she is
   competent to cope with. Not only will this empower and give
   him or her more job satisfaction, but you will only get passed
   important calls.

2. Cut short any calls where a lot of information should be sent
   by letter or fax.

3. Don't gossip.

4. Make it known that you prefer to receive calls on certain days only.

5. Pass on quickly any calls outside your sphere of expertise.

6. Keep all relevant information to hand if expecting certain calls.

7. Learn the art of saying 'good-bye'. Finish calls by saying 'I have to go in two minutes'; 'Now that's arranged, I'll say good-bye'; or simply 'good-bye'. Having said 'good-bye' don't get caught up in another round of conversation. (See *Tame that Phone* by Polly Bird, 'Further Reading', p. 224.)

Contingency plans

To some extent you can plan for emergencies. Work out which of your friends and relatives you can turn to in a crisis. Keep a list of emergency numbers by the phone, and let a neighbour know your and your partner's work phone numbers. Leave a spare set of keys with a neighbour or relative. Keep the fridge and freezer full of food. Have the number of an agency who can send someone to help at short notice. Make sure that your children's school has the name, address and phone number of someone who can collect your child in an emergency.

At work crisis management comes into play. If you have made a mistake admit it, put it right and try not to do it again. Don't pretend it hasn't happened or hope that nobody will notice – they will, and if you haven't warned them they will be annoyed. Companies with good crisis management teams face problems by getting their story in first, publicly admitting the fault and promising swift action to correct it. This is what it makes sense to do at your level – whatever that may be. When the crisis is over evaluate what went wrong, and work out how you can avoid something similar happening again.

WHERE TO GET HELP

Don't rely on one person at work or home to support you, as they may be unavailable or unable on occasions to do so. Work out whom you can ask for help and support in different situations, and be generous with your support in return.

Friends

Old friends can become neglected and new friends difficult to meet if you are too busy or too tied up to accept invitations. Conversely you may feel obliged to accept invitations from people you don't want to see out of a sense of duty or because they may be useful to your work.

Again, prioritise. Say 'no' to everyone except people you really want or need to see. Revisit old friends. Go out to different places and meet new people.

Paid help

If you can afford paid help you may need one or more of the following:

- babysitter;
- cleaner;
- gardener;
- house-sitter;
- au pair;
- nanny;
- child-minder.

Personal recommendation is the best way of obtaining paid help. That way you know that someone you respect has used and trusted the person you hire. If you have no-one to ask, try advertising in the local paper or on shop boards or in libraries. If you want a nanny the weekly magazine *The Lady* is a traditional place to put an ad. If having a nanny seems off-puttingly expensive, consider a nanny-share arrangement with friends or neighbours.

Before you advertise, write a job description so that you have criteria by which to judge applicants. These will consist of the hours to be worked, duties, qualities and skills needed, where the work is to be done, whether smoking is acceptable. You should ask around to find out the local rates of pay for the work. When interviewing applicants look for enthusiasm and good language skills (or acceptable ones in the case of an au pair) and ask for references. Always follow up references and check work permits where applicable.

When you choose somebody make sure that the duties, holidays, pay, days off, etc. are made clear before the job starts. Write them down if necessary. If the help will be looking after children or an elderly person let them meet first to see if they will get on together.

If you are hiring a nanny, remember that she will have to pay tax, and both of you will have to make National Insurance contributions. To find out more about this, contact the Contributions Agency (see your local telephone directory).

If your children are pre-school age, you can find out about local nurseries (state and private) from the council. Visit them more than once before deciding.

See Chapter Seven for more detailed information on childcare options, and 'Useful Addresses' pp. 213–214 for helpful contact addresses and telephone numbers.

MAKE LIFE EASY AT HOME

You will feel more relaxed and better able to deal with your work if you can run your home without undue stress. There are several ways you can do this.

Elimination

Take a few minutes to look at how you run your day. Could you reduce the workload if you had more machines – a dishwasher perhaps? Can some things be left? Can you reduce bed making by using duvets? Are your children old enough to make their own beds and get their own breakfast?

Do you need to drive the children to school or can your partner do it? Can a friend do it if you look after her child on Saturday afternoons?

Dealing with mess

One of the main causes of wasted time and temper is mess in the house. If you are naturally disorganised and/or have nowhere to put your belongings then you will be constantly tripping over things and it will take longer to clean the house. Keep things in a regular place and close to where you use them, and put them back afterwards.

At home invest in some large cheap plastic boxes or even cardboard boxes covered with wallpaper. Put one in each room and put everything into it that you find on the floor. See what reaction you get if you tell your family that if no-one has claimed what is in the boxes by the end of the week they will go in sacks for the dustmen. Provide shelves, boxes and hangers in all bedrooms. A wastepaper basket in every room, a wardrobe or hanging rails in each bedroom should cut down on the mess.

Easy options

Consider having lino or wood flooring instead of carpet for a quick brush or wipe over instead of hoovering, and keep all curtains and furniture coverings easy to clean. Get things repaired as soon as possible.

Put your work clothes away as soon as you get home and then put out only what you need for the morning on a chair so that you don't need to rush. Have your bag, coat and keys ready and set your alarm to allow you plenty of time to get to work or your appointment. If you are a sound sleeper then buy a large, loud alarm clock and check that you set it each night.

Put out the breakfast things the night before or delegate the job to one of your children.

Stop the paper chase

At work paper can take over the whole office as well as your desk. You don't need the hassle of hunting for vital bits of paper in a mess – nor will it help your efficiency. A mess of paper is not a sign of creativity, but of a lazy mind.

Have a large waste bin by your desk. Look at each piece of paper and either file it, act on it, pass it on or throw it away. Handle each piece of paper only once. Start with the paper on your desk now and then get your secretary and subordinates to tackle their offices. Keep everything off your desk except the phone/answering machine, pen, diary/notebook and a computer if necessary. Anything else can go in your drawers, on a shelf or on a pinboard.

Buying clothes

The secret of a good wardrobe is to choose one or two basic co-ordinating colours and plan your clothes around them. However, you don't have to choose the usual black, navy and grey unless your work requires it. Be adventurous and pick a bright colour that suits you for one of your choices (see Chapter Eight, 'Image', for more on this).

Lots of women have far too many clothes both for work and home. Take everything out of your wardrobe that doesn't suit you, is the wrong size or that you haven't worn for two years. Use what remains as your wardrobe basics. If you are still at a loss, then buy a good jacket in one of the most common colours of your remaining clothes. This will upgrade your wardrobe in one go.

Make a list of basics you need and go shopping armed with that list. Do not buy anything not on the list. Many working women in managerial positions go shopping for clothes only twice a year and some use the services of professional clothes' advisers (see Chapter Eight).

Keep styles simple, but add a shirt or accessory in an up-to-date style. Accessories are more easily changed than your basic clothes. Try everything on so that you don't waste your money. If you find something you look wonderful in in a classic style consider buying two of it. Try to keep buttons to a minimum and don't use too much jewellery. Try and avoid buying anything that is not on your list – particularly important during sales. If you find a catalogue with clothes that suit you and you are sure of your sizing then consider shopping by mail.

Cleaning your clothes

Clothes need to be kept clean so that they are ready to wear for work each day. Together with your family's washing this can take up considerable time. Organise the washing sensibly. Everyone can have their own laundry basket, and older children can learn how to use the washing machine and tumble drier. You may be able to get dry cleaning collected and delivered by a local firm. Investigate local ads for ironing services.

Choose one evening a week to do all mending. That way it only takes a few minutes rather than mounting up and ruining clothes. However much washing you have, sort clothes by colour and cloth type and do one type each evening. While the machine is on you can be doing other things.

You need a lot of tights, underwear and shirts because you wear clean ones every day, and you may have to buy more of these items to ensure that clean ones are always available.

Household shopping

One of the most time-consuming and exhausting tasks of any woman's day is shopping. Working women have to fit this into their lunch-times, after work or at weekends.

The way around this is careful planning. Take an evening to plan a fortnight's worth of meals that you can repeat each fortnight. Keep the meals easy to prepare and do not feel guilty about using prepared frozen meals some of the time. Invest in a microwave oven too, then even your children can prepare a meal if you're out or late.

When you have your list of meals write out a shopping list covering a whole month's worth of the menu's. Include regular basics such as loo paper, shampoo, dishwasher powder, etc. Armed with your list shop only once a month. Your partner or children can buy fruit and vegetables and any extras once a week. Include foods for a special meal which you can keep in your store cupboard or freezer in case of unexpected guests.

Entertaining

It is important to keep up your social life, otherwise you will become isolated and miserable and your work will suffer, as well as your home life. But entertaining does not have to be a chore. Instead of having friends round for a meal, why not just have a coffee, or a visit to the theatre or a few drinks early in the evening?

If you are providing a meal you may be able to afford outside caterers for one-off special occasions. Otherwise, unless you enjoy long hours in the kitchen, use ready prepared food of good quality or prepare the food a few days beforehand and freeze it.

If they are good friends ask them to contribute a dish or help prepare the food. Or why not take people out for a meal? The important thing is not to overdo the preparation so much that you end up not enjoying the occasion.

KEEPING ON TOP

Having made your plans to organise your life, don't put it off. If it all seems too daunting, then break your task into bits and reward yourself for each complicated piece of work. The whole idea is to take the guilt and anxiety out of running your life (and the household too), so that you will have more and better leisure time.

CHAPTER 3

Pay and Promotion

A WORKING woman's pay is one measure of her status, worth and independence. Unfortunately, in spite of the Equal Pay Act of 1970, even today women earn only 80 per cent of their male colleagues' salaries. Coupled with this is the still invisible glass ceiling on promotion, which means that women do not reach the higher levels of their jobs in the numbers they deserve. According to The National Management Survey of 1995 women still make up only 10.7 per cent of managers. So not only are women in many cases still denied the equal pay they deserve, but they are also prevented from increasing this pay by being denied promotion. Women as a whole are therefore underpaid and under-represented at the top of their professions.

Women tend to work in what are termed 'women's jobs' and are often underestimated as well as underpaid. One reason why women's wages remain low in comparison with men's is because the majority of women work in low-paid, part-time jobs and they have few opportunities for overtime or bonuses. Even women in managerial positions tend to be encouraged towards 'people' jobs such as PR or personnel work.

Unfortunately the trend in the recession for employers to flout the equal opportunities legislation and get rid of low-paid part-time workers (usually women), means women are in an even worse position. This is going to be exacerbated by the fragmentation of pay bargaining and the abolition of the remaining Wages Councils.

In 1984 Britain introduced regulations for equal pay for work of equal value. But the complexity of the law and the length of time it takes to conduct a legal battle has meant that there has been virtually no effect on the inequality gap (see Chapter One for more on this).

Women in full-time manual occupations earn less than two thirds of men's average weekly wage. Even women in full-time manager-ial positions earn only approximately 85 per cent of men's pay. Part-time professional women earn on the same basis as full-time women workers in the same job. But part-time managers and administrators earn 87 per cent of the average hourly pay. Women managers and professionals take home lower average earnings than their male counterparts. Women make up 32 per cent of managerial and administrative workers and 40 per cent of professional workers. But then again, some professions such as teaching are largely women-based and yet secondary headteachers tend to be men. (In primary education about half the headteachers are women.)

Women are also behind when it comes to gaining promotion because of lack of training and family responsibilities which take them out of the workplace. They may get paid the correct rate for the job they are doing – but that job may not be equal to the one which they would have had if they had not taken time out. This is why many women are in jobs which under-utilise their skills and intelligence.

THE WIDENING GAP

Britain's economy depends more and more on women to produce goods and provide services. The number of women in part-time work is set to increase for the rest of the century. But women still do not have appropriate pay and conditions of employment, and are disproportionally represented amongst the lowest paid. Women are also worst affected by the increased tendency for workers to be employed on a casual basis, as well as contracting out and alignment of pay with local labour market rates.

The pay gap between men and women in Britain is wider than in most EC member states, and is a major obstacle to women's economic independence.

A form of minimum wage should be a priority with any government. With the abolition of Wages Councils there is no pay protection for the lowest paid (with the exception of agricultural workers). The female/male gap was narrower in former Wages Council industries than it is in industry as a whole.

Although legislation on equal pay for equal value has been in force in all EU member states since 1975, women are still earning between 65 per cent and 85 per cent of men's hourly wages, between 54 per cent and 70 per cent of men's monthly wages, and on average 25 per cent less than men throughout the community.

In addition to the pay gaps between men and women managers, women are less likely to get company perks as they climb the promotion ladder. In 1995 the average female manager earned

£28,642 and the average male manager earned almost £5,000 more. Only 46.5 per cent of female managers have company cars compared with 59.4 per cent of male managers.

The wage gap is the result of:

- *labour market segregation.* Men's work/women's work culture in a limited number of jobs and sectors.
- *traditional women's employment* is still undervalued in terms of pay and social security.
- *work patterns* e.g., shift work/night work/bonuses are still treated as men's and generally result in higher salaries.
- *lack of detailed research* on salary differences at national level makes it difficult to implement the principle of equal pay for work of equal value.
- *under- or non-representation* of women at senior partner level means they are absent during wage negotiations.
- *statistical discrimination.* Staff are judged by the characteristics of the group to which they belong, e.g., statistics claim women are ill and change jobs more often than men and are generally less available.
- *discrimination* in work evaluation and job classification systems which means that women's contributions to the workplace are undervalued.
- *difficult and complicated legal proceedings* in court cases dealing with equal pay for work of equal value with the burden of proof in favour of employers.

Discrimination in work evaluation

This is the crux of the problem, because in the EU it is responsible for up to 8.5 per cent of the 25 per cent average wages gap. Jobs, not the workers, should be assessed in an 'asexual' way and should be used as a basis for salary negotiations. When you apply for a job try to evaluate the job description in these terms. You can raise any discriminatory points at the interview. When writing job descriptions yourself keep this in mind. You can give other women a fighting chance of promotion by making sure that the job description gives all candidates – men and women – an equal chance.

Even in 1995 female managers earn less than their male counterparts. According to a 1993 EOC survey the gender gap in earnings was narrower in professional than in managerial occupations. The earnings gap is wider in Scotland than in Wales or England for both managers and professionals.

For full-time workers the gender gap is particularly wide for general managers and administrators in national and local government, large companies and organisations. Although the gender gap for these groups is relatively narrow in the public sector, male general managers and administrators in large private companies continue to earn much higher average salaries than their female counterparts.

Lower rates for part-time workers are common and discriminate against women as they make up the majority of part-time workers.

PROBLEMS WITH PAY

There are several reasons why women do not get the pay they deserve. The first is that educationally they fall behind their male counterparts if schools do not take steps to ensure that girls have equal access to science and IT equipment. Girls can also be overlooked in class if they are not encouraged to speak out. Although girls now do well overall, they still tend to avoid maths and science subjects at A level and in higher education, which puts them at a disadvantage in the workplace. Not only do they still miss out educationally in the school system but when training and courses are available at work men are more likely to get on them.

EQUAL OPPORTUNITY COMMISSION (EOC) AIMS

The EOC has clear aims for improving women's pay. It wants to:

- get government commitment to narrowing the pay gap between men and women by tackling root causes;
- get the government to adopt the EOC's proposals for amending the law and introduce institutionalised protection for the lowest paid;
- find means of changing people's perceptions of the value of so-called 'women's work';
- obtain pro-rata treatment and valuation for part-time work;
- the integration of non-discriminatory pay determination and assessment by employers into their equal treatment policies assisted by the Code of Practices prepared by the EOC;

- policies to help men and women reconcile the demands of work and family.

The EOC has had a noticeable success with these aims in the new law giving equal rights to part-time workers (see Chapter One).

PAY RIGHTS

You have a right to be paid a decent salary for your work. Unfortunately because there is still no minimum wage, what you are paid depends on what your firm is prepared to pay and the effects of any trade union bargaining. Restrictions are also laid down by the government wage limits, which affects any increase your employer might want to give. If you are working from home, your wages will depend on what you can get for your work and what your employer is prepared to pay. Unless you are forceful you can find yourself working for a less than acceptable wage. If you are running your own business then what you pay yourself will depend on what profits you can make each year.

WHAT YOU CAN DO ABOUT LOW PAY

You might think that you are not being paid fairly for equal work to that of the men or being denied promotion because of your sex. In times of recession, restructuring of firms means you might also find yourself unfairly demoted. If you believe you have been discriminated against you can use the legislation for equal opportunities.

If you can prove that you are doing broadly similar work to that of a man in your workplace and are getting paid less then you may be able to take your case to an Industrial Tribunal to get your pay increased. The difficulty is in proving the similarity. You will need to enlist the support of other women in your sphere of work and your union. Cases for equal pay can take a long time to be heard and be complicated to prove. But once a case is won it sets a precedent for other similar cases and does an immense service to other women.

If you believe you have a justifiable grievance, do not wait to see what happens but complain to your line manager, the personnel officer and your union straight away. As your company is responsible for ensuring that women in their workforce are not discriminated against, it may settle the matter quickly and fairly without any need for you to take them to court.

If you get no satisfaction then you may want to contact the EOC with the support of your union representative and start legal proceedings through a tribunal or the courts.

If you do go to court make sure that you have kept written details of all cases of discrimination and any documentation which is relevant, such as dismissal letters, etc. The case could take up to two years to get to court and although you may think that you have been unfairly treated or dismissed you will remain in that position until the case is resolved. That means you will not be reinstated by the firm until and unless you win the case, and probably not even then. You can, however, expect compensation from the company if you win.

If you settle out of court and if the EOC is involved the firm may be asked to change its equality practices.

What you can do:

- Help other women. If they are nervous about complaining give them your support and if necessary back them up as a witness;
- go with them to talk to their employer, and if that fails accompany them to see their union representative and line manager;
- make notes about the discrimination you have seen and be prepared to stand up in court and back it up.

Claiming your perks

If you are getting paid as much as your male colleagues then check whether you are getting the same perks as they are. If your company does not give you the perks that they give a man doing a similar job then you may be able to claim sex discrimination.

PROMOTION

Promotion poses another problem. It brings increased pay and responsibilities, and enhances your attractiveness to prospective employers. However, several factors bar women from this passport to a better salary.

The first is the reluctance still of some companies to put women forward for promotion. Then there is the lack of company training opportunities which would give women the vital qualifications. But sadly, it is women who do themselves down when it comes to promotion.

Is there a glass ceiling?

According to many women aiming for the top there is still a glass ceiling, invisible but solid enough when reached. This barrier puts an effective stop to promotion and higher pay levels. The discrimination that forms the ceiling can often be subtle and indirect, so it may be difficult to prove that women are being discriminated against. You may be given training, interviews and oral encouragement, but still fail to overcome prejudice and fear from men in positions of power. It is possible to break the ceiling, but it takes determination and sometimes the willingness to resort to legal measures if discrimination can be proven.

When and if you reach your company's glass ceiling, three things can happen. You can:

- fail to break it;
- break it and pull up other women after you;
- break it and leave other women to struggle on.

If you have taken the courage to get to the top in spite of difficulties, then be generous to other women. Once a glass ceiling is broken it needs to be kept open by a steady stream of able and confident women reaching for the top. They need the training, support and encouragement you can give them to achieve their aims.

Company discrimination

No company should encourage their male rather than their female employees to try for promotion. But some companies do manage to get away with this kind of discrimination by letting their male employees take advantage of training courses, giving them more interesting work and opportunities to demonstrate their abilities. There is also the danger of prejudice from a male boss to a female employee, resulting in poor personal reports and a downgrading of ability.

It is difficult to prove this kind of discrimination. You risk being labelled as envious, unrealistic about your abilities, or even paranoid.

If you think you are being denied training opportunities then discuss this first with your immediate boss then with your personnel manager. Insist on being allowed to take part in training courses for which you are qualified.

Confidence

Many women do not have the confidence to put themselves forward for promotion because they think 'I would never get in anyway' or 'I don't think I could do that job'. Even women who have been encouraged by employers to try for promotion do not take the opportunity.

This stems from a culture which still imbues women with a sense of servitude. It can take a lot of encouragement and assertiveness training to reassure women that they are capable of doing a job and that they have every chance of getting promotion.

When they get to an interview, however, many women fail because they do not assert themselves. A senior manager who took part in many panel interviews in an organisation which encouraged women to apply for promotion, and was keen to appoint women to senior positions, expressed disappointment that none of the female candidates could be appointed. This was not for lack of qualifications but because they appeared to have no opinions of their own. They were, he said, too afraid of disagreeing with the interviewers, coming over as subservient and lacking in drive. The male candidates expressed their opinions clearly, even when they did not follow the orthodox line, and so appeared more confident and full of ideas.

GETTING PROMOTION

To improve your pay you can either get promotion within your company or a better paid job elsewhere. Bear in mind that the earnings gap between male and female managers is wider in the private than the public sector.

What you can do

To improve your chances of promotion within the company you need to do a number of things:

- take any training available (see Chapter Four);
- network (see Chapter Six);
- socialise with your colleagues – you need to be known as a friendly person;
- dress for the job above (image is discussed in Chapter Eight);
- learn as much as you can about your company;
- be prepared to accept change, and be flexible in your thinking;

- be creative, but have a sound basis for your ideas and decisions;
- keep up with your area of expertise;
- be prepared to market yourself – make yourself visible;
- be committed, honest and reliable;
- look ahead – plan for the short and long term;
- be independent – take responsibility on your own for getting things done;
- work well with others – don't be stand-offish or hog the work;
- offer something extra – perhaps an unusual but much needed skill;
- be realistic – don't expect to be boss overnight.

MOVING ON

To get a job elsewhere you need to make sure that you are known and that you apply for jobs appropriate for your skills. This is where networking comes in, as most people get jobs through personal contacts.

If you have a senior managerial position you might also want to make yourself known to a head-hunting agency. Head-hunters act on behalf of companies wanting to recruit a particular type and calibre of person. Contact the Federation of Recruitment and Employment Services for advice (see 'Useful Addresses', p.204).

Your curriculum vitae (CV)

Prepare a CV and ensure that it is up-to-date and professionally presented. The important facts are your name, age, address and telephone/fax number; your qualifications – i.e., GCSEs, 'A' levels, degrees, diplomas, certificates; your work history in reverse date order with dates and employers' addresses; the names and addresses of two referees. You may also be asked to fill in an application form. Don't do this without writing it out in rough first and checking your spelling. If your handwriting is poor type the form or fill it out in block letters.

If you are asked to write about your achievements and aims do so in a positive manner. Be positive about time taken out of the workplace. If you can afford to, ask a professional CV writer to help you – it may be worth the money. But there are many books which will show you how to present and write a CV (see 'Further Reading', p.224).

It must look professional. If you haven't got a computer, ask a friend with one to set your CV out for you, and print lots of copies.

Your covering letter to each company is very important. It must be specific to each individual job, and stress why you think you would be able to do the job and what you would bring to it. Both it and the CV should be entirely without errors – get a friend to proofread it for you.

Interview skills

Interview skills can be learnt on training courses, and you can help yourself by practising with a friend. Seeing yourself on video can be a very good way to spot bad habits and help you to improve your technique. Answer questions honestly, but be confident. Don't be afraid to ask your own questions. If you disagree with the interviewer, you should feel free to put your point of view clearly.

Don't be discouraged if you don't get the first job you apply for. Each time you get as far as an interview your skills will improve.

CHAPTER 4

Training for the Top

WOMEN need to train throughout their working lives regardless of the stage they are at or the level they have reached. Training is a key requirement for progress at work, both to enable women to update their skills and to re-enter the job market.

Women do not in general progress at the same speed and to the same level as men. One reason is that they lack the skills necessary for promotion.

EDUCATION

Training starts with education. This is important for women because it can improve job prospects in later life. But boys may have crowded girls out from technological and science lessons.

The aim is to ensure that all children get the same educational chances and choices. However, special efforts have to be made to ensure that girls actually get the same educational choices. Girls should not be discriminated against by being denied access to technology and other specialist subjects or ignored in class discussions.

Schools are now doing their best to overcome this by making sure that all pupils are asked questions in class and get a chance to show their skills. In computer and science lessons work is done in small groups, and where appropriate girls work together so that they are not overshadowed by boys. In some mixed-sex schools a few classes are held as all-girl classes. Many parents choose all-girl schools in the hope that this will allow their daughters to make academic progress without being overwhelmed by boys.

The EOC (Equal Opportunities Commission) would like gender to be one of the criteria for the accreditation of initial teacher training, with teachers being taught about gender differences in education. This has yet to be implemented.

ADULT TRAINING

As adults women usually have a much more broken work pattern than men, which inhibits long periods of training. Women are not put forward as often for training schemes – nor do they put their own names forward. Woman tend to be more self-effacing than men and not as confident in their own abilities.

Women who do take training courses benefit immeasurably, but many need to supplement training by assertiveness classes, or take part in all-women training in order to realise their full potential.

As in any kind of education, men tend to be more forceful and take natural command of technology such as computers. Lecturers and teachers can fall into the trap of directing their message to men rather than women.

The result is that not only do women lack the practical and work skills needed to progress but they also miss out on interpersonal skills, so vital in today's workplace. Managers interviewing men and women for promotion say they are struck how often able women fail to do as well as mediocre men because they are afraid to disagree or present their own ideas.

Another reason for the discrepancy between men and women's skills is that the cost of training courses is out of the range of many women. Some organisations do pay for students to take courses, others do not. More and more women are having to find the money and take courses at their own expense in order to boost their career prospects, although there now are a large number of flexible ways training can be obtained.

Managers have a poor record of obtaining qualifications, and yet well trained and qualified managers not only increase their own career prospects but improve the performance of the company.

Many women want to move from a regular job to controlling a business, and national trends show that more of them are doing so. They need training in order to make the move and to gain confidence in a new work sphere. This chapter explains what training choices you have and where to go for information.

WHAT DOES YOUR COMPANY NEED?

In order to progress in your organisation you need to keep up-to-date with skills and knowledge relevant to your present job and the wider aims of the company. Managers who are well trained and qualified increase their own prospects and that of their company.

Training also keeps your mind working and the ideas flowing. Even if you don't agree with the latest thoughts on your subject you must know enough about them to argue your case.

Keep up-to-date with your professional or trade skills and information by reading the appropriate trade and professional journals, reports and books and by reading relevant newspaper and magazine articles. Your company may keep copies of these in a central library section for staff circulation.

Keep an eye on what your company's requirements may be a year or eighteen months hence. For example, if it will need people with financial skills then now is the time to take training so that you are well-placed to fill future vacancies. Your firm may also want to recruit more diverse types of people. If they are in the market for those with confidence and public speaking skills rather than good administrators then now is the time to take the relevant courses. It makes sense to practise these skills within the company so that you will be noticed.

The firm may be planning an expansion in a year or two which will involve increasing the size of the computer section. See if you can utilise what skills you do have and extend into a new area. Perhaps if you are skilled at word processing on a PC you could take a course in spreadsheet management so that you are ready for the new posts that will be created.

Is your company looking towards more overseas business? Learning a language now could put you in the front line for promotion when the new business starts.

Consider courses which have a general usefulness, such as assertiveness training, dress confidence and public speaking. Although these do not lead to a qualification they can increase your confidence and give you a new outlook on your work.

Law and accountancy are so important to any company that large organisations employ specialist accountants and lawyers. If you have not yet decided on a career route, studying either of these subjects will give you a head start in career terms because they are always needed.

You may not want to take on the full training to enter either of these professions, but a knowledge of one or both of these subjects will not only improve your skills at work but also improve your job prospects. You can take short courses to build up your knowledge. Your company may well provide courses covering the basics of these subjects as they relate to your work.

Women who train in these areas and can bring specific expertise in these subjects to companies will be highly valued. The woman manager who understands budgets and can talk to the company accountant in his or her own terms has more control over her work and more chance of involvement in the business. Information about training in these two subjects follows later in this chapter.

WHERE CAN YOU START?

The first thing to do is decide what skills you actually need. These may be practical skills specific to your job, personal skills such as assertiveness or public speaking, or managerial and business skills. Remember to consider the company's future plans.

WHERE TO GET HELP

Many companies provide courses for their employees, and if yours does you should go on these if possible because they will be geared to your company's needs. Courses may be during lunch-breaks or after work and paid for by the company, or you may be given time off to attend them.

In some companies you may be given the chance to take longer day or week courses, or lecturers may be brought in to give lessons to staff in groups during work time.

Whatever the method of study, it is important that you do not feel inhibited about going on training courses.

DAY RELEASE COURSES

Day-release courses are when an employee is given one day off a week to undertake training leading to a recognised qualification. This often takes place at the beginning of someone's career, when an employee needs certain qualifications or training to be able to do the job. Other options include being allowed to take paid or unpaid leave for anything up to a year to pursue study.

SECONDMENT

Secondment is becoming more popular as a way of increasing skills. This involves your being 'lent' to another employer for a period of time – perhaps several years – in order to experience new ways of working and obtain a different view of your original job.

You may be seconded to a related company to experience different aspects of the company's work. Employees in the public sector may be seconded to the private sector.

When you return to your job you will bring new ideas and ways of looking at things to the benefit of your colleagues and the company.

Women may be worried that they will reduce their promotion prospects by taking time out in this way. This is far from the case. Nowadays firms are increasingly looking for people with a wide range of management skills and experiences, with a broad knowledge of the workplace as a whole. Far from reducing your prospects you will be in greater demand, not only from your own company but from others.

Take the chance of secondment if possible. If you are worried about not keeping in touch with your previous job make sure you get together with your original colleagues occasionally and phone for news of what is going on. Your salary will be paid by your original employer.

PART-TIME DEGREES

Some colleges and universities allow mature students to take a degree part-time or in the evenings. Birkbeck College in London is one college which not only provides a comprehensive series of short courses which can lead to certificates and diplomas but also full degree programmes taken in the evening. Its extra-mural programme of short courses and degrees is part of the University of London. Local universities and colleges will provide details. (See 'Useful Addresses', pp.204–206, and for a full list of higher education courses visit your local reference library.)

If you do well in any subject do let people know. You don't have to brag, but it does no harm to let people know that you have skills in particular areas. Your bosses will get to hear of it and it will be another point in your favour when you are looking promotion.

If you are taking a first degree then you may be eligible for a mandatory grant. But if you are earning above the limit then you will have to find your own fees. Courses for some institutions only attract discretionary grants. Local authorities award these as they see fit. Unfortunately, recent financial restraints have led to a sharp decrease in the number of discretionary grants awarded.

DISTANCE LEARNING

One of the most popular ways of gaining extra qualifications nowadays is to do so by correspondence or its more extensive form, open and distance learning. Even if you are working from home you still need to keep up-to-date with training and skills. Open distance learning courses are particularly suitable for women working from home. Organisations such as the National Extension College, The National Council for the Training of Journalists and many others offer distance learning courses leading to a qualification in a variety of subjects. Before you enrol for any course remember to find out what the fee is, what success rate they have and whether they can provide recent references from satisfied customers.

Wolsey Hall, Oxford is a distance learning centre which is helping Oxford Brookes University to run a long-distance MBA programme for students world-wide. In this course teleworking and long-distance computer conferencing are an important part of the teaching structure. Students are connected to the MBA host computer by means of a 'conference connection' pack which enables them to connect up with their own PC (see 'Useful Addresses', p.206).

In the West Midlands there is a women's training organisation called The Business Team, which is part of the New Opportunities for Women programme funded by the European Commission. It will link up with a number of Women's Business trainers in Spain, Germany, France and Greece. Teaching will take place for 40 women via laptop computer, and The Business Team will maintain lines of communication with their European counterparts via the IRIS network.

BUSINESS SCHOOLS AND MASTERS OF BUSINESS ADMINISTRATION (MBAs)

Business schools offer a wide range of courses, including first degrees and postgraduate study. The most usual qualification sought once a person has started work is an MBA. This is a post-experience degree in management studies at master's level. Traditionally it is used to prepare for a senior management position. Some people take it early in their career if their original degree is not relevant to their job.

To do an MBA you need to have a first degree or an equivalent qualification, as well as some work experience. If you do not have these qualifications enough work at a suitable level may make you eligible to take the course. Most business schools also require a GMAT score. This is like a GCSE examination, except that it is taken at speed.

MBAs can be taken full- or part-time or by distance learning. They can also be work-based. The costs vary from a few hundred pounds upwards depending on the length of the course. You may be able to get sponsorship from your company. AMBA (The Association of MBAs) publishes a world-wide guide to Business Schools and *The Economist* publishes an annual survey of MBA programmes. Information about business school courses can be found in the advertisements in the broadsheet press financial pages, particularly the *Financial Times* or in management magazines. *TOPwoman* magazine is a good source of information about MBA courses.

The number of women studying for an MBA has increased; Manchester Business School, for example, recruited 28 per cent women on its 1995/1996 courses. These courses give women more confidence in their own abilities, as well as the straightforward learning content. They also open up new horizons and opportunities. Studying for an MBA gives you the chance to review career options or move in a new direction. Many women take an MBA to help them establish their own business. Not everybody believes that an MBA is necessary to do well in management, but the qualification at least shows commitment and is an extra lever to your way into management. An MBA also gives an international dimension to your thinking about work.

It is possible to do all or part of an MBA course abroad. The University of Bristol's MBA course – which is run by a woman – gives students the opportunity to study in Paris for the third term of their course. (See 'Useful Addresses', p.206.)

THE INSTITUTE OF MANAGEMENT (IM)

The Institute of Management runs short courses of one or two days duration which can also be run on an in-company basis; this is cost-effective if there are five or more people to train. The management development courses are longer – up to five days.

If you want to follow one of the IM courses it is worthwhile asking your company if it can take place in-house. There are no courses particularly for women, but all are useful and cover personal skills and effectiveness, interpersonal skills, performance management, quality and customer care, management and business education. There is also a management development programme.

If required the IM can tailor courses to your company's requirements. There are also courses for senior management and NVQ (National Vocational Qualifications) courses taken in modules which lead to the Certificate or Diploma in Management.

In addition, the IM publishes a range of books and reports in areas of interest and importance to managers.

ACCOUNTANCY

Accountancy training leads to a qualification as a chartered accountant. People with good 'A' levels can start by taking the Foundation Course. If you have a degree in a relevant subject you may be exempt from this. Alternatively students can take the Association of Accounting Technicians (AAT) exam, preferably gaining a pass with credit, or take a BTEC Higher National Diploma or Certificate.

Once you have the relevant qualification you join an accountancy company for three to four years training, which includes practical work. Study patterns vary from residential, block release or full-time sessions. First time costs for examinations are met by your employer. Larger companies usually have their own training department and counsellor; smaller firms may group together to provide the same service.

Because applications are made to individual firms, mature students need to check the likelihood of acceptance before applying. If you are already working you may be able to study accountancy with your own firm or a related company, or be supported on a residential or day release course.

If you have a relevant degree you take a three-year training contract and take two professional examinations to end up with an ACA in addition to your degree. With a non-relevant degree the training is the same, with the addition of the Foundation Stage. If you are a non-graduate you will take a four-year training contract and the Foundation Stage if appropriate, and two professional examinations to get your ACA.

Accountancy may involve you in accounting, auditing, taxation, financial management, insolvency, information technology, corporate finance or management consultancy. Help for women in accountancy comes from the Women in Consultancy group, which is made up of representatives from the six major accountancy bodies. Also there is the Workplace 2000 group, run by the Institute of Chartered Accountants of England and Wales (ICAEW), which gives advice and assistance to female chartered accountants and helps to establish local support groups and networks.

Accountancy students can now train part-time, which is a great help to female students. Once qualified you may be able to work from home or in a job-share or flexitime situation. You may eventually be able to do consultancy work.

THE LAW

There are two careers in the law – as a barrister or a solicitor. Both involve the same basic training, but the difference is that barristers are called to the Bar and can be advocates in a court of law. Solicitors' training comes under the auspices of one of the law societies. Solicitors may now also represent their clients in court.

The Bar

The General Council of the Bar is responsible for barristers, and training for barristers is organised by the Council of Legal Education.

You usually need to have an upper second-class degree or above. If your degree is not in law you must take the Common Professional Examination of six core subjects, which is the examination also taken by solicitors.

Intending barristers then join one of the four Inns of Court – Lincoln's Inn, the Inner Temple, the Middle Temple, or Gray's Inn. Once a member you must keep a certain number of dining terms. These relate to the divisions of the legal year; students must attend a certain number of dinners on certain dates. For students who intend to practise as barristers there is a Vocational Course run by the Inns of Court School of Law. Students who are not going to practise at the bar but are intending to be part of the employed bar, perhaps in commerce or the Civil Service, take a different course at other institutions which leads to the Bar Examination.

After passing these exams the student is called to the Bar. The non-practitioner is then qualified. An intending barrister must complete a year's pupillage, however – that is working with a barrister in a set of Chambers or with an employed barrister. During this time there are other short courses to take.

Solicitors

Students taking a law degree need to have taken one which covers the six common core legal subjects. If your degree was not in law then you must take a one-year, full-time or two-year part-time course leading to the Common Professional Examination (CPE) or a Post-Graduate Diploma in Law. Once you have completed your academic training you must apply for student membership of the Law Society. You then take a full or part-time Legal Practice Course, and spend two years on a training contract. This is paid employment, under the supervision of a solicitor, and undertaking your own work. During this time you must complete the Professional Skills Course.

People without a degree can qualify through the Legal Executives route. You should gain employment in a legal office, join the Institute of Legal Executives (ILEX) and over one or two years take the Institute's Part I Examination. Over the following one or two years you undertake the Part II Examinations, which should include three of the six core subjects. If you pass you become a member of the Institute of Legal Executives. You must then wait to be 25 and have served for five years (two after membership) in a legal office so you can become a Fellow of the Institute. During this time you should undertake the remaining core subjects, and can then enrol as a student member of the Law Society and attend the Legal Practice Course. Where a Fellow of the ILEX has been in continuous employment prior to commencing a Legal Practice Course there is no need to serve a training contract. Members of ILEX can take the Legal Practice Course but must serve the training contract.

THE OPEN UNIVERSITY (OU)

The Open University, with its wide range of courses taught by correspondence, tapes and video with seminars and summer schools, is the best known and the largest organisation offering such courses.

Established by Royal Charter in 1969 the OU has over 150,000 students registered with it in 1995. Courses are carefully designed to meet the needs of home-based students. The courses are provided in the form of units (textbooks) linked with radio and TV programmes, audio and visual tapes, home experiment kits and computer software. The multi-media aspect of the courses is particularly suitable for disabled students.

Support is given by a local tutor and counsellor and meetings at study centres throughout the UK. There are also weekend or summer residential schools, which provide extended periods of tuition and contact with staff and fellow students. Undergraduate students must attend at least one summer school.

The courses are wide-ranging and include units which can be studied for pleasure and interest only and those which form part of a degree or higher degree.

The OU is open to everyone over the age of 18. Almost half the students are women – the highest proportion of female students of any university in the UK.

Women can and do take any of the courses on offer, but certain courses which have particular relevance for women deserve special mention.

OU Computing

The OU has a strong technology and computing programme and many women take their first steps into computing through the OU. This is important in a world where knowledge of technology and computing can make the difference in terms of career progression and understanding how a company works.

Open Business School (OBS)

This is part of the OU, and teaches courses which reflect the current requirements of employers and managers. The courses can be used to further specific development or taken to gain an award. The OBS makes Certificate, Diploma and MBA awards.

Approximately 70 per cent of those taking certificate and diploma courses are sponsored by their organisations, so if you think one of the OBS courses would be useful it is worthwhile asking if your company will sponsor you or provide part of the fees and/or time to study. Even organisations which have never done this may be receptive if you are the first to ask them. Companies benefit because of the higher level of expertise of their managers. Employers expect results, and the OBS makes sure that they get them. The units cover all aspects of modern management. There are also two study packs specifically for women. *Women into Management* concentrates on developing women's self-awareness and confidence, and makes them aware of problems women managers face. Part of the pack involves developing skills and strategies to overcome barriers. It is designed to lead on to the management training course. The other study pack *Developing Women Managers* is for women in management who want to advance their careers and to look at their position in relation to future management positions. Also of interest are the management courses specifically geared to retail management.

OU and OBS fees

The cost for an undergraduate course is in the order of £288 plus £188 if there is a residential summer school to attend. Each successfully completed and examined full course earns a full or half credit. One credit equals 60 points in the Credit Accumulation and Transfer Scheme (CATS) widely used in UK higher education. Six credits (360 points) are needed for a BA or BSc degree. For honours, two credits (120 points) must be at a higher level. Fees for a nine-month course not in the undergraduate programme range from £320 to £505. For management and business courses in the OBS fees start at £655. The price for packs for short interest courses start at £10 and are typically about £40.

OU undergraduates are not entitled to mandatory grants. Some local education authorities may provide discretionary grants, particularly for summer school fees. See if your company will bear part or all of the cost.

Courses which contribute to NVQs or Scottish Vocational Qualifications (SVQs) may be eligible for tax relief.

OPEN COLLEGE OF THE ARTS

This is affiliated to the OU, and uses similar teaching methods to offer a range of practical subjects in such things as painting, photography and creative writing. The courses are stimulating and have the advantage that an interest can be pursued in a more flexible timetable than conventional adult education classes.

PRIVATE COURSES

These are run outside the main business school and educational institutes and are run as businesses by private individuals. The courses range from long management courses to short courses on things like time management run by specialist firms such as Invicta Training Ltd which runs the Time Management Course and a number of short courses on management techniques (see 'Useful Addresses', p.205).

EVENING CLASSES AND ADULT EDUCATION CLASSES

One obvious route to improving your skills is to go to evening classes. Now that government cut-backs have reduced these the choice is not as wide as it was. The tendency in some areas is to provide only courses which lead to a qualification.

Fees are payable but these are reasonable, particularly if you live in the area. They are certainly cheaper than any private course. The range of courses available can still provide a choice of useful skills. Details of courses can be obtained from libraries, councils and through local listings such as London's *Floodlight* magazine. Local colleges usually produce their own adult education prospectuses. Enrol early, because popular courses are often over-subscribed. Courses usually start in September or October and continue until July. There are also day schools, usually on Saturdays, and weekly courses.

In addition to courses specific to your work and career prospects, don't neglect your other interests. It may not seem to you that learning history or taking a painting course is relevant to your job, but it stimulates your mind and makes you a more interesting person. This spills over into work and your attitude towards it. A lively person who has outside interests and can converse on a range of subjects is an asset to any organisation.

Adult education classes can take place in the evening or during the day, and can lead to awards. There are also full- and part-time courses available. The termly fees are moderate in order to attract a wide range of students, so they should be well within the range of a working woman.

SELF-HELP

Don't forget the simple things that you can do to train yourself. There are numerous educational programmes, including the OU on TV, and a great variety of educational videos and audio tapes. Libraries often lend both kinds of tapes. Reading books from the library has stimulated many a person to pursue a different interest. These can be self-help books, books to keep up with your own sphere of work, general books about management or industry, or books on a completely new subject to gain new insights and skills.

Newspapers and magazines provide an abundant supply of informative and (often) intelligent articles on virtually any subject you can mention. You may be able to talk to friends or relatives who are experts in their fields. Your trade union or professional organisation may hold talks and seminars you can attend.

COMPETITIONS

Some business schools run competitions with business magazines or women's magazines to attract more women. The prize is usually a place at the business school with all fees paid. In *The Guardian* there is an annual *Guardian* Women in Business Scholarship competition which sends one woman to Manchester Business School full-time and one on a part-time basis. Also *Cosmopolitan* and other women's magazines run occasional business competitions aimed at giving women the chance to study business.

CONFERENCES

Conferences held for people from many organisations are in theory learning places where you can hear the latest ideas on your subject as well as meeting your opposite numbers from other organisations. They can be very useful, but not if you take the attitude – as many unfortunately do – that they are just an excuse for a few days socialising.

To make the most of the learning opportunities at conferences read advance material and make notes of any comments or questions. Turn up at all the relevant lectures – apart from being useful to you, your company will expect you to attend and report back. Ask questions of the lecturer at an appropriate point. Make written notes at the time or tape the talks if this is permitted, and make written notes when you get back to your room. Make particular note of anything useful which you can put into effect in your organisation when you get back to work.

Even if your company does not require a full written report, writing one when you return home will keep all the important points in your mind and act as a reminder and reference for the future.

Make a note of the names and phone numbers of anyone you meet who has specialist knowledge which may be useful to you in future. Keep all the conference literature and read anything given to you at the time in the quiet of your room or when you get home. Bibliographies are often provided so you can follow up the conference subject by reading about it in your own time.

You may like to browse through the 'Useful Addresses' and 'Further Reading' sections at the end of the book to find organisations and publications that will be helpful to you whatever your training needs.

CHAPTER 5

The Working Woman's Finances

IN GENERAL women do not take enough care about or notice of their finances. Even women in managerial positions do not give enough consideration to the financial implications of old age, redundancy, long-term illness or death. Women who help in their husband's business for wages and self-employed women also need to make their own financial arrangements.

Many women rely on their husbands to provide at least pension and insurance cover for the whole family. Unfortunately this has left many women and their families under-insured and without adequate financial cover. Women lose more than men if their partner dies: more than 50 per cent of women lose over half their income in widowhood.

Women are just as adept as men at handling their finances, but they do have special needs as far as pensions and insurance are concerned. This chapter will tell you what financial choices you have and where to go for advice.

WOMEN'S NEEDS

Working women need to consider their financial situation in several basic areas. They need the following:

- an adequate pension;
- personal life assurance;
- mortgage protection;
- income and redundancy protection;
- to make the best use of savings;
- to make a will.

Only five per cent of women have private medical insurance; just over one per cent are covered by a personal accident policy; four out of ten women have no life assurance at all. Only a tiny percentage of women take out a policy to safeguard their earnings, in spite of the low level of sickness benefits. It also makes sense for them to arrange savings in their own name. Women should know their rights as far as maternity and childcare benefits are concerned.

WHAT YOU CAN DO

As a working woman, take a look at your financial arrangements and make sure that you and your family have adequate and appropriate financial protection.

To ensure you make the appropriate financial arrangements you will need independent advice from an expert. Even if you have to pay for it, the advice will be worth it. Be wary of 'free' advice which may mask the fact that the adviser is working on commission and therefore has a vested interest in promoting certain companies.

Financial help

Banks have financial advisers who will talk to you and suggest ways of dealing with your finances. Obviously they hope you will want to use their services, but you can shop around until you find a bank which gives you the kind of advice you feel happy with – and which has a sympathetic person to deal with you.

Most of the major banks say that they do not have any services or products aimed specifically at women because they deal with customers as individuals. They do offer particular services to make asking for advice easier, however. For example, Barclays has a number of initiatives for all its customers such as Personal Bankers, Personal Sector Managers and the Premier Banking Service which are designed to make using banking services easier for all its customers.

Abbey National does not provide services specifically for women because they believe that women might consider it odd to be singled out as requiring special advice, and might even find it patronising. They do have Personal Financial Advisers (PFAs) who deal specifically with mortgage advice and a Financial Planning Service (FPS) to help customers with life assurance, pensions and long term savings plans. Their advisers recommend the products of their own Insurance Company, Abbey National Life plc.

Lloyds Bank has Black Horse Financial Services, which are able to conduct a free full financial review. Their consultants may recommend products from a range of Black Horse Life and Lloyds Bank Unit Trust products.

The Bank of Scotland does not provide any financial advice targeted specifically to meet the needs of women. It does, however, provide a range of distinctive financial service tailored to meet the specific needs of all existing or potential customers.

The Co-Operative Bank has a non-discriminatory policy and therefore does not provide any financial advice particularly aimed at women alone.

National & Provincial Building Society has a free Financial Services for Women helpline for independent telephone guidance. If they cannot answer your query immediately they contact an expert and ring you back. The service is supported by a series of booklets specifically for women.

Legal & General provides a pension guide for women. The Midland Bank provides useful guides for women and sponsored *Women and Money* by Marie Jennings (see 'Further Reading'). See 'Useful Addresses', pp.206-208, for contact numbers for these organisations.

Advice for women by women

Some companies have realised that finance is daunting for many women and have tried to make it more user-friendly. Towry Law, for example, provides a pension service for women with individual consultation if needed, and with female consultants available if required.

National & Provincial Building Society has an independent information service, Financial Services for Women (FSW), and is a joint founder of the Financial Forum for Women (FFW) with the National Council of Women. The FSW provides a useful newsletter.

If you feel more comfortable talking about your financial affairs to a woman then it should be possible to do so.

Women-only firm – Fiona Price & Partners

The independent firm, Fiona Price & Partners (FP&P), is an all-women firm of independent financial and tax advisers who advise business and professional women and other women with an independent income. They start by providing an assessment of your existing financial arrangements before dealing with your particular financial problem. FP&P's approach embodies the principles of impartial advice, impartial remuneration, regular reviews and no jargon. They are authorised by PIA (Personal Investment Authority). (See 'Useful Addresses', p.207, for FP&P's address and phone number.)

WOMEN'S PENSION NEEDS

Women have their own special pension needs. On average women live longer than men and so their pension has to support them for longer. The increase in divorce has meant that more women are at risk over a pension income. Although divorced women can claim a pension on the basis of their former husband's state pension, they are not entitled to any part of their husband's State Earnings Pension Scheme (SERPS).

Women also often have shorter working lives than men because of time taken out to start a family. This means that they will have a reduced pension if they don't make extra pension provision while they are working. They may end up without the necessary length of service to enable them to take part in a company pension scheme.

Part-time working women who work eight hours or more can now join company pension schemes; women who work less than eight hours a week will have to make their own arrangements.

Freelance working women, women who work at home, or temporary workers often have no pension provision at all. It is unwise to rely either solely on your husband's pension or your own state pension when you retire. It becomes even more important if you are not married or are self-employed.

When can you collect your pension?

Recent changes mean that women born after 5 April 1955 will not collect their state pension until they are 65. This will make the state pension age equal to that of men, but it will be phased in over ten years. Women born before 5 April 1950 will still receive their state pension at 60. Women born after that date but before 5 April 1955 will get their state pension at earlier ages on a sliding scale. The equalising of the ages at 65 will occur in 2010. The phasing in period started on 6 April 1994 with women aged 38–43 who had an extra month added to their state pension age for every month after 5 April 1950 that their birthday falls. This leaves working women with three options:

- continue working until 65;
- retire at 60 without a pension until 65, perhaps relying on a partner's income;
- replace the state benefits lost between 60 and 65 and retire at 60 as planned.

Obviously simply replacing those five years will not give you a reasonable retirement pension. The basic state pension is not good enough to provide a reasonable income (despite the fact that so many women end up having to try and live on it), but it is a start. You may want to consider a Personal Pension Plan as discussed later in this chapter (see p.56).

State pensions

There are two pension schemes operated by the State. The first is the basic State Pension Scheme and the second is the State Earnings Related Pension Scheme (SERPS). The basic state pension is paid for by National Insurance contributions, or if you become unemployed, by credits. Everyone with a full record of contributions can receive their basic state pension from the State Pension Age. But only 78 per cent of women receive the full basic pension.

Your company will pay your National Insurance (NI) contributions. If you are self-employed you must make the contributions yourself either by paying a quarterly bill, sent to you by the Contributions Agency, or by direct debit from your bank account. Married women who have chosen to pay the cheaper so-called 'small' stamp do not qualify for retirement pension.

SERPS is an additional pension linked to your full-time or part-time earnings. You cannot join SERPS if you are self-employed.

If you are an employee you will automatically pay into SERPS unless your company has contracted out of it, you pay the small stamp as above, or you have chosen to opt out by paying into a Personal Pension Plan. In this last case your SERPS contributions are redirected into this plan.

If you reach 60 before the year 2000 your SERPS pension will be 25 per cent of your average earnings of the best 20 years of your working life adjusted for inflation. If you are 60 after the year 2000 the maximum percentage is reduced over a ten-year period to 20 per cent in 2010, and it will be based on your average lifetime's earnings. Because many women have interrupted work patterns this will act against them, because they will have a lower average lifetime's earnings.

You can arrange not to be part of SERPS if instead you contribute to your company's final salary pension scheme. This must be at least as good as SERPS and offer a Guaranteed Minimum Pension (GMP). If you have contracted out you pay reduced National Insurance. You can also contract yourself out by contributing to a Personal Pension Plan (PPP). Part of your own and your employer's contributions are paid into the plan at the end of the tax year. At present the government adds a one per cent contribution to plans of people over 30 who contract out in this way, but this will be reviewed in 1996.

You can also contract out into the company's money purchase scheme, although there is no incentive contribution from the government. The payments are made directly and not through the Department of Social Security (DSS).

There is no guarantee that benefits through the latter two schemes will match SERPS. But it may be to your advantage to contract out of SERPS, depending on your age and level of earnings, because in certain circumstances a contracted-out personal pension scheme may get you a better pension. Women, with their disjointed careers, may find this an advantage.

If you are among women who joined the earlier State Graduated Pension which ran from 1961 to 1975 you will get a small amount of graduated pension at State Pension age.

Company pension schemes

There are three types of company pension schemes:

1. Final Salary Scheme (or defined benefit scheme);
2. Money Purchase Scheme (or defined contribution scheme);
3. Hybrid Schemes.

1. Final Salary Scheme. This guarantees you a proportion of your final salary. It depends on how many years you work and how many years you are a member of the scheme. You can often 'buy in' years to make up for those you have missed on the scheme. Typical contributions are five per cent of your salary with the employer paying the extra. There are also non-contributory schemes where the employer pays the whole cost. Some schemes exclude overtime or bonuses from the final salary. Some schemes increase in line with inflation. A widow's pension is usually separate from the scheme. You can usually exchange part of the pension for a lump sum.

2. Money Purchase Scheme.   You and your employer pay contributions at a specified level. These are invested and build up over the years. Your contributions and those made on your behalf are identified separately. The problem is that your retirement benefits are not known in advance. They will depend on the size of your fund and the cost of purchasing a pension when you retire. On retirement part of the money can be taken as a lump sum and the rest used to purchase a pension with an insurance company. The schemes usually provide benefits for dependants if you die in service. If yours does not you will need to purchase a dependants' pension.

3. Hybrid Schemes.   These are rare, and combine both the previous schemes. You get a pension based on a proportion of your salary or based on the fund build-up, whichever is greater, but subject to any limits imposed by the Inland Revenue. Your individual fund is a notional amount consisting of both your own and your company's contributions plus interest, whether at the rate earned by the fund as a whole or at a guaranteed nominal rate.

Points to note
If you are part of a company scheme you cannot also have a Personal Pension Plan unless you have two different sources of income, for example from two separate jobs. The only exception is if you are in a contracted in company pension scheme in which case you can have a rebate-only personal pension. A rebate-only PPP is used solely to contract out of SERPS. You and your employer only pay in the NI contribution (the rebate) which is transferred from the DSS to your rebate-only PPP. Tax relief on your part of the rebate, and currently a government one per cent incentive if you are over 30, is also paid into the plan.

Personal Pension Plans (PPPs)

Personal Pension Plans allow you to pay contributions into a policy in your own name. This fund is then invested in the way you wish, and in theory grows until you retire. Unfortunately, interest rates can go down as well as up. If the rates go down you may not end up with enough money to buy a pension. When you retire you can take part of the fund accumulated in cash. The rest of the fund provides you with a pension. You do not have to buy your pension from the same company to which you contributed. When you retire you can choose whether your husband will get a widower's pension. You can choose within limits a guaranteed rate of pension increase. If you choose either of these your own pension will start at a lower level.

Rebate only PPPs

If you are not part of a company pension scheme or part of one that is not contracted out, you can choose a PPP just to opt out of SERPS. You and your employer pay NI contributions which the DSS pays into the plan. If you are over 30 you get the government's one per cent incentive at present.

Group PPPs

These are a cross between Personal Pension Plans and Money Purchase Schemes. Your employer arranges with an insurer for a group of employees to take out pension plans under an umbrella contract. Your employer may or may not contribute to the scheme. Administration charges are lower, therefore more of your contributions can be invested to earn you benefits.

SELF-EMPLOYMENT RETIREMENT ANNUITIES

If you are self-employed then you may have started paying into an annuity before 1988, when Personal Pension Plans were introduced. Annuities are similar to PPPs, hence have the same tax advantages. You cannot start this type of scheme now. Contributions and receipts are usually higher, and it is possible to take out the money as early as the age of 50. You can take out a PPP as well, which could give you the advantages of both schemes.

Pensions for part-timers

In 1994 part-time workers won a European Court ruling that they are entitled to take part in company pension schemes if it can be shown that their exclusion amounts to sex discrimination.

Not all companies let part-time workers join their company schemes, but now more will have to do so. It can now be considered discriminatory if part-timers are excluded because most part-time workers are women. If you work part-time and can join a company pension scheme, your contributions and final benefits will be based on your part-time earnings. If you do take full-time work, then only that period will count towards full-time benefits, the rest part-time.

If your employer does not run a company scheme then you should consider a PPP. But your employer will not contribute to this if there is a company scheme available. If you go into full-time work you can increase your payments to a level appropriate to your salary.

Early retirement

You cannot take your state pension early but you can usually do so under other pension schemes.

Returning to work after a break

Many women have broken records of work because of years taken out to raise a family or look after elderly dependants. If this applies to you, you will have missed out on working years and possible promotion leading to increased salary, and so increased pension benefits.

If you can join a company scheme you will then need to pay higher contributions to achieve a worthwhile pension. You can also pay additional voluntary contributions (AVCs), which if you can afford it is a tax-efficient way of increasing your pension. You could also consider a PPP.

Maternity leave and pensions

When you receive Statutory Maternity Pay (SMP) you will receive notional NI credits. So you should still receive the basic state pension. But this will not be the case if you take a longer break from work. Most companies will treat time when you are receiving SMP as pensionable service. Some will require you to continue to make the normal payments, but as a percentage of SMP. Others will only give you credit on SMP if you return to work within the statutory time limit. Good schemes will ignore time you were absent without receiving SMP.

Other schemes treat you as a new member after SMP with the decrease in benefits that entails. This means that the period of service before a birth is not linked to your final salary.

You cannot make contributions into Personal Pension Plans if you are not receiving pay, which you will not when you take maternity leave. So this will lower your benefits. This is because when you are not earning you are not paying NI contributions. You can start paying into a personal plan when you return to work, if possible at a higher level to make up for the loss of time.

If you have less than a full record of NI contributions you can contact the DSS to find out how much it would cost you to make up the arrears. Or in a company scheme you could pay AVCs.

Some companies have provided cover for career breaks. For example, Private Patients Plan has added career-break income protection to its policies, maintaining full cover for up to 12 months. This is useful for women who want to take longer maternity leave than usual. It is resumed without health or medical questions being asked. Norwich Union Healthcare also offers income protection through its new Safeguard policy for up to 75 per cent of earnings up to £45,000 a year and 40 per cent above this.

AVCs (Added Value Contributions)

These are extra contributions you can make towards your pension if you are a member of your company pension scheme. These can increase your benefits on retirement to cover a break from work, part-time work or early retirement. Your contributions can be up to 15 per cent of your salary including your company scheme contributions. Contributions are normally collected directly from your salary by your employer.

There are also free-standing AVCs which are paid after tax at the basic rate to an insurance company or other financial institution who reclaim basic-rate tax on your behalf. If you pay a higher rate you must claim the difference on your tax form yourself.

Changing jobs

Most people change jobs at least once during their working lives. Women with Personal Pension Plans are unaffected, but those in company schemes need to be aware of complications.

If you have less than two years pensionable service then you may get a choice of having your payments refunded or taking a deferred pension. If the schemes are contracted out any refund will be reduced by an amount paid to the state in order to reinstate you in SERPS. If you get a refund then you cannot have any further benefits from the scheme in future.

If you have more than two years pensionable service your new company's scheme must offer you benefits to be retained in the scheme until you retire.

If it is a Final Salary Scheme your pension will be based on length of service and the final salary at the date you left. This may be increased to take some account of inflation until normal retirement age, depending on when you left. If you left this kind of scheme after 1 January 1986 part of your salary must be increased in lieu of deferment. If it is a Money Purchase Scheme, your contributions will remain invested from the date of leaving until retirement.

Instead of keeping the benefits from your old scheme you can have a transfer value paid to your new company's scheme or make some arrangement such as a buy-out policy or Personal Pension Plan. A transfer value will be used to buy extra pension or a number of 'added years' of pensionable service. In Money Purchase Schemes or an individual arrangement this is invested and the accumulated fund used to buy your pension.

When deciding whether to make the transfer, take into account pension increases, lump sums payable on death, widower's and children's pensions as well as the amount of initial pension offered. There are also more risks attached to PPPs than company schemes.

MATERNITY LEAVE AND ALLOWANCE

All women, even those who have just started a job, are entitled to 14 weeks maternity leave. If you have worked for your employer for two years you can take a total of 40 weeks away from your job with entitlement to return, that is 11 weeks before the birth and 29 afterwards.

Twenty-one days before you want to take maternity leave you must inform your employer in writing and state what date you intend to return. Your employer must reply by post by 49 days after the date of the expected confinement date. You must reply within 14 days or lose your right to maternity leave. You need to write to your employer again no later than 21 days before you expect to return to work to inform him or her of the exact date of your return.

Statutory Maternity Pay and Allowance

All women are entitled to at least 14 weeks' maternity leave, regardless of their length of service or hours of work. In addition, depending on your length of service, you may also be entitled to further maternity absence up to the end of the 28th week after your baby is born.

Statutory Maternity Pay (SMP) is governed by different rules. If you meet the conditions based on your length of service and average earnings, SMP is paid for up to 18 weeks. If you qualify, you get SMP at the higher rate (90 per cent of your average earnings) for the first six weeks and then at a flat rate for up to 12 weeks. If you only qualify for 14 weeks' leave you will be paid SMP for that period only. SMP is subject to tax and NI contributions.

If you have been employed for less than 41 weeks when the baby is due you will not qualify for SMP. But if you have made enough NI contributions you may be able to claim Maternity Allowance at the SMP flat rate for 18 weeks. This is not subject to tax or insurance and your employer will pay you directly. If your baby is premature the payment will start the week after the birth.

The starting date of the maternity pay period is flexible, but the core period is for 13 weeks starting the sixth week before the expected week of confinement. The remaining five weeks can be taken before or after this period or split.

If you don't qualify for any maternity payments you automatically qualify for sickness benefit. You can present your maternity certificate as evidence of inability to work and get benefit from six weeks before the birth until 14 days afterwards.

For more information about the new regulations, contact the Maternity Alliance (see Useful Addresses, p.207).

INCOME AND REDUNDANCY PROTECTION

There are two main aspects of this part of financial care. One is income protection, which includes the need to maintain cover during long illness as well as in retirement, and the other is income protection in the case of redundancy.

Income protection

In a 1993 Abbey Life survey, Families at Risk, it was discovered that women with families who do have cover have on average less than two thirds of the amount men have. On average women have cover of £41,000 compared to £68,000 for men. That means that when a woman dies or is seriously ill her family is at greater risk than if a man dies. One in three women have no personal life cover at all, compared to one in five of men. Only two per cent of women with families have enough personal life assurance to produce the average level of income required – £17,500.

Women tend to have more concerns than men about health risks. This is important when you consider that one in three people in Britain will get cancer at some stage in their lives, and at least half of those who do will survive. So you need to consider the effect of long-term illness or disability as well as death cover.

Income protection – redundancy

The effects of redundancy and long-term unemployment can be devastating, especially where the woman's income is vital to maintaining living standards in the home. It is important that women recognise the need to get cover for this possibility. Self-employed women should consider taking out their own insurance against the possibility of long periods without work.

INSURANCE PLANNING

All those in retail financial services are regulated by the Personal Investment Authority (PIA). There are two kinds of advisers on life assurance, personal pensions and unit trust products – either independent or representatives of a particular company. Both kinds should only recommend products if they are suitable to your needs.

An independent PIA adviser will usually get a commission from the company whose plan they sell you – but they act on your behalf.

PIA's rules mean that the representative recommending a product will explain to you the main features and details of costs and benefits. You will be told you have the right to change your mind before you commit yourself, and that you may lose money if investment values fall.

You will get full details of your policy in writing, details of the adviser's commissions, and with a life policy you will be told how much money you would receive if you stopped the policy within five years of starting it.

Life insurance

Eighty per cent of people interviewed in an Abbey Life survey thought that they would need a yearly sum of £10,000 or more to maintain a reasonable standard of living. The average sum quoted was £17,500. As a guide the insurance industry advises that life cover should provide a lump sum equivalent to ten times the annual income required. This should give you the same as if from a good pension.

Each month you invest a sum in your chosen insurance plan. This pays a lump sum which you can invest to provide a level of income suitable to your needs. Assurance companies assume a basic rate of interest, and tax at the basic rate. They assume that at the end of the period for which the income is required the capital will have been used up. Payments are assumed to be monthly in arrears.

Do not cash in your insurance policy if you take a career break or you will suffer severe penalties. Take advantage of your own tax allowances, such as capital gains, and your own tax relief as with Personal Equity Plans (PEPS) (see p.65).

House insurance

You should keep up your house insurance because it is a requirement of your mortgage. If you are having problems paying either your mortgage or insurance then contact your building society and discuss the problem. Building societies are not keen to repossess property, and will often agree to your paying part of the payments or the interest only until you are back on your feet.

Mortgage protection policy

You should have insurance to cover redundancy or long-term illness, so that you can get enough money to live on and pay your mortgage.

Look carefully at your mortgage agreement. A joint endowment mortgage will be difficult to deal with if you split from your partner. Unless your name is on the mortgage you won't inherit anything if your partner dies without leaving a will. If you are not married to your partner, make sure you are classed as joint tenants rather than tenants-in-common so that one can inherit if the other dies. Tenants-in-common have no rights of inheritance.

Shop around for house contents and mortgage protection insurance. Ask about extra discounts you might get, for example as a member of a Neighbourhood Watch scheme.

Car insurance

If you use your car for work as well as pleasure you will need to make sure that it is insured correctly. Consult one of the insurance brokers about car insurance. Some insurers give better deals to women drivers. For example, Norwich Union has a Lady Motoring Contract which is designed for women and recognises their better insurance risk. It provides a special range of extra features such as accident recovery and legal advice services at a specially reduced premium. Over the age of 23 the policy can relate to the policy holder and two named drivers 23 or over if female, 25 or over if male. It is designed for women who have the car registered in their name, have no serious accidents or driving offences and where the main driver is female. Of particular interest is the priority response from the RAC in the case of calls for help from women drivers. It will also pass on messages to your friends or family as you require. The policy can be extended to include breakdown recovery.

You may not need a policy especially for women, as many companies offer the same package to everyone. Insurers of company cars and general motor insurances often specify a lower age limit of 23 or 24 for female drivers (other than the car's owner) compared to 25 for men. This recognises women's safer driving record. However, only 18 per cent of company car drivers are women.

SAVINGS

Women's savings are usually at a lower level than those of men. Many are unable to save at all. Working women often have to pay for childcare and contribute to the family finances to the extent that there is little or nothing left over for them to accumulate. If possible, every working woman should have a bank or savings account in her own name so that she has some independent money. This is important not only for self-esteem but also to provide a safety net in case of emergencies or the breakdown of a relationship.

Banks and building societies all offer savers different terms and conditions. With some accounts you can take your money out on demand; with others you have to keep a certain amount in for some time before you can withdraw it without penalty. There are also schemes for regular savers.

The only way to decide which organisation and account is best for you is to ask for details at several different branches. You will need to take into account such things as bank charges and interest rates too. Ultimately a lot will depend on the ease of access to the institution you have chosen and the service offered by the staff. These may seem mundane, but it is no good choosing what seems like an excellent bank or building society and then discovering that there is no branch nearby.

All these institutions will give you advice about their own

savings plans, but if you want independent advice you should pay for it from an independent financial adviser. This is particularly important if you are lucky enough to have a substantial amount of money to invest in stocks and shares.

Savings plan

Investing a lump sum each month in a savings plan is a good way of making your money work for you. The important thing is to save regularly. You can arrange for payments to such a plan to be paid by banker's order so that you do not miss a payment.

Some plans will give you a higher rate of return, but you may have to give longer notice before withdrawing the money. Some plans can generate an income, while others will provide you with a lump sum. You can also make savings with banks and building societies simply by paying money into special accounts with higher interest than basic accounts.

Investment schemes such as TESSA or PEP may be what you need. TESSA means Tax Exempt Special Savings Account, a scheme which allows you to make regular savings without paying tax. You can only have one TESSA account and there is a limit on total savings. You will get a tax-free return as long as you don't touch the money for five years.

Another way of saving is to buy shares as part of a Personal Equity Plan. You can buy shares in unit or investment trusts this way without paying income tax, and you can invest up to a certain limit each year.

Being paid in cash in the 'black economy' will not help you in the long run because your NI may not be paid and you will have no job security. It is not a good idea to borrow money to 'tide you over'. If you are in financial difficulties ask your Citizen's Advice Bureau (CAB) (see your local telephone directory) for sensible help in budgeting and repayments. Try to pick a savings scheme to suit your situation and not what banks, building societies and financial institutions try to sell you.

Many women put their income straight into the household budget because it is an important part of maintaining basic living standards. Others may have enough to save but be unaware of the best way of doing so. Whatever the size of your savings you owe it to yourself to make the best of them – even if all you want to do with it is take a well-earned holiday!

MAKING A WILL

Many people do not think about making a will, or know the problems that are caused by not having one. If you die intestate, that is without a will, there may be serious difficulties if you leave an estate worth over £75,000. There are even more problems if you are married. If you leave a husband and children and assets of more than £150,000, and die intestate, then your dependants could be liable for inheritance tax.

If you die intestate, your husband will get all your personal effects and £125,000 (or the entire estate if this is less), plus a life interest in half of the remainder for his lifetime. The residue is shared between your children, or if any of them have died, your grandchildren. If you have no children, your husband gets your possessions plus £200,000 (or the entire estate if this is less) and shares the balance with your parents, or if they have died, relatives in a set order. If you die leaving no close relatives, your husband will inherit all your estate.

Many working women will laugh at these amounts. But if you own a house or part of one then your assets could be more considerable than you realise, even if you have little in the way of savings.

You can make a will without consulting a solicitor by using a will form, which you can buy from a stationer's. If it is correctly signed and witnessed it will be legal. If your wishes are not straightforward, however, you should ask a solicitor to draw your will up. It does not cost a great deal, and is quick to do. It is vital that your wishes for the disposal of your estate are made entirely clear. The solicitor will keep a copy of the will and give you one. You should go to a solicitor to have your will drawn up if you are not married to your partner and want to leave anything to them, or if you have children. Otherwise the intestacy rules will apply.

CHAPTER 6

Networking

WOMEN have always guided and supported each other, but without calling it networking. The woman who pops round to a new neighbour and gives advice about the best window cleaner in the area, the friend of a friend who can babysit at the last minute, the single woman who has a heart-to-heart with a distraught niece are all part of a network. The difference between men and women when it comes to supporting each other is that men have taken it into the workplace and called it networking.

Men know that a word here or a question there to the right person will be useful to them both. Now women have woken up to the fact that it is time they joined in and took their natural skill of forming networks of support into the market-place. Men are not afraid to make use of contacts to further their progress, and most jobs are still advertised by word of mouth. Women who want to get on need to network so that they can grasp opportunities in the same way.

This chapter will tell you what networking is, how to do it and how to get the best out of it. There are also a number of organisations in 'Useful Addresses', pp.208–212, which you can 'read through' to see which ones are most relevant to you.

WHAT IS NETWORKING?

Women often misunderstand the concept of networking, even those who have been doing it for years.

Networking is talking to anyone who might be useful to you in your work and who might benefit from your expertise. It is making use of your contacts as a resource for help and advice. It gives you a collective backing where you might have struggled on alone, and it also gives you a pool of experienced people at your disposal. Networking covers all kinds of mutual help, and can include such things as:

- socialising;
- making contacts;
- help with lobbying;
- advice and help with careers;
- obtaining business;
- advice about promotion prospects.

This is not necessarily a direct exchange – you help someone one day, they help you the next. It can be a circular process in which you help someone, they are then in a position to help someone else and someone else altogether helps you. The point is that there is someone to turn to for advice, and you in turn can give what help you can to others.

Networking is not confined to talking to your colleagues or opposite numbers in other related companies or businesses. Everyone you meet is a potential part of your network. Your contacts can be friends, neighbours, colleagues, boss, subordinates, fellow professionals or trade members, people you meet when you go to the shops or to the doctor, friends of friends or your children or your partner, relatives, friends of your relatives, strangers you meet when you travel – the list is endless.

Networking takes place outside the formal rules of work. Attending a formal departmental meeting and discussing changes at work with all your colleagues is contact, but everyone has the advantage of hearing what everyone else says. On the other hand, a chat in the women's loo about a new job opening in a colleague's department is networking because it takes place informally.

Should networking exclude men?

Although many women feel more comfortable contacting other women, especially if they have never met, there is no reason why someone in your network should not be male. The important thing is whether you and he can talk together in a friendly fashion and you can ask his advice. If you feel uncomfortable, threatened or patronised by a man then he is not likely to be helpful as a contact.

This formalising of the networking process is new to many women and so they often prefer to network in all-women situations. This is not only for ease of mind, but because they feel that another woman can more easily understand the particular problems that women still face in the workplace or in running their own businesses. In some ways women who work at home are off to a better start because they have to network if they are not to become isolated and out of touch.

WHY DO YOU NEED TO NETWORK?

You don't need to network. You could struggle up the career ladder without asking anyone for help or guidance – but you would be most unusual. You have heard of the PO-PO principle that declares that people who take no part in office politics get Pissed On and Passed Over? The same applies to networking.

In theory, hard work and talent get their just reward. In practise these alone are not enough. You need to let it be known that you are doing a good job, and are suitable for promotion. You need to find out quickly where jobs are created and which often go unadvertised. You also need to know what upper management is *really* looking for. Contacts can help you do this.

People who you think have attained their position by merit alone have almost certainly also sought out others from whom to ask advice and find out about appropriate job opportunities.

Is it fair?

Women with a heightened sense of fair play may be uncertain about networking because they think that it is unfair to others to obtain promotion or enhanced job prospects by this means.

But it is not unfair. In essence it is doing the research that everyone should do if they want to do well at their job. In itself it will not guarantee you a job or promotion – your own qualities and abilities have to do that for you – but it can point you to an opening and provide advice about how to tackle it.

It is also useful for other women if you get a step up. You can in turn help others, men as well as women, to make changes that they might not otherwise have been able to make.

WHY WOMEN NEED THEIR OWN NETWORKS

Traditionally women have been excluded from the networks men have taken for granted. We all know about the 'old boy' informal networks of ex-public school men, but men have also formalised their networking in several ways. First there are the gentlemen's clubs, which are still legal. Although doing business is frowned upon officially in such places, deals are still made and help is given there. Then there are organisations such as the Freemasons, which exclude women except for occasional celebrations. Sports clubs are another well-trodden networking ground for men, where women are often excluded or separated from the men. Private clubs too can legally exclude women.

Women have not had access to these traditional networks that men take for granted. Women's networking has therefore tended to be more informal, and at a social rather than business level. But this is changing as women increasingly understand the importance of contacts in business life.

WOMEN'S NETWORKS

There are two kinds of women's networks, informal and formal. Both have their uses and are not mutually exclusive – many will overlap. The important thing is to find out how you like to network and to make the most of what each kind of networking has to offer.

Informal networks

The majority are informal and based on a loose network of friends, acquaintances, colleagues, etc. Even the few 'old girl' networks of women who perhaps attended the same public school or were in the same year at college have not had the same prominence as the male equivalent. Women may well keep in touch or recognise each other enough to make contact if they need information or help. For most women, however, there has been no specific informal network they can plug into, although this is now changing.

Formal networks

In recent years a number of specific women's network groups have been created. Many formal women's networking groups have sprung up and these can add an extra strand to your overall networking. Some women will welcome an all-female grouping, others will be uncomfortable about such separation of the sexes.

It does not make good sense to exclude men from your personal network. Apart from being unfair, it is a fact that more men than women are in positions of power and can help you. However, an all-women group may make you feel able to talk more freely about problems that affect working women in particular.

Distinguish between network groups and campaigning groups. While you can network in both groups, the latter have a particular aim with which you may not agree. (See 'Useful Addresses', pp.208–212 for a list of women-only networks, and see also 'Further Reading', p.225.)

Some women's networks and groups relate to specific spheres of work such as Women in Music, Women Architects or Women in Publishing. Others are in-house groups set up by large companies to help women employees improve their chances of promotion. There are political groups such as Labour Women's Network, Emily's List, the 300 Group and Women Into Public Life. Some groups relate to unions. Then there are organisations such as the Women's Institute or the Townswomen's Guild which are general meeting places for women.

Computer networking: the Internet

There is now a new way of networking. The Internet is a world-wide informal network of computers. You gain access via a 'gateway' by joining a subscription service such as Demon. There are other similar, but less intimidating networks such as CIX and CompuServe. You can now access Internet from within CompuServe. Using these services can be expensive but will give you unrivalled access to information and individuals. Using the Internet can be complicated but there are many books to teach you how to use it. Both individuals and commercial on-line services provide women's areas and opportunities for contact and exchange of information with other women. It makes sense to use computers for such contacts, given their increasing importance to late twentieth-century society.

Going on-line

You can use your PC to communicate with other people via their PC by using a telephone line. This is called going on-line, and sending letters from screen to screen this way is called Electronic Mail or E-Mail. To go on-line you need to connect your computer to a telephone by means of a modem. You will need some communications software, and also a 'card' that fits into the PC itself. This can all be tricky to set up correctly, so you may need to ask your supplier to do it.

Once set up, you can send messages to people or extract information from data bases directly from computers and computer networks elsewhere using networks such as CompuServe. You will pay the cost of the phone time and, if downloading data (putting the data into your machine or printing it out directly) for its cost per page. Some information centres or E-Mail groups may charge you to join them as well. Faxes can be sent directly from PC to PC by E-Mail.

All this can be expensive and time-consuming, but invaluable if you need to communicate with people across large distances or have access to vast stores of information quickly.

It can be complicated to work out how to access the Internet as this informal network of computer information is known, so you will be wise to ask someone to show you how it works. Look in the many PC magazines and see if there is a PC user club in your area. Enthusiasts there may be glad to help. If you still have trouble working out how to use the Internet, try asking for help from one of the individual PC trouble-shooters who advertise. These people will come to your home if necessary and show you what to do and their fees are reasonable.

There are many new books about the Internet and reading one will show you how to find your way around. An extra piece of software called a gopher may be a useful addition to your PC. It makes finding information easier, by taking you through a series of on-screen instructions and searching out the information you want wherever it is.

The Guardian has a useful weekly section called 'On-line' every Thursday that gives help to newcomers and experts alike.

MENTOR SCHEME

The mentor scheme is closely related to networking and can be part of it. A mentor is someone in your company in a more senior position or more experienced than you who can act as a focus for discussion about ideas and ways of tackling problems. They can advise you how to approach people and your work as well as listening to what you have to say. They are there to give you support and a helping hand.

If your company does not have an official mentor scheme where someone is allotted to you to help you, then you can find your own. It should be someone you respect and who has similar values to you at work. Choose someone who is a success. Listen to their opinions but make your own judgements. The advice and help of someone who has succeeded in your field can be invaluable.

A mentor can introduce you to an already existing network and help establish you as a contact. From there you can branch out on your own to other networks.

HOW DO YOU START?

Talk to people whenever you are in a new situation. Find out what you have in common, what your differences are and how they relate to your working life. They may become a friend, remain a stranger, be of no use or help a great deal. The point is that you have made contact and that you feel able to call on them if you need to.

When you make a new contact, arrange to have lunch or a drink with them. Chatting in an informal setting gives you both a chance to get to know each other better, and to discuss matters of interest to you both without the pressures of work to curtail your conversation.

Don't be shy about letting people know what you want to achieve. If you tell enough people your words will eventually have a good chance of reaching the ears of someone who can help you. In the same way if you hear of someone's aim and you can help, do so. For networking to be effective and beneficial there must be give as well as take.

Contact with your peers

Networking with your peers is a vital source of help and advice. Try not to abuse people's generosity with their time, and make sure that you put your case objectively.

Your ability to network with colleagues will diminish rapidly if they take against you, so avoid hassling people for help. Networking can be used to effectively block someone's career as well as advance it. A dismissive word in a few ears if you have badly offended someone might be enough to stop your chances of promotion. Equally, don't ignore your colleagues to concentrate on networking with higher ranks. It makes sense to keep on good terms with all the staff.

Listening – the vital skill

Networking is not just about talking and questioning but listening. What are people really saying?

Understand how management structures, systems and operations in your company work. This can be learnt by watching and listening to the people around you as much as by talking to them.

Business cards

Men are used to carrying business cards, handing them out and receiving them. It is a quick way of getting all the details about someone or providing them with your details without holding up the conversation. You may lose the impetus and friendly atmosphere of the moment if you have forgotten your notebook and pen or have to rummage around for the back of an envelope to jot down someone's name and phone number.

If your employer does not provide you with cards, arrange to get your own printed. Business cards are not expensive and you can order some from any local printer, who will usually have a range of stock styles. Keep to standard size cards and do not use the oversized ones from machines that look like and are often used as tradesmen's cards.

Do not clutter up your card with irrelevant decoration. The cards should be printed with the words parallel to the long sides (landscape position) and should clearly show your name, business address, phone and fax numbers. Your job title should appear as well. You can personalise cards by adding your home phone number for some people, if you want to.

Always keep some business cards with you and hand them to anyone with whom you might want to keep in touch. Ask for their card in return and as soon as possible afterwards annotate the back with the date and situation in which you met the person and anything memorable or useful about the meeting. Otherwise it is easy to end up with a pile of cards from vaguely remembered meetings, making it difficult to contact people again.

GATHERING INFORMATION

Francis Bacon said, 'For knowledge itself is power'. The way to succeed is to gather as much useful information as possible and to extract the most meaningful nuggets. Networking is a way of obtaining this information. But if your circle of contacts is limited then you can obtain information from other sources. You can also use these sources to get in touch with new people and to give them a chance to get in touch with you. Some of these sources are:

- *distribution lists* for organisations that interest you or which will be useful;
- *your company's magazine/newsletter/leaflets* to keep you in touch with other parts of the organisation;

- *departmental newsletters/reports* – and not just from your own department;
- *the firm's annual report* and reports from other related companies. These are useful for the names of executives you may want to contact as well as for information about the direction other companies are going in.
- *membership of groups.* As well as being a member of your own professional or trade organisation, consider joining related organisations.

Using these information ideas

Read the magazines, lists, and so on, to discover new contacts – these might be people mentioned in articles, or the authors of articles themselves, who could be helpful to you. Letter writers are another good source of information.

Try writing articles for your professional and company magazines and newsletters, and write letters too, and offer your name as an expert on your areas of the company. If you feel you don't have the writing skills necessary for articles, then write letters commenting on other people's work. Comment on articles in the magazines and offer your own views. This is one way of getting your name noticed throughout the company and by rival and related organisations.

When you join a group try to take an active role – you could contribute in many ways. Take your work and hobby expertise into the group – perhaps you can offer help with accounting, publicity or social organisation? If you find that it is difficult to penetrate a cliquey atmosphere, offer to do the most hated job (there is always one!) or tactfully offer to help someone already doing a job.

Getting onto the committee of any useful organisation is important if the opportunity occurs. It boosts your visibility, shows your commitment and makes you visible and available as a contact. The press may contact you too as an expert representing the organisation. This again will boost your image and give you a face as a contact. If it is a formal group try to take some administrative role or contribute in other ways.

Events such as conferences and exhibitions, courses or social occasions can be very important for making new contacts. Networking can take place at breaks or over a meal.

Don't overdo it

Don't be obvious about 'grabbing' new contacts. If your eyes are constantly wandering and you are not listening to people you are supposed to be talking to you could lose as many useful contacts as you gain. If you are genuinely interested in people you will find that contacts come naturally – and people will take you more seriously.

Networking can demonstrate loyalty and usefulness to your company. You gain by:

- helping others and letting them help you;
- sharing information, ideas and problems;
- helping your thought processes adapt;
- helping you get your message across in the workplace in an objective and tactful way;
- helping you practise points you want to put over to other relevant people;
- developing more confidence;
- widening your horizons.

START YOUR OWN NETWORK

You may find that in your work and local community you have enough contacts, but you can also make a decision to start your own network group. You only need a few friends with a similar aim to create an effective informal group.

You can influence people, but you need to network to do so. Take a lot of trouble with genuinely friendly contacts. Time after work spent on a drink, a chat or a meal can be well spent. A group of you can influence policy more effectively than one person alone.

OTHER NETWORKING OPPORTUNITIES

If you are offered the chance to be an assistant to a more senior manager for a period, do take it. You can learn more about the job you aspire to and take the opportunity to network at a higher level.

Secondment is also a way of extending contact in related industries. In spite of what some people think, employers see employees who take secondment as an asset to the company because they return with new ideas, work practices and networking contacts.

TRY NOT TO BE SHY!

Don't be nervous about making the first move to get to know someone. Most people are only too pleased to find someone with whom they might have something in common. Contact means just that: get in touch.

CHAPTER 7

Childcare Choices

IF YOU ARE a working mother you have difficult choices to make. Do you work from home? Do you hand over childcare to somebody else? Do you work part- or full-time? What happens when the children are ill or there is a school sports day? Whatever your reason for working, there is no need to feel guilty – your choice is the right choice for you and your children.

Even among the best equal opportunities employers women are still expected to look after the families. The Automobile Association allows paternity leave of five days, but only if the dates are agreed by prior arrangement with the appropriate manager. Even where facilities for childcare at home are offered, it is the women who make the overwhelming number of enquiries even if the workforce is predominantly male. The British government in 1994 vetoed an EU proposal to give men three months statutory paternity leave. The expectation still seems to be that British fathers should pay for their children, not care for them.

Some men use the excuse that they work late and in managerial positions need to socialise in the evenings. This makes no concession to the fact that women in equally demanding work may need free evenings too.

There are many practical problems. Without adequate and afford-able childcare facilities many women are in the trap of remaining financially desperate or risking their child's well-being by leaving them with inappropriate carers in order to earn more money.

Looking for childcare causes problems whatever the ages of the children. State provision for the under-fives is still woefully inade-quate, and so is before- and after-school care for older children. Voluntary or private concerns provide much of our under-five care.

WHAT ARE THE CHOICES?

Childcare choices facing a working mother are care by relatives;

78

care by friends; registered child-minder; council day-nursery; private day-nursery; voluntary nursery; community and partnership nursery; nanny; au-pair; nursery class; nursery school; primary school; nursery/primary school with pre- and/or after-school care; playgroup; parent or toddler group; workplace nursery; latch-key kids; part-time work; job-share; house 'husband'; mother's help; babysitter; maternity nurse; or a combination of more than one of these.

RELATIVES

Many women live too far from relatives to ask them for help. For those who do have willing and able family nearby the advantage is that the children are with people who are close to them and whom the mother knows and trusts. The disadvantage is that the children can put great strain on the relatives, particularly grandparents. There can also be conflict if the parents' ideas of discipline and theirs do not agree. A wider family support group willing and able to help with childcare can provide one way round the problem.

FRIENDS

Friends can and do help with childcare on occasion, but you have to be on very good terms and to come to a clear understanding about what it will entail.

Parents of young children can look after them for half a day or take and collect them from school. Parents of older children often arrange to share car travel and after-school care on a reciprocal basis – taking your turn at the traditional 'school run' is very common. Others share walking the children to and from school or providing tea afterwards.

This can only work if the job you do allows you time to do your share. If one of you is not working then the arrangement can become one-sided. However, the care is free and the children usually have others of their own age to play with.

REGISTERED CHILDMINDERS

A registered childminder is a person not related to her charges who cares for them more than two hours a day for payment. She must register with her local Social Services Department, and must be over 18 and under 55. There are strict rules she must comply with about the condition and safety provisions on her property. Once registered she may care for two or more children up to seven in number.

How to find a registered childminder

Start looking for a registered childminder before your baby is born. You can obtain a list of childminders and their vacancies from your local Social Services Department.

Most registered childminders also belong to the National Childminding Association (NCA) (see 'Useful Addresses', p.213). This has 34,000 members, who care for a quarter of a million children in the childminders' homes. An offshoot of the NCA is Childminding In Business! which is a consultancy for employers. Childminders usually use the NCA's standard form of contract that will set out the terms and conditions for the childcare and allow both to agree on matters such as discipline and holiday arrangements. Visit a prospective childminder more than once, with your child, and remember to take up her references.

Unregistered childminders

Unregistered childminding is illegal, and you should not use an unregistered minder. The motherly woman down the road who will look after your children for an affordable price may satisfy you, but might not pass muster with the local authority if she applied for registration. Without registration there are no safeguards for your child's well-being.

LOCAL AUTHORITY PROVISION

Under section 18 of the Children's Act of 1989, local authorities *must* provide appropriate day care for under-fives 'in need' and *may* provide it for under-fives not in need. The problem is that the term 'in need' was not defined, and so provision varies widely. Provision includes a number of schemes, some provided by the council and some voluntary, such as holiday play-schemes and nurseries.

Local authority day nurseries

Local authorities fund these directly and parents pay lower fees because of council subsidy. Children of single parents or who qualify in other ways as being 'in need' have priority. It is rare for children from two-parent families to get a place.

The age range is usually nine months to five years, and the nurseries are open from 8am to 6pm. The local Social Services Department of the local authority supervises these nurseries and there is usually a long waiting list

Community and partnership nurseries

These operate in a similar way to local authority day nurseries except that they are set up and run by the community. The local authority helps by giving a grant. In return it expects the nursery to set aside a proportion of places for children 'in need'. Organisers can charge lower fees, but the grant cannot subsidise these, and so this type of nursery must arrange for other sources of funding. Fund-raising activities are important to maintain the nursery and to keep fees low.

Local authority nursery schools and classes

Local authorities provide either nursery schools that operate separately from primary schools or nursery classes attached to primary schools. Provision is uneven between authorities and within individual authorities. Places are highly sought after, and it is not yet the case that all three- to five-year olds can get a place.

Children can enter a nursery class or school from the age of three, if there is space, and stay until the age of five when they transfer to primary school. Most nurseries will give priority to a second child from one family.

Nursery classes and schools are staffed by nursery teachers and nursery nurses. Schools usually admit children from a surrounding catchment area, and priority for a certain proportion of places is given to children 'in need'.

Many nursery schools and classes operate a half-day session for all children or for part of a child's time in the class. These sessions are usually from 9am to 11.30am or from 1.00pm to 3.30pm. Sometimes a school or class will operate a part-time week where a child will attend for a combination of full and half-days.

Although nursery education is important for a child's educational progress, the provision for this is still poor. In practice many children do not get a place in a nursery class or school until the age of four and then perhaps for only a part-time place. In practical terms it may not help a working mother who needs full-time provision for her child.

PARENTS' CLUBS

Parents sometimes organise their own schemes during the holidays, where they take it in turns to organise a group activity for the children of other parents as well as their own for a small fee. This can be successful, but you must be able to take your turn at providing a day's activity.

Holiday play-schemes

Many local authorities have well-established holiday play-schemes. They provide premises for five days a week during the holidays where children can play and take part in organised sport or social activities. Volunteers, usually qualified play leaders, run these schemes. You can find them by asking at your library, primary school, council leisure section or by looking for ads in the local papers.

Commercial holiday schemes

Commercial holiday schemes charge parents, and can be expensive. Children take part in sports, computer lessons and social activities. These schemes often use school premises, usually providing transport to and from the centre and operating a longer day. Some open on a daily basis, some weekly and some let the children board.

Pre- and after-school care

Some authorities let schools look after children before and after the normal school day. Parents drop their children off to school on the way to work. Qualified leaders, not teachers, look after the children. They give them a basic breakfast and keep them occupied until the start of the school day. After school the leaders look after the children again until they are collected.

Volunteers sometimes give children the same provision in other premises such as a church hall. In that case parents drop and collect the children at the care premises and the leaders arrange to escort the children to and from school.

After-school activities

Some schools run after-school activity sessions for their pupils, and perhaps homework or hobby clubs for older pupils. This can be useful for a working mother who needs to make sure that her child receives care until the end of her working day, but who can arrange for someone to take the child to school.

WORKPLACE NURSERIES

The ideal choice for working mothers with jobs outside the home is a workplace nursery that takes children from babies upwards. Unfortunately, although the government encourages this in principle, it has not given the financial help that would encourage all companies to provide workplace nurseries.

Some large organisations – such as parts of the civil service and the Midland Bank – do provide workplace nurseries. Either the company pays for the nurseries and asks for a subsidised contribution from the parent or they are run by outside agencies.

Workplace nursery places are coveted where they do exist. They usually take children from a very young age, often from birth, to five years. The ratio of carer to child is high, with one adult to three babies or one adult to five toddlers. The mother or father has the security of being able to visit the child during breaks, knowing that if there is a problem nursery staff can call her or him at once.

Childcare Vouchers

There is a subsidiary of the Luncheon Voucher scheme called Childcare Vouchers. This lets employers help parents finance childcare at either a workplace nursery or another agreed form of childcare acceptable to the scheme. The parent chooses the childcare. The carer, who must be registered legally with the local authority, then signs an agreement with Childcare Vouchers. The parent and carer sign the vouchers, which are then returned to Childcare Vouchers for payment.

The advantage of this scheme is that although the employer can use the vouchers to subsidise childcare the mother can choose the form of childcare that suits her family best, as long as the carer is registered with the scheme. Until all companies provide workplace nurseries it is worth asking your company to join this scheme.

PRIVATE DAY NURSERIES

Private day nurseries have qualified staff in the statutory staff to child ratios. They usually take children from birth to five years and must be registered with the Social Services Department of the local authority. The disadvantage is that most of them are much more expensive than subsidised state or workplace nurseries. Again it is children with a special need for a place who get first priority.

VOLUNTARY NURSERIES

These are day nurseries entirely run by volunteers. They rely on donations and fund-raising activities to pay for equipment and premises, but do not pay staff.

PLAYGROUPS

These are either private or run by volunteer parents. Organisers can if they wish choose to join the Pre-School Playgroups Association. Each playgroup has a playleader who may have taken a playleaders' training course. The sessions are usually two-and-a-half hours in length, with a session each morning and each afternoon. A child can attend for up to five sessions each week.

The cost to parents is a small fee for providing drink and biscuits for the children and, in many groups, a commitment to help one session a week or month. Playgroups can be very useful for mothers who work part-time and/or whose children are waiting for a place in a nursery class. They are, however, very often open only during school term-time.

PARENT AND TODDLER GROUPS

These are voluntary non-profit making groups where mothers, fathers, carers and guardians can get together to enjoy each others' company while their children play together. The parent or carer must stay with the child. These sometimes take place in schools or church halls or similar places. Clearly these groups are not geared towards parents who work outside the home, although they will serve a purpose for those who work part-time.

NANNY

Today many working women use nannies as their main form of childcare, and not only those women in well-paid executive jobs. Some women have a daily nanny, some have a live-in nanny and others share a nanny with other working mothers.

What is a nanny?

A nanny is an independent employee who, being in demand, can state her own conditions. She will wash, clean, iron and shop but only for the children she cares for. Likewise she will clean up after her charges, but not after you. A nanny will take the children to and from school, and will also expect to take them to and from social events and to arrange the children's social life during the day.

If your nanny lives in she will expect to have her own room, a colour TV, her own bathroom – or a bathroom shared only with the children – and the use of a car. Explain her duties carefully and be fully in agreement about what time she will have off. A nanny will probably have her own contract for you to sign. Norland nannies, for example, have a standard contract produced by the Norland agency.

Many of the more expensive nannies now live out and will work for you from 8am or 8.30am to 6.30pm. If the nanny lives in then the hours are likely to be 7am to 7pm. You must agree beforehand who will get up if the children need someone in the middle of the night.

Your nanny may agree to work for a friend on a shared basis as long as the homes are close, the children are virtually the same age, there will be no increase in hours worked and you and your friend pay the appropriate wage between you.

Some nannies find this acceptable, others may feel that they wish to concentrate on one family only. In any case, don't assume that your nanny will help out with a friend's children just because you think your nanny has time to spare.

Where to get a nanny

You can get a nanny by advertising in papers or magazines, such as *The Lady* and *Nursery World*. Or use one of the agencies that supply nannies, although the disadvantage with an agency is that you will have to pay them a fee for placing the nanny with you, and then pay the nanny.

The advantage of an agency is that if there is a clash of personalities it can replace the nanny or iron out the problems. It can also provide emergency cover. Nanny agencies must be licensed by the Employment Agency Licensing Office, which is part of the Department for Education and Employment.

How to find a good nanny

A nanny from an agency will be a safe bet. You can ask if she trained at one of the well-known nanny colleges, such as Norland. Ask for references which she will have from her college if she has passed the National Nursery Examination Board (NNEB) tests. Otherwise ask for references from previous employers, and do follow them up with a phone call. In return you should give your nanny the names and phone numbers of your previous nannies, if you have had any, so that she can check you.

MATERNITY NURSE

A maternity nurse will come to you for the weeks after the birth and will stay from four to six weeks, and no longer than three months. Her job is to look after newborn babies, and she will not take on the care of older children. She will look after your baby for 24 hours a day six days a week during that time.

Such a person is expensive but could prove worth the investment if you simply must get back to work immediately after the birth, or need extra help during that time. Qualifications for maternity nurses vary between agencies, and again you can advertise for one through *The Lady* or *Nursery World* or look for one in the *Yellow Pages*.

AU PAIR

Au pairs are a popular way of obtaining help around the house. Au-pairing is an arrangement under which an unmarried person aged 17–27 inclusive, and without dependants, may come to the United Kingdom to learn English and to live for a time as a member of an English-speaking family. They must be a national of a western European country or other country specified by the Immigration Office, which can provide a list of permitted countries. The employer has an obligation to an au pair to allow the person to live as part of the family, and to allow them to study English at a college.

What do au pairs do?

An au pair will work for you for five hours a day or 30 hours per week. He or she will do light housework and care for the children. In return they will expect to have their own room, time off to study English and some pocket money (not a wage). As this pocket money may seem very little to them, especially if they come from well-off families, you should carefully explain how the accommodation, food, laundry etc, that you provide counts financially as part of their pay. Find an English Language School as close as possible to your home and let him or her know beforehand how much the fees will be.

Regulations

Non-European au-pairs must register with the police if they will be staying for more than six months. EU nationals must apply for a residency permit if they stay for over six months.

You need to give your prospective au pair a letter of invitation from you stating what duties he or she will be expected to carry out, what free time they will get and what pocket money they will get. The au pair must, of course, have a valid passport.

Problems with au pairs

Taking an au pair is the luck of the draw. You may get an efficient worker who gets on well with your children, or someone who has never done any cleaning before and cannot use a washing machine. It makes sense to sit down right at the beginning and explain their duties carefully, and let them know how you like things done. Organise a written timetable so that there is no mistaking what you meant. Problems are most likely to arise if what you expect of them is not made clear from the start. Bear in mind too that they may be homesick, and encourage them to keep in regular contact with their family – without making your phone bill exorbitant! Let the au pair know how and when you would like them to join you for meals. If you want them to do babysitting, then you must let them know well in advance so that time off can be rearranged.

Meet them when they arrive and let them phone home to reassure their parents. Introduce them to some other au pairs locally, but do not expect that they will necessarily get on with them – they are more likely to meet friends at college. Do include them in some family outings, not only to make them feel at home but also to give them a chance to see something of the UK.

MOTHER'S HELP

This is a British person who is a live-in help but who is not a trained nanny. They will be over 17 and employed to help with the children and domestic chores. If they are non-commonwealth members they will need a work permit.

It is easy to exploit such young and untrained help, but it is not good either for them or the children. Neither is it possible to expect the same standards of care as a nanny would give. It is unlikely, for example, that a mother's help would have sole charge of your children every day while you go out to work. Having a mother's help works best if you work from home. To find one, advertise locally.

HOUSE 'HUSBAND'

You may be lucky enough to have a partner who is willing and able to stay at home to look after the children while you work. This can be a very good solution, but only if you are both fully aware of the drawbacks it may entail. If your partner works from home this arrangement will only succeed if the children are elsewhere for a large part of the day.

You should be clear about who is going to do the chores and cook the meals and when. You are going to feel resentful if you come home from work and find that you still have to do all the housework and cook the dinner. Your partner may need home help as much as you would have done.

Some partners relish the chance to spend more time with their children, but many find that the natural networks that mothers use such as toddlers' clubs or playgroups are off-putting for men. These groups may be non-sexist in theory, but still make men feel like outsiders. Partners may also find themselves teased by other men. If your partner is a woman this may be less of a problem, however unfair this is.

Do resist the urge to criticise the way your partner does things – folding the sheets differently or leaving dust behind the clock is hardly vital. You will need to agree on such things as discipline and treats, however, so that the children cannot play off one partner against the other.

If both of you can work part-time and share the chores and childcare this can be an ideal solution.

JOB-SHARE

One couple I know successfully arranged a job-share between them at their place of work. This worked very well, except that they found they were both doing more than their half-week and it became very difficult to leave work behind when they got home. Employers sometimes expect job-sharers, whether domestic partners or not, to do more than their fair share.

For a job-share like this to work you must agree strict hours with your employer, assuming the employer is willing, and agree who gets the wages. This couple had to negotiate very hard before their employer finally agreed that husband and wife should receive their pay separately. This can be very important for the esteem of both partners. Although this kind of arrangement is very unusual, one of you may find a job-share that at least enables that partner to work part-time, thus cutting down on childcare costs.

BABYSITTER

There is no legal minimum age for a babysitter but if an accident happens to anyone in your home while the babysitter is under 14 then you will be held responsible. In any case, few young people under 14 are responsible enough to look after small children. The Children and Young Person's Act advises that babysitters in charge of young people in your home should be 16 or over. In Scotland it is illegal for under 16s to babysit.

Use someone you know or whom a friend personally recommends. Pay them the local going-rate per hour. Make sure there is a full list of emergency numbers by the phone and that they always have your phone number.

Your expectations of a babysitter should be no more than that they will keep the children safe and content until you come home.

Provide transport to and from your house if your babysitter needs it. No youngster should travel home late at night on their own, so arrange to give them a lift in your car or another form of safe transport. If you are out after midnight then you should expect to pay more.

Babysitting circle

A variation on the babysitting scheme is the babysitting circle. Everyone in the group starts off with a certain number of points which they can then accumulate or use as payment for baby-sitting services. This is fine except that couples sometimes find that in order to accumulate enough points to go out they are babysitting too often. Some people also babysit but rarely go out themselves, so upsetting the balance of the circle.

An informal method is to get together with another family and arrange to babysit for each other on alternate weeks. This means you can definitely go out once a fortnight, with any extra babysitting needed being up to you. No payment or tokens change hands. I used this arrangement for many years with good friends and it worked very well. It came to a natural end once both sets of children were old enough not to need a sitter.

LATCH-KEY KIDS

Most parents do not wish their young children to become latch-key kids, children who take their door key to school, make their own way home, let themselves into the house and make their own meal while waiting for their parent to return from work.

There are many dangers: children can wander the streets for hours; they may be abducted while wandering the streets; they may have an accident if unsupervised in the home; a stranger may gain access to the house and harm them. Only once a child reaches secondary school age is it reasonable to expect them to be able to cope. Parents do occasionally have to let young children do this, but it is dangerous and unsatisfactory.

If there is no childcare available locally try asking a neighbour if they would be willing to take your child in until you return. At the very least the child should have your phone number for emergencies, and you should phone as soon as you expect them to return home so that they feel obliged to return straightaway.

The police or Social Services will certainly take an interest if your child seems in distress and they are alerted to the fact that they are in the house alone.

COMBINATION TACTICS

In practice most working mothers use a combination of the above childcare options whether together or one after another depending on the children's age and need and their own work situation. The juggling that has to go on is preferable to the anguish parents feel if they are worried about their children in their absence.

It makes sense, whatever you decide to do, to take these sensible basic precautions and provide your carer with:

- the child's medical history and doctor's number;
- any special medication;
- work and home phone number of yourself and partner;
- school's phone number;
- phone number of a friend or neighbour who has agreed to take the child in an emergency;
- list of food likes and dislikes;
- favourite book, toy, music or video;
- expressed or bottled milk (for baby);
- spare clothes.

CHILDCARE FOR CHILDREN WITH SPECIAL NEEDS

For a working mother with a child who has special needs and cannot be left with an ordinary carer there are further problems. It is more difficult to find childcare, because not only does the carer have to be specially qualified and perhaps willing to work harder, but there is not enough specialist care around. Unless you can get voluntary help the costs too may be more than you bargained for.

There are nannies or trained nurses who will work with special needs children as well as local authority specialist minders. You can advertise for such help in the *Nursing Times*, *Nursery World* or *The Lady*. State Enrolled Nurses (SENs) may be available to give you paid childcare.

There are voluntary organisations, charities and self-help groups who will help you to find the appropriate carer for your needs. One such agency is the Council for the Disabled (see 'Useful Addresses', p.213). The DSS provides leaflets about allowances to help care for disabled children.

People who work with children with special needs should themselves have support. The Special Care Agency (see 'Useful Addresses', p.214) supports nannies who work with handicapped children and will recommend nannies willing to work with children with special needs. Societies for children with particular disabilities will also give help and advice.

CHAPTER 8

Image

IT MAKES GOOD SENSE to think about your image in the world of work. Your image will decide how high you go in your job, whether you receive the rewards you deserve and the amount of respect others give you. It will also affect how other people view the importance of the job you do. This chapter will explain what image is and how you can change it to your best advantage.

WHAT IS IMAGE?

Image is not just the way you dress. It is the perception people have of you and consists of the total picture you present to the world. Other people will form their opinion of you from a number of different facets of you as a whole person – your looks, speech, dress, actions, skills, attitudes, posture, body language, accessories, surroundings and even the company you keep.

If you present the wrong image in any one of these areas it could affect your promotion prospects or how keen people are to do business with you.

Of course, you don't just have one image which you present to everyone regardless of who they are or in what situation you find yourself. You will not behave or dress in the same way for your boss or customers in a formal business situation as you would relaxing at home with your family. These images are simply different aspects of your own personality, however, which you can adapt depending on the circumstances.

This is not as confusing as it sounds. Once you have worked out what your image is, then you can adapt it accordingly. You will not need to become Jekyll or Hyde – just yourself.

HOW IMPORTANT IS YOUR IMAGE?

In most jobs probably 50 per cent of your work will be concerned with image. You will need to project yourself to your boss, colleagues, subordinates, customers, the general public, prospective clients and perhaps shareholders and advertisers as well as the people in related or supporting trades or professions.

Each of these groups of people will make a judgement about you, and that judgement will reflect on your work and your organisation. If your image is acceptable then you as an individual will be regarded with respect and therefore so will the work you do. That in turn will reflect on the organisation you work for or the business you run. A well-perceived business will prosper and lead to increased prospects for you within it.

Self-promotion

You are therefore in the business of self-promotion, with all the rewards that can accrue to you and your work if you are perceived to have a good image.

Some large organisations have already realised the rewards of cultivating and enhancing the images of individuals within their companies. Many use individuals from the workforce instead of actors to appear in their television commercials for just that reason. Midland Bank and Abbey National are two organisations which have done so.

DOES YOUR IMAGE NEED CHANGING?

Look long and hard at your image, and decide whether you need to change it. In some companies you will have a yardstick to go by because there will be a definite company ethos; this will be explicitly stated and laid down through rules for dress and behaviour which you will need to adhere to. Others have an equally defined ethos which is not specifically laid down but which is maintained by group conformity. Yet other businesses will leave personal image up to the individual.

Being your own boss

Women who work at home or who run their own businesses are not as free as they might think to project any image they like. While they can, if they wish, dress and behave how they like, particularly in the privacy of their homes, they do have to deal with customers either face-to-face or on the phone.

If you go out to meet customers or they come to you then you will need to conform to their expectations of you, depending on what your business is. You are more likely to gain the confidence of your customers if you look capable of doing your job well. People will generally expect an accountant to dress soberly and formally, for example, but may be disappointed if a designer does not dress flamboyantly. A saleswoman would impress by dressing neatly, but customers might be suspicious of a landscape gardener who does not wear boots on a muddy site.

Dressing to expectations does not mean that you should abandon the good manners of ensuring your clothes are clean and tidy.

DECIDE ON YOUR IMAGE

Before you do anything else, make sure that you are not a square peg in a round hole. If you are desperately shy are you happy trying to sell things? If you are outgoing are you unhappy stuck in a back-room by yourself?

If you are in the wrong job then your first move should be to find somewhere more appropriate for your personality, which will make better use of your image. But if you are going to stay in your present job, then there are ways of making sure that your image is the right one not only for the job but for the company.

You can change your image by improving your good points and playing down or changing your bad points. If you have a good speaking voice you can take part in seminars and discussions which will give you a chance to show it off. If, on the other hand, you are inclined to mumble then you can tape yourself speaking into a tape recorder and practise until you have learnt to speak clearly.

Take some time to decide what kind of person you are, and then adapt this to the general image expected of you at work. If you are naturally flamboyant and extrovert but are expected to behave and dress in a formal way, then you cannot turn up in loud shirts and be exuberant all the time. But you could perhaps indulge in a passion for unusual jewellery, and tell a few jokes at appropriate times.

If you are used to formal dressing and are shy, but your organisation expects you to spend a lot of time talking to customers and to wear bright clothes, then you can choose a classically cut outfit. Ensure that what you do say is clear, and cultivate the neglected art of listening.

Image objectives

You should have certain objectives for your image.

1. You should be clean with neat nails and an updated neat haircut.
2. You should keep your clothes in good repair and regularly cleaned.
3. Buy a few decent sets of clothes for quality and one or two good accessories.
4. Use accessories to keep up to date.
5. Improve your diet.
6. Keep yourself fit and healthy.
7. Keep abreast of the news.
8. Keep an eye open for trends in your organisation.
9. Update your 'image extras' (see p.97).
10. Take part in talks and other group activities where you can meet other workers.
11. Meet the public.
12. Take part in a community activity.
13. Learn new skills.

IMAGE AND DRESS

Although dress is not the only part of your image it is very important. However unfair it may seem, most people are going to make a judgement about you within the first three minutes of meeting you. They will make that judgement largely on your looks – your physical attributes and your clothes. It is therefore important that you do not confuse people by giving off conflicting images.

Expectations

Everyone has expectations of how they expect other people to look. Bankers and accountants are supposed to wear suits and creative designers to wear something more outrageous. However outmoded these ideas may seem, these expectations remain fairly fixed.

This pressure of expectation is what forces many women to adapt the suit-and-tie work image in many jobs. If a woman works in a business dominated by men in dark suits, then the expectations of the company and the public force her into the same role.

Women often find it difficult to act their rank. When a certain position is reached, the holder of an office is expected to precede subordinates through doors, for example. Women find it difficult to stride ahead and assert their rank, but if they don't then their colleagues become confused because they expect high ranks to take precedence.

To conform or not?

You have the choice of conforming to the men's style or being distinctive. You can adopt elements of men's fashion – perhaps by wearing a white shirt but in a looser style and coupling it with a loosely knotted scarf as a tie. Or you can be blatantly feminine and wear dresses and skirts in brighter colours.

Dressing too informally, except in certain creative professions, will mean that you project an image of not taking your work seriously. Both men and other women will subconsciously downgrade you. This does not mean that you should always wear a suit, but it does mean that you should be wary about wearing a mini skirt and high heels!

In most jobs men wear much the same thing every day, often a suit, shirt and tie. Women who do not want to follow the same trend have a more difficult problem simply because they have a much wider choice of garments. But there is a simple answer to the problem – a jacket. Whatever you are wearing, a jacket worn over it will give you a more formal look when appropriate.

If your superiors wear grey suits and flashy watches you could tone down your clothes and buy a decent watch, so that you look promotable. You don't need to follow fashion slavishly, but a good haircut and up-to-date accessory can update your image overnight.

Office policies

Be careful of office policies. If you decide to go out on a limb in terms of looks and behaviour then you are likely to be regarded as unsuitable for the company rather than a loveable eccentric. You need to decide whether more subtle nonconformity would be wiser.

IMAGE AND BEHAVIOUR

Image is not just a matter of dress. It is how you behave and how you react to other people. Whatever your work involves, there are some rules for image building which are applicable to all.

1. Adapt yourself to the situation. People react better to the familiar, they will respond better to you if they can relate to something about your looks and behaviour. It could be as simple as both being formally dressed in suits, or the fact that you wear similar watches. If you go into a meeting and everyone is in shirt-sleeves (or the men are!) then you can make yourself look more casual by taking off that indispensable jacket. If the meeting is run strictly then conform, or if everyone chips in in a casual way then do the same.

2. *Stress points of contact not differences.* Perhaps you both have small children, or perhaps you both enjoy working out in the company gym. Anything that brings you together as people will improve your image in the other person's eyes. Stressing differences will drive you apart. People like to be with positive people.

3. *Don't hide your disagreements.* If, however, you know that there are certain business disagreements between you, do not try to hide them. Mention the differences so that they are out in the open. By making sure that everyone is aware of the obvious you are eliminating the chance of resentment building up.

4. *Live up to people's expectations.* This is an important part of your image. If you are expected to start the discussions at the regular team meetings, do so. If you are expected to look like everyone's idea of a manager, then do so. (The only thing you should not do is make the tea if everyone expects a woman to do so, unless you are the tea lady.)

'IMAGE EXTRAS'

Women do not take seriously enough the image extras that men take for granted. What men do without thinking to improve their image, women have to learn to think about. For example, do you use your business cards effectively (do you even have any?) or do you write letters to the papers?

Think about the following:

- *Letters.* Do you use a ball-point or fountain pen, sign your full name or first name only? Letters signed in ink with your full name will give a more formal image than your first name written in ball-point pen.
- *Telephone manner.* Do you speak clearly? Do you always give your name and department? Do you always keep your temper? Telephone contact may be the only indication of you and your company somebody gets. Be polite and speak clearly. Be honest about your ability to help, and pass the

caller to someone more useful if necessary. Don't get angry with complainers – listen and find constructive suggestions to make. Anger on your part will be remembered – your image is hard-won and easily lost.

- *Office machines.* Have you got your own personalised fax sheet? Is your answering machine message clear and helpful? These may be the only indications of your image other people get. Make sure that they are clear, and not flashy.
- *Free time.* Do you do something to improve your health, or only related to your work, or make time for your family? You need a life outside work not only to relax and revive you but to make you a more interesting and lively person.
- *News.* Do you regularly read a daily broadsheet and a Sunday heavyweight paper? Do you read your trade or professional magazines and journals? You need to keep up with the latest ideas even if you do not agree with them. You also need to be able to make general conversation intelligently when socialising in the course of your work.
- *Writing articles or reviews on your specialism or hobby.* This is a good way of making your expertise known without blowing your own trumpet.
- *Contributing to a department newsletter.* The more you are known in your department as a person with ideas, the more likely you are to be remembered when jobs come up.
- *Writing letters to or articles for the house journal.* This will ensure that you are known throughout the company, not just to your immediate colleagues.
- *Keeping cuttings of any published work.* These can be used to help you get other work published, act as an introduction to editors and impress prospective customers and employers.
- *Well designed business cards.* Do you carry them at all times and hand them out when appropriate? Cards act as a useful reminder of you to people who may be too busy to recall you otherwise.
- *Networking.* Do you make the best use of personal contacts? (see Chapter Six.) It is no good cultivating your image if you don't meet other people on whom to impress it.
- *Social life at work.* This is not only enjoyable but brings you into contact with members of the company from all departments and ranks. If the director remembers your skill in playing the piano for the staff concert for example, he will have a good impression of you.
- *Volunteer to give talks or go to conferences.* Skill at public speaking can be learnt and the more you put it into practice the more you will be remembered.

Any and all of the above can enhance your image both within your workplace and when you are out meeting customers and others from your profession.

MEETING THE CUSTOMERS

Your image will be of little practical value to you unless you meet customers and prospective customers. They are the people who will be keeping the business going with their custom and who can improve your work chances.

Your image can make or break a company. How often have you encountered a sulky receptionist, for example, and thought 'I don't want to go there again', or met a helpful and pleasant salesperson and come away feeling that you enjoyed the experience?

If you project a good image to your customers word will get back that clients like meeting you. If you are particularly good at this then there may be opportunities for you to talk to the press on behalf of the company, or take part in company advertising.

There are many ways to meet the public. These include: giving talks to organisations, schools, clubs; showing visitors around the workplace; meeting VIPs who visit the company; attending presentations; attending trade fairs; taking part in local social events, charities or sports and selling to clients. Make the most of opportunities to meet the public.

Community action

One way to improve your image with the public is to take part in some local organisation – a sports club, church, charity, or club for example. There is no point in doing this cynically, however. If you do not care about what you are doing it will soon show, and do you and your company no good. But to be a person who joins in and gets things done reflects well on you and your work.

Meeting colleagues

Joining your trade or professional association will give you a chance to meet other people in the same line of work by attending meetings, conferences, seminars, lunches and talks as well as trade fairs and similar events. (See Chapter Six, 'Networking', pp.67–77, for more on this subject.)

Spotting trends

If your knowledge of your subject is outdated and you are not aware of what the company is looking for then your image will be held back by the perception of you as not moving with the times.

Speaking skills

Good communication skills improve an image and make work easier. If you do not have these skills to the necessary extent (you may be good at writing reports, but hopeless at public speaking) do not give up. These skills can be learnt if you apply yourself.

If your company provides courses on various aspects of work skills such as public speaking then go along to them. Or else practise yourself at home with a partner or a tape recorder.

Communication skills are very important so practise your own by talking to as many different people as possible.

Listening carefully is as important as saying a friendly 'Good morning'. Your image will do well if you listen constructively to others. Comment to show you've understood. Ask appropriate questions.

In group discussions make a note of a point you want to make then attract the eye of the person chairing the meeting and when allowed, make your point. Speak clearly and keep to the point. You may be brilliant as a scientist, archivist or whatever, but unless you can put your thoughts over to others your talent will be submerged in bumbling mediocrity.

PUBLIC SPEAKING

You are most likely to use public speaking skills when you are asked to give presentations. Don't turn down these opportunities, because if you do them well your image will be greatly enhanced both within and outside the company. If necessary ask your company for training in giving talks.

Presentations

Presentations are occasions when you stand up in front of other people and give a talk about your work, product or company. For example, you might give a talk to a few colleagues about how your work is progressing or new proposals; to the directors about how your department is doing; to a large audience of your colleagues throughout the industry about your company.

Both content and presentation must be good; skill at one and not the other will not impress anyone.

The basics of good communication in presentations are those which apply to your everyday speech, whatever your accent: that is clarity, good grammar, honesty, acceptable language, sincerity, enthusiasm and humour. Your audience must be able to understand what you are trying to say.

Preparing for a presentation

Good preparation for a presentation will give you confidence. Find out who you are to give your talk to and decide what you want to say. Pitch your talk to your audience so that, for example, you don't bore a group of salespeople with a detailed technical analysis when they want broad sales points.

You need to know:

1.   Who your audience will be.

2.   What they are expecting to hear about.

3.   Where the presentation will take place.

4.   When it will happen.

Your talk will succeed if you:

1.   Know your subject.

2.   Prepare thoroughly.

3.   Check illustrations.

4.   Visit the venue, if possible.

5.   Check equipment to be used.

6.   Practise using the equipment.

7.   Practise your speech.

8.   Dress appropriately.

If you are not used to giving talks then write your speech out in full using lots of headings, subheadings and underlinings as guides. (When you are more experienced you can just use notes and headings.) Read your speech into a mirror to judge the timing and to watch for over-use of hands. Tape your talk as well to hear whether you have any linguistic irritations to remove.

Giving the presentation

Take a few deep breaths beforehand. Your audience usually wants to hear what you have to say so assume they are on your side. Tell them whether they can ask questions during your presentation before you begin. Start with a joke if you can – something simple and not bawdy and not well-known. Follow this with the classic structure of a talk which is to 'tell them what you're going to say, say it, tell them what you've said'. Keep to a few main points and speak clearly by 'speaking to the clock at the back of the room'. This keeps your head up and helps to project your voice. This is important if there is no microphone.

Coping with the audience

Most of the audience will be on your side. Hecklers are not usually loved by the rest of the audience, and you should be firm with them. If interrupted say 'You are entitled to your opinion. Now the rest of the audience wants to judge what I have to say.' If the heckler is abusive or physically violent do not hesitate to ask the organiser or some of the audience to remove him or her.

You may also encounter clever-dicks who use a question as a chance to show off by giving a long speech themselves. Simply interrupt and say: 'I'll stop you there. I want to answer your first point.'

It may also be that they have a perfectly valid point to make, so listen carefully and answer it as well as you can.

There is no reason why your talk should not go well but if it does go badly, perhaps the audience have been at lectures all day and are tired and bored. Do not assume it is your fault. If you can't get their attention with a well-timed joke or interesting fact then wind up the talk and put it down to experience. If you do give a good presentation then you will undoubtedly be asked to give more and your image will be immeasurably improved.

Papers

If you are asked to provide a paper for the meeting prepare a copy of your talk with any additional information needed as well as references and a heading. Give copies to members of the audience before or after your talk.

DON'T HIDE YOUR LIGHT . . .

You may get noticed if you work quietly and never communicate with anyone, but it is much less likely than if you create opportunities to show your worth.

If you have done something worth talking about make sure that people know. Even if it is nothing to do with work it will show that you are an achiever in some sphere and will get you noticed – a sporting award, an article in a newspaper, a mention about your work in your professional journal – these are all worth drawing to your colleagues' and bosses' attention. You don't need to boast about it but a quiet mention can help.

WHO CAN HELP YOU?

There are a number of different organisations which claim that they can help working women change their image. These vary from dedicated clothes dressers to colour and style consultants. There are also consultants who will visit your home and reorder your wardrobe, or who will give you a complete makeover from head to toe and talk to you about how to walk, speak and smile to your best advantage.

Whether or not these organisations have any influence depends on your point of view. Some people have told me that they have noticed a miraculous transformation in people who have used image consultants. Others say that they have tried them and found them of no help. Among those who approve are the politicians who rely on image consultant Barbara Follet and others to improve their public persona. Margaret Thatcher famously improved her image by following a consultant's advice to soften her hairstyle and clothes and lower her voice.

What you get out of them will depend on what you learnt. Most of us can probably gain some insight into our needs by reading the fashion pages in magazines and observing our colleagues and friends. But those with less confidence or time will benefit from an outsider's appraisal of our needs. Other organisations offer courses on assertiveness, communication skills, colour consultancy, etc (see 'Useful Addresses', pp.214–215).

Health and Safety

ALL THOSE women who work are entitled to do so in safety, and to have their general health taken care of. Not only are there the traditional dangers of working with machinery or chemicals to consider, but this is the era of new technology and their accompanying dangers and stresses. There are also the particular health problems of working women. How long can you work during pregnancy? Can you get enough rest? Whom can you go to for help with health problems at work? Can you get health screening at work? How can you avoid getting RSI (Repetitive Strain Injury)?

Health and safety go hand in hand. Both employers and employees have rights and responsibilities in regard to health and safety. But responsible employers want to keep their employees working and reduce absenteeism due to sickness. Therefore they make provision for their employees' general health while at work.

This chapter will tell you what health and safety provision you can expect to find at work, and what to do about your general health. It also looks at women's specific health needs at work.

HEALTH AND SAFETY AT WORK ACT

Employers have a duty at Common Law and under the Health and Safety at Work Act 1974 (HWSA) to take reasonable care of the safety of their employees. The HWSA 1974 explains the duties of both employer and employees. As a result many companies will appoint someone competent to deal with health and safety issues. The Act doesn't guarantee that an employer will prevent injury to employees, just that reasonable care should be taken to prevent it. All employers must follow the Management of Health and Safety at Work Regulations 1992, and other Regulations, and take steps to ensure effective health and safety management. There are now six additional supplementary Regulations implementing European

Framework Directives and five additional 'daughter' Directives.

The Common Law understanding of employers' responsibilities is that they must take reasonable care to avoid injuries, diseases and death of employees at work. They should provide a safe place of work with safe means of entering and exiting; provide and maintain safe appliances, equipment and plant for doing the work; provide and maintain a safe system of work; and provide competent people to do the work. Failure in the above features in the general law of negligence.

Overseeing health and safety at work is the responsibility of the Health and Safety Commission. Among its statutory rights are to require information, initiate an enquiry and investigate any accident or occurrence which it feels useful to do. After consulting the Secretary of State for Education and Employment it can issue and approve Codes of Practice.

The job of carrying out the work of the Commission falls to the Health and Safety Executive. It has six inspectorates – Agriculture, Alkali & Clean Air, Explosives, Factory, Mines & Quarries, and Nuclear Installation. It also has the Employment Medical Advisory Service. The inspectors appointed by the enforcing authorities have wide powers to enter, search and inspect premises.

The regulations are detailed, but to a large degree are common sense. If there are no instructions or safe means of operating machinery; if the entrance or exit is blocked enough to make access difficult; if the nature of your job is making you ill – then work practices are inadequate.

Information

The Health and Safety Information for Employees Regulations 1989 require that information in a prescribed form of posters and leaflets is made available to employees. Your employer must display a poster which explains what you should know about the law. Copies of these are obtainable from the HMSO (see 'Useful Addresses', p.215).

Employers of more than four people must provide a written statement of Safety at Work policy, which should be brought to employees' attention. This should contain a general statement of intent, the organisation of health and safety at work, and arrangements for carrying these measures out. It is usual to add information about specific legislation concerning the business where attention needs to be drawn to details. These might include such things as individual responsibilities of management and employees; specific company policies concerning such things as smoking, AIDS etc.; possible hazards at work and what steps can be taken to avoid them; joint consultative procedures; health and safety information system; fatal and major injury procedure; and procedures to protect visitors.

Find out what your company's health and safety statement says, and make a particular point of reading the items that govern aspects of your work.

HEALTH AND SAFETY PERSONNEL

Some companies may provide health and safety officers and first aiders. Others may provide a medical centre complete with doctor, nurses, physiotherapist and other health professionals. Here are some of the people who may represent your health and safety interests in the company and/or provide practical health assistance.

Safety Representatives

You need to know who your Health and Safety Representatives are. These are appointed under the Health and Safety Committees Regulations (SRSCR) 1977 from among the employees by a recognised Trade Union. They represent the workforce in consultation with the employer, and their aim is to develop and promote measures to ensure employees' health and safety at work. They also check the effectiveness of health and safety measures. Your employer should allow safety representatives to take time off during work – with pay – to do the job. They are entitled to inspect the workplace if they give written notice, but can only do this at three monthly intervals. They may also do it when a notifiable accident has occurred, or a notifiable disease has been contracted.

Find out whether one of the representatives is a woman, and whether they present women's concerns adequately to your employer.

Health and Safety Managers and Officers

Larger companies sometimes have a two-tier system of Health and Safety Officers. A Health and Safety Manager reports directly to the board and advises on health and safety policy issues. Local safety officers specific to their workplace report to him or her and inspect and advise on unsafe plant and procedures.

Safety Committee

Your employer must form a Safety Committee (SRSCR) if requested to do so in writing by at least two Health and Safety Representatives. The employer must consult the workplace Trade Unions, post a notice giving membership of the committee, and establish the committee within three months of the request. However, it is up to the employer how the committee is run and what its role and function is.

The committee plays a part in reducing accidents and occupational ill-health. It is a forum for discussion, and a way of disseminating ideas and information. If your company does not have a Safety Committee, ask your trade union to put pressure on your representatives to set one up. Request that women's health and safety issues are specifically raised at the meetings.

Occupational Health Nurses

These are qualified nurses (e.g., SRN, RGN) with special qualifications in occupational health nursing such as the Occupational Health Nursing Certificate (OHNC). They provide health supervision; education and counselling; monitor the environment and occupational safety; liaise with other agencies; deal with unit administration and resettlement; and provide treatment centres.

Occupational physician (Company doctor)

This is a registered medical practitioner, preferably with a recognised qualification in occupational medicine such as one from the Faculty of Occupational Medicine. The doctor has overall responsibility for how the health of employees affects their capacity to work, and the effects of work on health. His or her role is therefore an advisory one, including inspection of health and hygiene of staff from such places as canteens and kitchens, as well as responsibility for practical health examination, treatment and provision for all employees.

Occupational Hygienists

These people deal with the identification, measurement, evaluation and control of environmental factors such as noise, radiation and contaminants. They enter the profession through the British Examination and Registration Board in Occupational Hygiene (BERBOH).

First-aiders

These are employees who have received first-aid training and hold a current first-aid certificate from an organisation or employer approved by the Health and Safety Executive. Your employer should also provide a first-aid room, especially if access to casualty departments or treatment centres is inadequate or distant. Consider having first-aid training yourself, whether you intend to act as the official company first-aider or not.

WOMEN'S SPECIFIC HEALTH AND SAFETY NEEDS

Women in the workplace have special health needs. They may become pregnant, be going through the menopause, need breast or cervical examinations, or have problems with menstruation. All these things can affect a woman's ability to work well. These are in addition to general health problems or work related health problems which may occur.

Pregnancy

Pregnancy is sometimes thought of as an illness rather than as a natural condition. There is no reason why a fit woman should not continue working up to six weeks before the due birth date, although firms will vary in whether they allow you to do this.

If you are pregnant and are working, it is important to get enough rest and to put your feet up occasionally. Try and arrange more frequent breaks, and rest somewhere at lunch-time where you can put your feet up. See if you can have some of your ante-natal checks with the company doctor or nurse. If this is not possible, you are entitled to time off with pay to attend necessary ante-natal appointments, as long as you show your employer proof of appointments.

Decide in good time whether you want to return to work after the birth and inform your boss as soon as you can. Failure to make the application in good time could jeopardise your job. It may make sense for you to say that you are returning, even if you are unsure, as you then have the option. You will need to know from the company if there will be financial implications if you decide after maternity leave not to return.

Pre-menstrual syndrome (PMS)

Many women suffer from PMS, which leaves them depressed, liable to mood swings, bloated or with a desire to overeat. This can last for up to two weeks before a period starts. PMS can present difficulties at work, and may prevent you from working properly. Men put down weeping and mood swings not as something needing medical help but a 'typical woman' mood. Doctors are now taking the condition seriously, and there is effective treatment for PMS. If yours does not take it seriously, ask to be referred to another doctor. You can help yourself by eating low fat snacks throughout the day and schedule important meetings for times of the month when you feel better or get a colleague to take the meeting. There are a number of books around on PMS (see 'Further Reading', pp.226–227.)

Menopause

Hot flushes, vaginal dryness and feelings of depression are common during the menopause, which can affect women any time between the ages of 35 to 50, sometimes earlier, sometimes later. Wear layers of clothing to remove when you feel overheated and take a shower at work if possible to combat sweating. Try to ignore flushes – you notice them more than other people will.

GPs are now more receptive to prescribing Hormone Replacement Treatment (HRT), which many women find transforms their lives by making them feel normal, although it is not appropriate for all women. If you cannot take HRT for any reason, then homeopathic treatment can be helpful. Consult a practitioner recommended by your doctor, or find one through an organisation such as the Institute for Complementary Medicine.

Breast examinations and cervical smears

Many companies are now making arrangements with hospitals and GPs to offer regular mammograph and breast examination sessions and cervical smears in company time. This is because women who need to attend such sessions cannot always do so because of work timetables. Women at all levels in the workforce can take advantage of this.

The advantages are clear on both sides. Women can get the necessary vital check-ups with the minimum of travel and inconvenience. The company loses fewer worker hours, and has a fit and healthy workforce.

If such sessions are not provided by your company then you should ask if they can be arranged. Such examinations and tests may be arranged in company time in co-operation with the local hospital or a local GP practice who can send in a team. These may be offered as part of a general 'well woman' check-up, together with urine analysis and blood-pressure checks.

CHEST X-RAYS AND MAMMOGRAPHS

One of the first company introduced schemes was regular chest X-ray screening and this is still a common provision today. If your firm offers this, then do attend the sessions. Women over 50 may also be offered mammography checks for breast cancer. The breasts are flattened one at a time between two boards and then X-rayed. Although slightly uncomfortable this does not hurt. It is a vital means of checking for the first signs of breast cancer, which may otherwise go undetected during a normal breast examination by hand.

You should do a regular examination of your own breast by hand just after each period and report any changes or lumps to your own GP or the company doctor immediately.

WOMEN'S CLINICS

Many GPs offer their patients services geared to their particular needs. For women this includes ante- and post-natal clinics and well-woman clinics. These give blood-pressure tests, blood and urine tests and a chance to discuss your general health needs. It is sensible to have a check up at one of these clinics at least at annual intervals – they are usually available by appointment at the surgery.

Some health authorities also provide well-woman clinics. The idea behind these was that any women in need of health advice could turn up without an appointment. An appointment is usually needed today, and can involve a wait of several weeks. This rather ruins the object, as it does not help women who may be apprehensive about seeing their doctor, or who perhaps have a male doctor and would prefer to be seen by a woman.

PRIVATE HEALTH CARE

Over six and a half million people now have private health insurance. If you are a member of BUPA or one of the other private health schemes, then you pay a certain sum of money each month. For this you will be covered for private treatment at certain hospitals. Some conditions may not be covered by certain policies, so check whether yours meets your expectations. Your firm may give membership of BUPA as a perk at a certain level.

Besides this, some health-care schemes and private doctors offer a health check for a fee. You will get the full range of well-woman checks as well as an X-ray and mammograph if appropriate.

RSI (REPETITIVE STRAIN INJURY)

RSI results from doing a repetitive task with your hands and arms for long periods. If affects people working in a range of industries, and those who work at a keyboard without adequate breaks are particularly prone to RSI. The soft tissues in the hand, wrist, arm or shoulders swell, resulting in severe pain in those regions as well as restriction of movement, which can be bad enough to stop you from working.

Many people use keyboards nowadays without having had proper typists' keyboard training. One magazine editor has observed that none of his typists ever get RSI because they have been properly trained in keyboard skills, but many of his journalists get RSI because they have not been taught how to hold their hands and wrists properly. However, some women who have been trained as typists do get RSI too.

RSI is now accepted as a genuine illness and large sums have been awarded to sufferers disabled this way in the course of their work.

Correct working conditions will solve most of the problems. Your VDU and keyboard should be at a comfortable working height, separated if necessary, and you should be sitting in a comfortable position with your fingers and wrists at a suitable angle.

The most sensible advice is to make sure that you use your keyboard safely and get proper keyboard training. Ask for such courses if your company does not provide them. Meanwhile you can take lessons at evening classes or secretarial schools. (See 'Useful Addresses', p.215 for the name of an organisation that can offer information and support on RSI. See also 'Further Reading' on p.226.)

Keyboard safety

Your company should supply you with equipment that reduces the possibility of RSI. Even managers who do not use their keyboard all day should make sure that they get suitable equipment installed. This includes a table and chair of appropriate height so that your feet and back are firmly supported and your arms are parallel, at right angles to, and just above keyboard height. As many keyboards are too high, this may mean raising your chair and using a footrest.

You should ask for a wrist support if you do hours of typing, and make sure that the keyboard gives the right amount of resistance. If you cannot adjust or lubricate it easily, then you may need to exchange the keyboard for another, or you may get the chance to test keyboards for stiffness before you acquire one.

Laptop computers

The advent of the laptop computer means that women can work anywhere. But beware of laptop computers with a poorly lit and small screen or cramped keyboard. You may find that you have a tendency to hunch over the smaller machine. Because batteries do not last more than a few hours on these computers, you need to save your work frequently and then transfer it to a desktop computer. Use the mains lead whenever possible.

Eye strain

Women often worry about eye strain from working with VDUs. There is a slight flickering on all screens, but on some more than others. If yours is particularly noticeable then ask for a replacement with less flicker.

The contrast on a screen is important too. You should have a VDU that allows you to adjust the contrast between the image and the background light on the screen to a comfortable level.

The Health and Safety (Display Screen Equipment) Regulations 1992 says that users and operators of VDUs, that is people who use a VDU habitually as a significant part of their work, should have a screen with a stable image (no flickering etc.) and easily adjustable contrast. It should be able to swivel and be tilted, have a separate base and screen and no glare. The keyboard should be tiltable and have a separate matt surface.

Get your eyes checked

Most eye-strain is probably caused by the fact that people do not get their eyes checked regularly enough. When did you last get yours tested? There is a charge nowadays unless you are entitled to exemption, but adults usually only need testing every two years if their sight is stable. This is a small price to pay for eye safety. Glasses can be expensive, but many opticians now compete to offer cheaper ones. If you have severe eye trouble then you may be entitled to a small amount of financial help from the government.

Women who wear prescription glasses may need a different pair for use at a VDU. You should not wear tinted glasses unless they are part of your prescription.

Resting is important too. Take a break from sitting at a keyboard and looking at a screen at regular intervals around every twenty minutes to glance away from the screen and stretch. This will reduce the strain on your eyes.

Managers who have to read a lot of documents for their work should also beware of eye strain and get their eyes tested regularly.

Radiation

Radiation from computers, particularly their screens (VDUs – Visual Display Units) has caused concern to many users. However, the Health and Safety Executive has found no proof that the small amount of radiation that comes from VDUs does any harm. If you are concerned, then ask for a screen to fit over the front of your VDU.

ACCIDENTS AT WORK

If you have an accident at work or suffer from a disease caused solely by the nature of your work you can sue the company for negligence and claim compensation, and you can sue your employer if you suffer because of unsafe plant or equipment. It is also your employer's responsibility to provide you with competent workmates. So if your colleague is negligent and you have an accident as a result you can sue your employer.

What should you do?

If you suffer illness related to your work, or an accident at your workplace you should first take legal advice from your union lawyer or your own legal adviser to see whether you have a basis for a claim against your employer. If you do have a basis to claim, do not be afraid of pursuing it. Your employer is insured against work-related accident or illness and so will not be making any payment personally. Make sure you also claim any welfare benefits that apply to your case.

If you are injured at work, write down the names of any witnesses, take photos of the scene if possible and report it to the employer as soon as possible. Enter the correct details in the company's accident book, and see your doctor as quickly as you can.

If the equipment is defective, keep it or make sure that it is not thrown away or repaired until your lawyers have photos taken of it. Find out whether any similar accidents have occurred within the company.

Make a note of all losses and expenses, including those of your family, arising from the accident as these will form a part of your claim. Don't accept any compensation until you have taken full legal and medical advice.

Your employer must notify the Health and Safety Executive if the accident causes major injury or death, or it is a major incident endangering everyone even if nobody was injured. This must be done within seven days of the incident.

Employer's liability

Your employer is only liable if he fails to take reasonable steps to ensure employees' safety in the light of current knowledge and practice. He must keep up-to-date with developing knowledge and apply it in a practical manner. The employer's duty is personal, and he cannot avoid liability by delegating duties or using an independent contractor. If the injury is due to defective equipment supplied by a third party it is deemed to be due to the employer's negligence.

To succeed in an action of negligence against your employer, you will need to prove that you are owed a duty of care by your employer and that a breach of that duty resulted in injury. The employee has to show that the employer did not comply with the code of practice under the HSWA 1974. It helps if the employee can show that the employer acted against the normal practice in the trade, and that the accident couldn't have happened unless there was negligence by the person managing or controlling the operation (i.e., the employer). It is therefore up to the employer to prove that he exercised all reasonable care, that the accident was due to a specific cause and that he was not negligent. The employer also has a defence if the employee consented to run the risk of injury. Some jobs are inherently dangerous and the employee knows this when they accept the position. Even so, there is still an obligation on the employer to follow the best possible working practices, and to assess possible risk to employees.

MAIN HEALTH AND SAFETY PROBLEMS

The most common health and safety problems concerning general occupational health relate to vision, posture, the layout of the work environment, comfort and the rate of working. If any of these are at odds with how you can operate, then you will be liable to ill-health and stress and so will your colleagues.

GENERAL HEALTH

Women are notorious for neglecting their own health in order to look after their families, and because they are busy and too tired to make the effort. But exercise can make you feel less tired, because it boosts your adrenaline as well as reducing stress.

Exercise

It is possible to fit a regular exercise routine in to a busy working day. Half-an-hour of brisk exercise three times a week is the minimum recommended for good health. Even once a week is better than nothing. A lot of health problems stem from a sedentary lifestyle, and many women have done no sport of any kind since they left school.

Why not walk or cycle to work instead of driving or going by bus? Take the stairs instead of the lift? Do press-ups in the office at break or go for a swim at lunch-time?

Some companies have their own sports facilities, in which case do make use of them. Unless you have to rush home, then take half-an-hour after work to swim, play badminton or go to a work-out class.

If you cannot fit these in, buy a video or a book of exercises; practising them regularly at home will keep you fit. Exercising for 20 minutes a day, three times a week, will keep you fit.

Food

So much contradictory information has been written about food that many women have little idea whether they are eating well or badly. First, it is exercise not dieting which keeps you fit. What weight you are is not important unless you are grossly over- or under-weight; what *is* important is that your muscle tone is good and that you are supple.

It is sensible not to skip breakfast, although many people cannot stand the thought of eating early in the morning. At least have a bowl of fibre cereal, a glass of milk or orange juice and a piece of toast or piece of fruit. You can have small meals throughout the day instead of a large cooked breakfast, lunch and dinner.

Take fruit and nuts into work as snacks and buy sandwiches and salads at lunch-time. Bread and potatoes are good for you, so you can fill up with these. Have a cooked meal in the evening.

Business meals

You do not have to eat too much yourself because you are taken out for a meal by a client or have to attend a dinner. If the menu consists of heavy food, then eat smaller portions and do not douse your meal in heavy sauces or cream. Restaurants usually offer healthy alternatives, and at fixed menu dinners nobody will even notice if you don't eat everything.

Drinking on such occasions is more of a problem, because it is tempting to drink a lot of alcohol at someone else's expense. But it can rapidly make you gain weight and help you lose concentration. If you have to attend a lot of dinners for your job then stick to mineral water. This is regarded favourably nowadays, and the best business people like to keep their heads clear while all around lose theirs. On the occasions when you do drink, do not drive but get a taxi home.

STRESS

Stress is now on the same footing as accidents at work or industrial diseases. In 1994 a social worker successfully sued his employer for stress from overwork. If you are overworked to the point of breakdown you now have grounds for a compensation claim.

The Abbey Life Stress Survey of 1995 found that 83 per cent of working women admit to feeling stressed. If we take into account that most of the population does not get enough rest because of the demands of work hours and other commitments you can see how dangerous this is not only to your health but your work.

Women adapt to an exhausting and over-demanding lifestyle by taking short cuts with their health. They often cut lunch-breaks to fit in shopping and other chores. Women also rise earlier than they would like in order to have time to deal with children and get to work. They can find themselves going to bed early because they are exhausted, and then have difficulty sleeping. They have less social life because they are trying to fit everything in, and when they are free, feel tired. Some are also very conscientious, bringing work home.

Work is good for psychological well-being, but bad when it puts such demands on a woman that she is stressed and exhausted. This is exacerbated where the woman is the lone breadwinner or with an unemployed partner. These are common experiences, and help and support can be gained from employers, partners and friends and the government. Childcare choices are dealt with in Chapter Seven and not every woman has a partner, male or female, with whom to share this workload.

Stress can be physical, chemical or biological. It results in the individual being unable to cope successfully, and in them responding in unwanted physical, mental or emotional ways. Although some stress can be beneficial and spur us on to do more things energetically, too much can be counterproductive and even dangerous.

The main causes of occupational stress are:

- too heavy or too light a workload;
- too easy or too difficult a job;
- too many hours at work – over 60 and you're in trouble;
- conflicting job demands;
- too much or too little responsibility;
- poor human relationships;
- incompetent superiors;
- lack of appreciation;
- feeling vulnerable because of middle-age, and so concerned with redundancy or lack of promotion prospects;
- over- or under-promotion;
- interaction with family and work commitments;
- not being good at 'people' skills.

Dealing with stress

You can deal with some of the things mentioned above straightaway if you set about it. If you are working excessive hours, then explain to your boss and ask for assistance, a longer time to complete the work, or different work. If you are lacking in personal skills then there are many courses (your company may run one) which will help. If there are conflicts between work and home, then sit down with your family and work out where the problems are and adjust your life. Middle-aged vulnerability is something that we have probably all felt or will feel. The important thing is to look at your options and decide whether the concern is justified or whether it is simply a symptom of getting older. If you think it is justified, then now is the time to learn new skills for a change in job or increased leisure. If it isn't, then you need to study relaxation techniques or discover new interests outside work. (See 'Further Reading', pp.226–227 for some books on managing stress and your lifestyle.)

The problem of over- or under-work, promotion or too difficult or easy a job is something only you can determine for yourself. If you wake up apprehensive each morning because you cannot understand or get to grips with your work, then you are probably in over your head. If you are constantly bored then you need more demanding work (but not so that you work excessive hours). First talk to your personnel officer to see whether there is a possibility of change within your present company. If not then you should actively look about for new work. Talking to your boss will help too, as he or she may be able to adjust the work so that you can cope, or give you more interesting things to do. Discuss your prospects of promotion realistically.

If you feel ill then find out from your union rep or the personnel officer about the company's sickness absence procedure.

The most important thing is to take a few minutes out of each day to unwind. It doesn't matter when you do it or how you relax, but twenty minutes on your own is vital. Perhaps you relax by reading a good book, taking a bath, having a nap or doing some yoga. The important thing is that you do it on your own, and that it makes you feel good.

EUROPEAN LEGISLATION

Health and safety conditions do need to be improved, but there is argument how this should be done. The European Parliament wanted to introduce basic rights for all workers called The Social Chapter, which was vetoed by the British government. This veto may well be reversed eventually. Included in the ten rights were a commitment to a safe limit to the number of hours worked, proper rest periods at work, time off for new parents and family emergencies and at least three weeks holiday a year.

SMOKING

Smoking is becoming an antisocial thing to do. If you do smoke then try hard to give it up, especially if you are or wish to become pregnant. Talk to your GP if you are having trouble giving up. Smoking can harm your unborn child. Passive smoking is also now accepted as a cause of lung cancer, and so you are actively damaging your colleagues if you smoke. Apart from that, you will have a greater chance of heart disease and lung cancer if you continue to smoke.

Smoking is increasingly being banned from the workplace, and most companies now have a policy on smoking. This is in addition to those work environments where smoking is banned because it is dangerous. If you don't smoke and want smoking banned, then encourage your employer to develop a policy on smoking at work, which should be circulated to all employees. A common solution is to ban smoking everywhere except in one small side room, or ban it completely. The policy should be developed in consultation with employees and unions.

YOUR RESPONSIBILITY

It is easy to think that your employer shoulders all the responsibility for health and safety at work. But as an employee you have duties as well as rights. You are obliged to take reasonable care of your own and others' health and safety at work. You should also do this when carrying out a requirement of your employer concerning health and safety. You are not allowed to recklessly interfere with or misuse anything provided for health and safety or welfare.

You can also take sensible precautions in the office environment. Keep your workplace tidy and safe, and do not block rooms or doorways so that people cannot move freely. If your employer allows you to arrange your own office space, then try to ensure that there is as much free floor-space as possible. Do not tamper with electrical appliances, and ask that qualified people check dangerous or non-working equipment or circuits. Lift and carry things in a sensible manner – bend your knees to pick things up and do not carry more than you can safely manage. Be careful of any dangerous substances or materials, and always follow the instructions. Ask for written instructions if you are not given any. Make yourself conversant with the fire precautions and do not drop matches or cigarettes on the floor. Be sensible about how you dress so that you can work and move about unhampered.

Your personal conduct involves health and safety too. Simple things can cause accidents, so look where you are going, don't run, use proper steps or other access equipment when getting things from awkward cupboards and open doors carefully. These may sound very basic, but can be the cause of serious injury.

WOMEN AT HOME

Women working from home must be equally careful of their health and safety. Keep your doctor and hospital casualty number near the telephone, together with numbers for a nearby relative or friend who can be contacted in an emergency. Have numbers for a local plumber and electrician handy.

Most accidents occur in the home, and if you work there the risk to you will increase. Try and keep papers to a minimum, and safely filed away. Turn off electrical appliances at night unless they need to remain on all the time, and keep wires tidy and out of the main pathways.

If you want to look more closely at health and safety practices, including the law, see 'Further Reading', pp.226-227 for some relevant books.

Travel in the UK

TRAVEL in the UK is an important part of many women's working lives. It might be only a few miles or a hundred, your regular journey to work or much longer trips. Whatever the distance, you need to know what travel choices you can make and how to travel safely. This chapter will explain how you can travel in the UK and what you need to know to make sure it is enjoyable and safe. International travel is covered in Chapter Eleven.

USING YOUR OWN CAR

You may need to use your own car to travel for work. If you don't have a car try getting an interest-free loan from your company to buy one. If you are thinking of buying a car first ask your company what they offer in the way of help for car buyers. They should at least give you a mileage allowance on travel connected with your work – that is payment of an agreed amount for petrol and wear-and-tear per mile. To claim this you will need to produce receipts at the end of each month. If your company asks you to use your own car for work purposes but does not have an agreed mileage rate, then ask the AA to recommend a mileage cost. This will depend on the make and age of your car.

Do make sure that your car is properly insured to use for work. See Chapter Five, pp.50–66 for further details.

COMPANY CAR

If you have a company car then some of the problems are removed. Unfortunately, the tax position for company cars as perks is not as favourable as it once was and the amount of tax you will pay will depend on the list price and age of the car as well as your yearly mileage. So bear this in mind if you are offered a new company car every year. The most expensive model may not be the best bet, and if your car is still in good condition at the end of four years consider keeping it for a bit longer.

Sometimes your company will expect you to choose a car more frequently and insist that it be within a certain price range. This is both to keep up the image of the company to the public and to underline the internal hierarchy. If your company operates in this way then you will just have to agree. Bear in mind that clients expect to see a certain level of show from a particular level of employee, so you would be letting the firm down if you did not co-operate.

Company car facts

When you have a company car you need to check whether certain things are to be included. Ask the following questions:

- Can your partner drive the car?
- Can your children drive the car? (If so, this is usually restricted to children over the age of 25 years.)
- Can the car be used for private as well as business purposes?
- Do you get mileage? If so, don't forget to claim.
- Do you get petrol free on a company card or must you claim separately?
- Does the company arrange for the car services through the leasehold company or must you do this and claim back?
- How often can you change the car? How often are you expected to?
- Is a car phone fitted? Will the company fit a phone at their expense?

I know people who have looked forward to having a company car, only to find that it cannot be used for private purposes or driven by their spouse, so it is important to straighten these matters out at the start.

If you are given a full company car deal you will be given a card issued by the leasing company. By presenting this at approved garages the price for repairs and services is charged directly to your company. You may also have a card which does the same thing for petrol. The company will take care of insurance and tax, but check these regularly in case there is a delay updating them. It will usually be up to you to arrange the annual service and any other service or repairs at an approved garage, but the cost will be borne by the company.

Car rules and safety

Keep an eye on tax and insurance and make a note in your diary well in advance for each annual payment.

Your MOT is important because without it you cannot get a tax disk or get your car insured. It also highlights any faults on the car which you must get repaired before you get the MOT certificate. Garages will sometimes give a reduced price if you get the car serviced and have the MOT done at the same time. If it is your own car, use a garage where you know the owner and/or a mechanic, or get a recommendation from a friend.

Become a member of a car rescue service like the AA or RAC – essential if you take long journeys.

Try to keep your car near your house or off the street in a garage or garden area. This is not always possible, especially in built-up areas, but is safer than leaving it several streets away. Your car is less likely to be vandalised if you park it in a safe place, and the safer you will be if you need to reach it at night.

If you have to leave your car in a street, get it fitted with a decent car alarm and try to park it under a street lamp. If you are ill, or go away on holiday and have to leave the car in the street for a long time, ask a friend to check that the tax disk is up to date and to move the car occasionally. If the car has not moved for several weeks, people may assume that it has been abandoned. Then they can ask the council to remove it. A removal notice is put on the car, sometimes weeks before it is moved, thus giving passing thieves a chance to remove your tyres before the council removes your car!

Thieves also take spare tyres, radios, mobile phones, etc. so the less ostentatious your car, the better.

When you use the car for work remove anything important, such as a briefcase, from the car before locking it. If you have a mobile phone put it under the seat out of sight or take it with you.

Safety on the move

When you travel by car on business keep your doors locked and travel by well-lit main routes. Leave a description of your route and your destination address with your secretary or a colleague and in your desk diary.

If you have to stop on a motorway do not leave the car unless you are near an emergency phone. If you are on the verge for any length of time the police will spot you. Remember not to get out of your car for anyone except the police or the emergency service or car rescue service you have called. Car rescue services such as the

RAC give priority to single women, so tell them you are on your own if you have to call them out. A mobile phone is useful in this situation, because it means you can call for help without leaving your car.

You can buy a plastic 'man' to put in the passenger seat to make it look as if you have a male companion with you. This may or may not be effective and whether you want to try it will depend on how foolish you feel ferrying a plastic companion about. Remember to deflate him before you leave the car!

Public car parks

The safest kind of car park is an uncovered one on ground level only. It is possible to see across the cars, and although your safety cannot be guaranteed, at least this sort of layout gives you a better chance of avoiding problems. Many women do not like multi-level car parks and although they are convenient they are often dark, with places for attackers to hide. If you have to use one try to park on the ground floor or as near to an entrance as possible. Hotels often have their own car parks with attendants to look out for your car.

Norwich Union has pioneered a Safe Car Park Award. This was begun in 1993, and is likely to become an annual event. It is aimed at promoting safety for women in car parks country-wide, and to highlight the growing menace to women driving alone.

Handbags
In recent years there has been an increase in the number of bags snatched from cars waiting at traffic lights. Keep your handbag out of sight (under the seat) and doors, windows and sunroof locked when stationary. If you can, choose a car with central locking, so you can lock all the doors by locking the driver's door only.

Mobile phones
These are a useful addition to your safety but they are expensive to buy and use. Cheaper rates are available from some firms for users who make few calls. Always make sure that you stop the car before you use your mobile phone as it is illegal and dangerous to use one while driving. Mobile phones are also a target for thieves, so take it with you when you leave your car, lock it in the boot, or put it out of sight under the seat.

Car safety

Never be tempted to skip or put off services or repairs. Many people drive dangerous cars because they cannot or will not pay for the necessary maintenance. This is not only potentially dangerous for them and their passengers but for the general public, because it increases the chances of an accident.

If you have a company car then the cost will be taken care of (see p.121), so it is just a question of remembering to get the work done. If you need to use your car while the work is being done on it, look into hiring an alternative or using public transport.

As far as your own car is concerned, if you are not prepared or cannot find the money or time to get such work done, then consider giving up the car. This will at least save you money. You cannot service your car adequately yourself unless you are a trained mechanic, even if you are good at changing the oil and cleaning the spark plugs, so let an expert do it.

Although garages will do major repairs, remember that firms such as Kwik Fit can change tyres and exhaust pipes and do your MOT very quickly, usually while you wait. An MOT, however, does not guarantee the roadworthiness of your car, so you yourself must make sure that tyres and so on are in good condition. If the police catch you in an unroadworthy vehicle you can be taken to court, which may result in you losing your licence, imprisonment or a fine.

TAXIS AND MINICABS

London and many of the major cities have systems of licensed cabs (black cabs), which are licensed by the police and have their licence number clearly displayed. Prices are fixed, and any cab driver reported for misbehaviour or underhand practices can have his or her licence revoked.

There are also minicab drivers who use ordinary cars. These are unlicensed, although many of the reputable firms follow a voluntary code of good practice. Disreputable minicab drivers do exist, and these tend to tout for business on the streets.

Your company may use a particular taxi or minicab company, in which case you sign a tab and the company pays the bills at regular intervals. If they don't have such an arrangement they may have a list of local reputable firms.

If you call a minicab do not give your first name, and ask for the driver to come to the door of the building you are in. Ask for the name of the driver, and do not get into any cab if the driver does not know your name. Never hail a minicab which is roaming the streets – only black taxis are safe to flag down. When using a minicab ask for an estimate of the fare beforehand.

The tip for taxis and cabs is between 10 and 15 per cent of the fare. For business purposes remember to ask the driver for a receipt.

COACHES

There are many companies offering coach travel on inter-city and local express services, the biggest being National Express.

National Express has the most comprehensive service and covers 1,500 cities in England and Wales. Two thirds of their seats are reserved for non-smokers and all seats have an individual reading light and personal ventilation and many recline. Some of the more up-to-date coaches have toilets and refreshments, but it is sensible to take your own food. If there are no toilets then regular toilet 'rest' stops are made.

You need to pre-book on the Rapide service. On other routes pre-booking saves time, but you can often buy your ticket on the day.

Booking can be done at any travel agent, but also at coach stations and some shops which display the National Express sign. Phone bookings can be made at National Express main centres – your nearest one will be listed in the phone book.

Scottish coaches

In Scotland there is the Scottish Transport Group, which consists of the Scottish Bus Company and Caledonian MacBrayne, which provides sea ferries services on the Clyde and to the Western Isles. You can make reservations for Scottish coaches at any travel agent.

Complaints
You cannot complain if your miss your appointment because the coach was late. If you have any other complaint about the services then contact the manager of the bus company, or in London, the London Transport Passengers' Committee (see 'Useful Addresses', p.216). You can also contact your local traffic commissioner whose address you can get from the local council offices.

TRAINS

You may be lucky enough to be able to travel first-class courtesy of your company. In that case all you need to do is turn up on time and take your seat.

Seat reservations

Seats can be reserved on all InterCity trains and this can be done from two months before the date of travel until two hours before the train leaves its first station; or the previous evening for early morning trains. On some trains reservations are essential and are provided free of charge; on some others reservations are highly recommended. Try to book as far in advance as possible because on some InterCity routes this too can get you a reduction.

Tickets

The only way to ensure that you travel the cheapest and most direct route possible is to enquire at a railway station or at your travel agent. Even the concept of one ticket office per station will be lost as BR is privatised; the privatised services may open their own ticket offices at the same station. This has already happened for the Heathrow trains, much to passengers' confusion. There can also be a price difference between the same service by different operators. There are plans to limit the number of stations which can sell through-tickets, although this had not been finalised at the time of writing.

Passengers' Charter

This gives passengers certain rights when travelling by train. Under the Charter you may be able to claim compensation if your train is late or fails to get to its destination on time, or is cancelled. The minimum you should expect is:

- a safe, clean, punctual and reliable train service;
- clean stations and clean trains;
- friendly and efficient service;
- clear and up-to-date information;
- a fair and satisfactory response when things go wrong.

You can arrange for Hertz car rental to meet you at many major railway stations. You can book cars in advance through Hertz branches and freephones or phone the Hertz reservation centres (see 'Useful Addresses', p.216).

Complaints
These should be addressed to your local Rail User's Consultative Committee and their address can be obtained from your local railway station.

Timetables

BR no longer provides full InterCity timetables at stations. You can get a free copy, with regular updates (see p.215 for phone number). You can pick up guides for your local services at your nearby station but you can also get these sent by post by contacting your local Regional Railways service. Your local station will tell you which serves your area. With privatisation, all services relating to timetables will of course change.

INLAND FERRIES

You are unlikely to use ferries in the course of your business travel in the UK unless you live in Scotland or use the water buses on the Thames. When you do use standard ferries they will take your car.

AEROPLANES

Inland air flights include inter-city flights and flights to Northern Ireland and the Republic of Ireland, for which you do not need a passport. Do take some form of identification, such as a driver's licence, in case you need to show some.

On internal flights you can in theory turn up shortly beforehand, buy a ticket and get on. In practice it is better to book first and to allow time beforehand – one hour is recommended.

You can drive to the airport and use its short-term car park if you are returning the same day. Otherwise it may be cheaper to use nearby commercial parks.

On business you may travel first- or business-class, which provide better facilities and food. British Airways has an Executive club which provides lounges with various facilities.

If you need a ticket quickly, then most large travel agencies can arrange for you to pick it up at the airport of departure. They can also arrange accommodation. Your travel agent should be a member of the Association of British Travel Agents (ABTA) for your protection.

Air Miles

Many airlines now have an Air Miles scheme, whereby you are given a card which records accumulated points gained by making flights with specific companies. When you have a certain number of points these can be traded in for plane tickets. You can also collect Air Miles points if you join the Shell Smart-Card scheme for buying petrol.

HOTELS

Hotels in the major chains are geared to business life, if not always to lone businesswomen. Depending on the hotel, you may expect to find fax, telex and mail facilities and sometimes secretarial help. There may be transport to and from the nearest airport. There should be quick laundry facilities and all-night room service, and in many hotels you will also find gym and swimming facilities.

Try to book your room as far ahead as possible. Let the hotel know you will be on your own, and ask for a secure room near a lift.

Your secretary may arrange the booking. Otherwise make your booking by phone and ask for confirmation in writing. Let the hotel know if you will be arriving after 6pm, which is considered late. Credit cards from the major companies are usually accepted at hotels. If in doubt check beforehand; some places take Visa but not Access, or vice versa.

When you arrive and check in find out where the lift and fire escape are and make sure that your windows are locked, especially if they have window ledges where prowlers could lurk. A ground-floor room is not a good idea unless there is no other room available. Check the fire instructions and that the lights and electricity work.

Get to know the head porter, who can arrange theatre trips and car hire for example, and tell you about shopping locally.

Check your bill carefully on departure even if this means not using the 'quick check out' facilities, because you cannot rectify bills later.

For help finding hotels where women feel comfortable, contact The Facilitator Service. This service networks female business travellers by highlighting hotels with a caring and positive attitude towards their women guests. (See Useful Addresses, p.215.)

Two major hotel chains also offer help for women on their own: Forte and Hyatt.

Forte plc

At 'Forte Crest' hotels business women on their own are specifically catered for with Forte's 'Lady Crest' rooms, which are available at no extra charge. They were introduced some years ago to ensure that female guests have everything they need in practical terms, and have safe and comfortable surroundings in which to rest or work. Ask for one when you or your secretary makes the booking.

Forte Crest includes staff writing down room numbers instead of saying them out loud; locating Lady Crest rooms nears lifts; and providing extra security for Lady Crest rooms in the form of an extra spyhole on the door. All Lady Crest rooms are equipped with an ironing board and iron; padded clothes hangers; a desk which converts into a dressing table complete with a mirror and hairdryer; business and women's magazines; extra bathroom lighting; and a bowl of fruit. (See 'Useful Addresses', p.216, for contact numbers for Forte.)

Hyatt International Hotels

Hyatt considers that women have different requirements but do not wish to be singled out. They offer patrolled car parking; services such as extended room service hours and valet services; bathroom amenities such as make-up mirrors and hair dryers; skirt hangers; extra electrical outlets; light food dishes; and a choice of informal venues where women eat without feeling conspicuous. These extras are included because of, but not specifically for, women business travellers.

Hyatts Regency Club is a 'hotel within a hotel', which is proving popular with women. It offers extra security and amenities, such as private key lifts and their own concierge in the exclusive lounge. Women find that the Regency Club lounge is ideal for small meetings, because it avoids any problems that might occur if clients are invited to one-to-one meetings in women's own rooms.

Hyatt staff give all travellers equal treatment. Restaurant staff put bills in the middle of the table and provide women who are entertaining guests with wine lists and menus. Small tables are distributed throughout the hotel restaurants so that all individual diners feel welcome. (Hyatt is listed in 'Useful Addresses', p.216.)

Many other hotels are also waking up to the fact that business-women are an important part of their trade, by making an effort to improve travel for women on their own with better security, making eating alone less intimidating and by providing extra services and amenities. Some hotels have video cameras to improve safety and have put proper locks on bedroom doors.

Often a small, secure hotel is a better choice than one of the large chains, if you have a choice. The family atmosphere can be more sympathetic to lone women. On the other hand, you may have no way of judging how welcoming or safe a small hotel is until you arrive.

Motels

Cheap overnight accommodation for drivers can be obtained from motels connected with establishments like Little Chef or Happy Eater. The accommodation is basic but comfortable; you do not necessarily need to book, although this is advisable. There are also nine Pavilion Lodges on major motorways at which you can book a room in advance. Premier Lodges in 29 locations combine hotel standards with pub informality. (See 'Useful Addresses', p.216, for phone numbers.) Motels and Lodges usually have a fixed fee per room regardless of the number of people sharing.

Dining alone

A quarter of all travellers on business trips are women, yet women still feel vulnerable in hotels, when having to go into bars, or when dining alone. It is all too common for staff to be patronising and to place a woman in an out-of-the-way corner – and for fellow male diners to assume that the woman is out to pick up a man.

Don't be intimidated. Ask to be seated at a more acceptable table, and complain to the manager if you are being harassed by staff or fellow customers. Nor do you have to sit at someone else's table if the staff want you to. If you want to dine on your own, say so. Take a book or newspaper to while away the time and ward off intruders. Remember to tip (10–15 per cent) if the service deserves it.

If you receive poor treatment, then make sure your company is told about it and that a complaint is made to the management. This may make the establishment improve its attitude, especially if your company represents useful business.

Conferences

These can be a particular hazard for women. Similar assumptions to those above about lone women by men can apply. Good companies take steps to ensure that their male staff do not take a sexist attitude to their female colleagues. But although you may feel relaxed and safe with men from your own company, you may not be so lucky with those from other firms. Also, the behaviour of your own colleagues may change out of the office. Some conference goers think that a conference is a chance for a free holiday and for having a good time, not working – including the assumption that women are there to get a man.

This attitude must be nipped in the bud. If a situation develops which you feel should be reported, then by all means feel entitled to do so, to your own colleagues, the management and the conference organisers, if necessary. You can also raise the matter with your union, if this is appropriate.

You could try and get a list of other people attending the conference, and maybe contact another woman on the list beforehand. Remember there is strength in numbers!

11

International Travel

THE WORLD is opening up for today's working woman. Since the removal of barriers to trade throughout the EU and the creation of a single market in 1992, Britain has increased business with Europe. The rest of the world is also opening its arms to enterprising businesswomen from the UK. This chapter will explain what arrangements you need to make to travel abroad and offers advice about how to conduct business in a foreign country. (See 'Useful Addresses', pp.216–218, for details of organisations that may be helpful.)

WHY YOU NEED TO GO ABROAD FOR BUSINESS

There are a number of reasons why you may need to conduct business abroad:

- to make new business contacts;
- to seek new markets;
- to consolidate business contacts;
- to check progress of business;
- to sign and finalise business contracts;
- to sort out problems.

It may seem as if all of these things can be done by a few phone calls or a letter and fax or two, but conducting business from a distance can have its pitfalls. If you do not meet your colleagues abroad regularly you may lose business to people prepared to make the journey. A contract is more likely to go to the company whose representatives have familiar faces and who make the effort to meet face-to-face.

You will need to keep an eye on problems and suggest solutions. It is difficult to do this if you do not go and visit the site first hand or talk to those involved in person. Second-guessing solutions when you have no first-hand knowledge of the situation can be a recipe for disaster.

Making personal contacts abroad means that people may be willing to go a bit further in helping you or easing your way. A quiet word from a contact can sometimes smooth a path that you might have found insurmountable otherwise. Attending international business and academic conferences, trade fairs and social occasions will help you to make contacts abroad.

PREPARING FOR TRAVEL

Contact the tourist office and/or Embassy or High Commission of the country you will be visiting for up-to-date guidance about customs and laws. The UK consulate in the country itself can give you more detailed guidance. Ask for the address of the national women or businesswomen's organisations. If you have time, contact them for advice about behaviour and business etiquette. For helpful information about foreign travel for women, have a look at the *Handbook for Women Travellers* by Maggie and Gemma Moss (see 'Further Reading', p.227 for details).

Commercial organisations can also give you advice about conduct in their area of business abroad. The Travel Advice Unit of the Foreign & Commonwealth Office issues advice notices relating to the safety of British nationals overseas where there may be significant risk. These travel notices can be seen on BBC2 Ceefax, and are regularly updated.

There is no substitute for talking to someone with direct experience. If you do not have a colleague who has been to the country, the Embassy may be able to provide you with names of British women who have business dealings with them. Otherwise contact one of the businesswomen UK networks listed in 'Useful Addresses', pp.216–218 and ask if there is anyone with direct experience.

Language

English is widely spoken as a business language, but this means that we are inclined to be lazy about learning another language. Being able to read and talk in another language, however, means that you can check interpretation, and there is less chance of misunderstanding.

Even if you are completely ignorant of the language of the country you are visiting do try to learn a few key phrases such as please, thank you, good morning, good evening, good-bye. Even if you don't get them right your efforts will be appreciated.

Better still, bring your foreign language up-to-date with a refresher course if you have done some previous study, or take a condensed language course. See if your company will pay for this. There are many language schools which give fast-track tuition, with some courses especially geared to business people. Longer courses can be taken at evening classes too. There are self-teaching audio tapes, video tapes with accompanying books, and language programmes on radio and television.

If some of your colleagues regularly visit the country concerned and can speak the language well enough to conduct business in it, see if they will give you a few minutes of their time regularly to talk in the language with you and correct your pronunciation.

Mistakes

If business is conducted in English, do not assume that you will always understand what is being said. Nuances of language are important and people in another country may put a slightly different interpretation on what is said. Get anything you are in doubt about clarified by an interpreter or a colleague who speaks the language. Do not sign anything unless you are sure of the document's meaning and you have been given an English translation and/or it has been checked by a solicitor versed in foreign law. Even if you are reasonably good at the other language you should double check anything that seems ambivalent.

Passport

You can get an application for a full passport from your local post office. (The one-year visitor's passports are soon to be phased out.) Allow up to two months to renew one or get a new one by post. You can apply in person at a Passport Office (see 'Useful Addresses', pp.217–218) if you need one quickly, but allow at least a full day for doing this.

Visas

In the Middle East, Israel and some other countries you will be expected to have a valid visa. It is safer to have arranged it beforehand, but if time makes this impossible you can in some cases get one at the border.

For EU countries and most other destinations a visa is not required unless you are intending to stay for a long time, in which case you will also need a work permit and or a resident's visa. Find out whether you should apply for these beforehand or when you arrive.

Allow plenty of time for getting visas in the UK if applying by post. You can get them from the Embassies by going in person, but their offices may be open for only a few hours on certain days.

E111 health form

You will need an E111 form in order to enjoy reciprocal health care in Europe. Get one from your DSS office or local post office. Fill in the form at the back, get it stamped at the post office and it is valid immediately. It can include all members of your family and is valid even when you move home.

Health and accident insurance

If you have an accident or need medical care abroad your health bill could run to thousands of pounds. Arrange for health and accident insurance every time you travel wherever you are going. The cost is small compared to the anxiety of being unable to pay for necessary medical treatment abroad.

Tickets

Your company may arrange tickets and accommodation for you through a local travel agent. If making your own arrangements, try to book your tickets well in advance. This can result in savings on fares, and you can reserve seats.

It is possible to get standby tickets for air travel at short notice but these will give you no choice in dates or time of travel and can involve waiting a long time at the airport. If you are attending meetings at specific times rather than making a general reconnaissance visit then you need to arrange travel that will get you there on time.

Travel with an experienced colleague or friend if you can. One manager travelling to Kazakstan on business relied on an experienced colleague to negotiate a dash across Moscow from one airport to another to catch a flight home the same day rather than wait another 24 hours – a changeover which British travel agents said couldn't be done!

Seasoned travellers will also know about accommodation, safety, customs and business procedures. Ask for help with these matters. This could make the difference between a successful trip or otherwise.

Injections

Go to your doctor and arrange to have any necessary inoculations done in good time. The tourist office or Embassy of the countries you are visiting will have up-to-date information about inoculation requirements. It is better to avoid having them done at the last minute.

You will need to take your certificates of inoculations with you, as some countries will not let you in without this proof of inoculation.

If you take any medicines with you, label them clearly and ask your doctor for a letter stating their content in case you need to show it to Customs. Your doctor can charge for certain inoculations and certificates.

AIDS

Casual sex is not safe in any country, as you run the risk of venereal disease or becoming HIV positive and developing AIDS. Infection can be passed on to other people on return. If you do have sex with anyone on your trip, make sure your partner uses a condom. If you anticipate having sex abroad then take some condoms with you. Sex with people living in Africa (but not Morocco, Algeria, Tunisia, Libya or Egypt) will disqualify you from being a blood donor for two years on your return.

ON YOUR WAY

Luggage

Keep a basic travel bag packed so that you can travel at short notice. It should be small enough to use as hand luggage on a plane so that you are not delayed at the ticket desk. Put another larger bag in very lightweight material folded up inside, and use it to bring any extra material home. As a general rule, the dimensions of hand luggage should not exceed 45" (115 cm) in total, and the weight should be no more than 11 lbs (5 kg).

A basic travel bag will need to contain:

- brush/comb;
- make up (in small quantities in plastic bottles);
- toothpaste/brush;
- flannel;
- small hairdryer with continental socket adapter;
- international bath plug;
- sun tan cream/after sun cream (in small tubes);
- sunglasses;
- headscarf or folding hat (to protect against heat and for wearing where women are expected to cover their heads);
- jumper (if required);
- sewing repair kit;
- two pairs of tights;
- knickers/bra;
- clean shirt;
- nightwear;
- towel;
- necessary medicines (malaria tablets, diarrhoea medicine, own medicines).

When you pack a larger pack for a long stay and you have more time you should include:

- spare skirt;
- trousers;
- spare shoes;
- extra shirts;
- camera (optional).

Experienced travellers pack small items into and around larger ones and roll rather than fold clothing. This keeps clothes fairly crease-free, and you can pack more into a smaller space.

Carry a lightweight coat and your briefcase. Your briefcase should contain:

- business documents;
- address and contact list (vital);
- passport;
- international driving licence and 'green card';
- inoculation certificates/doctor's letter/health insurance;
- pens/pencils;
- spare paper;
- writing paper and envelopes.

You may not need a handbag if your briefcase can double as both. Otherwise you can pack a very small handbag just big enough for the essentials.

Your own needs will dictate whether you can leave out even some of these minimal requirements. The trick is to eliminate everything that you don't need. You can survive with your briefcase and a toothbrush, but most women will feel happier with a little more than that.

Wear a suit whether you usually do or not. A trouser suit is ideal and you can pack a skirt. This eliminates the need to travel with a lot of clothing. A bright shirt with your skirt and some evening jewellery will see you through any dinner. Remember that in some Muslim countries you will be expected to keep flesh covered up, and so your clothes should have long sleeves and high necks. Wear long skirts or trousers too. See the *Handbook for Women Travellers* (p.227) for information on etiquette for women abroad.

Money

Travellers' cheques or foreign currency are available from travel agents, banks or some main post offices. This can take several days or more depending on where you are going, so allow time to order what you need. Bear in mind that travellers' cheques are safer than cash.

You can get cash quickly at airports or bureaux de change but this will cost you more, especially if you use your credit card to get it.

Money safety

Keep a good hold on credit cards, money and travellers' cheques, which can be easily stolen. Carry as little cash as possible and use your credit card; most international hotels will accept these nowadays, but take enough money in travellers' cheques to pay for your bills if you are unsure. Carry Access or Visa as well as your usual credit card because some hotels still don't take other cards. Never leave your cards with anyone else and try not to allow them to be taken out of your sight when paying in foreign shops or restaurants. Some travellers have returned home to find extra items ordered on their card which they knew nothing about.

Check your credit card statement carefully, because there can be discrepancies in charges which can be increased by the difference between the buying and selling rate of foreign currency. Where extra charges result from different buying and selling rates, Barclays, for example, will refund the difference to its own customers if notified.

If going to a country where thieving is rife, buy a lightweight plastic wallet which can be worn around your waist under your jacket or even under your shirt. If your hotel has a safe you can keep your important documents in it.

Taking a car

You are unlikely to take your own car abroad on business unless you are going to be away for some time. If you do, you can arrange to travel by ferry with the car or use the Channel Tunnel link.

It is cheaper and quicker to hire a car on arrival if necessary, which you can arrange with one of the major car hire firms that operate both in the UK and abroad (see 'Useful Addresses', p.217). You can either hire a car in the UK and pick it up on arrival or you can hire one when you get there. Hiring when you get there may be cheaper because you can use a local firm and pay local rates.

In some countries your UK licence alone will not be enough and you will need an international licence, which can be obtained cheaply from the RAC or AA by members and non-members alike, and is valid for one year. You will need to supply a passport photo and allow five days for issue. Check with your insurance company what extra motor insurance is required for abroad. You will also need a green card, and although it is not necessary to carry this in Europe at present it is useful to have it on you in case of an accident. You can join one of the motoring organisations such as the AA or RAC, and get their cover for foreign travel.

Le Shuttle

As an alternative to taking a car by ferry, you can now go from Folkestone to Calais in 35 minutes on the new high-speed rail link. From Calais you can load your car onto the French Motorail to avoid the stress of long days of motorway driving.

As a foot passenger you can also get on a train at Waterloo Station in London and travel straight through to Paris or Brussels just by turning up and buying a ticket half-an-hour before the train leaves. The journey takes about three hours.

Safety en route

Basic safety precautions should not be overlooked when travelling abroad. Take sensible precautions. Don't carry a lot of cash or wear expensive jewellery. Avoid walking down side streets alone, particularly after dark. Try to travel with someone you trust. Leave Miss, Ms or Mrs off your luggage label – just put your initials.

Many countries are appreciably safer than ours; others more risky. If you do travel about, leave your destination, address, and expected time of arrival and departure with someone who will raise the alarm if all does not go according to plan.

Accommodation

Try to pre-book accommodation so that you do not have to worry about finding a hotel when you arrive. Your travel agent can recommend hotels or bed and breakfast accommodation in an acceptable price range in a safe and convenient area.

Do not ask the local taxi driver to recommend a hotel. The one he takes you to will probably be cheap (and run by his brother-in-law!) but may well be on the outskirts of town and at some distance from your business destination. Personal recommendation from a friend or colleague is best.

Customs

Customs officers are entitled to ask to see your luggage. They can search you – including an intimate search – if they have reason to believe that you are hiding drugs or other contraband. If they want to search you they must inform their senior officer, and you have the right to be examined by a woman.

Women travelling on their own are often subjected to searches of this kind. If this happens to you in spite of complaining at the time, then raise the matter with your MP, the senior Customs officer, the Foreign Office and the police. Unfortunately, at the time there is little you can do but submit to the search.

DOING BUSINESS ABROAD

Countries as different as Bulgaria and Japan, Kuwait and Kenya are potential markets for the working woman to explore. Whether you are venturing abroad on behalf of your own business or for the company that employs you, you will need to know how to cope with business life across the sea.

What do they expect of you?

Most countries expect of businesswomen what they expect of anyone they do business with – respect, professionalism, courtesy and friendliness. You will need to have some understanding of how your business works in the country you are visiting. Unless you are an expert on the subject, you will not be expected to have a complete understanding of foreign business law, commercial practice or the entire import-export system.

If you are already fluent in the appropriate language then you will have no problems. Otherwise, many business people in other countries speak English. Do not rely on this, however. Ask for an interpreter if you need one. Also, before you leave the UK, arrange for any documents to be translated into the relevant language or languages and have them available in both English and the translations.

You should dress professionally, always bearing local traditions or requirements in mind. As in any business situation you should dress to afford respect from your opposite numbers.

Women are not always taken seriously in business, wherever you are. It is therefore up to you to demonstrate your ability.

Business cards

Do not overlook business cards when working abroad. They are an indication of status and serious intent, and also act as a useful ice-breaker. Most foreign business contacts will give you a card and expect you to proffer yours in return. If in doubt, ask them for theirs and give yours in exchange. If they are likely to contact you at your hotel remember to write your hotel phone number on your cards.

Cards are a great help in countries where you find the names difficult to understand. If you are visiting a country where the names are particularly difficult and the script is not Roman, then the cards may be printed in English on the reverse. Arrange to have cards specially printed before you leave the UK bearing your details in English on one side and in the appropriate language on the other. This is particularly important in Japan.

Communications abroad

Modern communications are reasonably good the world over, but do not rely on them in out of the way places. It is not easy to send a fax from Khazakstan, for example, unless you know someone working for a company with a satellite link. If you take your own PC and modem, then make sure that you have an adapter for the local electricity supply.

When in Rome . . .

Each country has its own quite distinct traditions and social customs that visiting foreigners should respect.

It is sensible and polite to adapt your behaviour to that of the country you are in. You should keep your body covered in Muslim countries, join in the spirit of a German *Bier Keller*, try local food and be prepared to attend meetings at what might seem unsocial hours.

Never lose your common sense – in other words you should try to accommodate local customs and try the best of what the country has to offer without going out of your way to do something dangerous or against the law of the country. If you are in any doubt about what you can and can't do or what is acceptable then ask, even if you feel foolish doing so.

International conferences

Be prepared to attend the necessary number of seminars and readings. If you are giving the paper or leading the talk make sure that you have all the facts and papers with you – don't forget slides or overheads if these are needed. Ensure that all papers are translated into the relevant languages if the organisers have not arranged this already.

You can give your talk in English, but check that translations and/or interpreters will be provided. Keep humour simple; unless your audience is adept at English the jokes could get lost in translation. Giving a paper at a conference can confer status, so do not refuse to do it if asked. (See Chapter Eight p.100 for help on public speaking. See also p.132 for more information on conferences.)

WHAT THE COUNTRIES SAY

Although most countries claim that businesswomen are treated the same as men, common sense and experience tell us that this is not always the case. Few countries give specific guidelines for foreign businesswomen but general advice can be obtained from the relevant tourist office or embassy. It may also be worth approaching the British Embassy or High Commission on arrival for advice. Rapidly changing political and religious situations in some countries make it imperative to get up-to-date advice before you travel.

Don't just read tourist brochures or guide books which are

designed to promote a country to foreigners. If you read books by authors native to the country you are visiting you will get a more realistic view.

Try to cultivate an aura of confidence and untouchability; women who look and feel vulnerable make themselves so.

On the whole you should find it possible to conduct business in most countries as long as you use your common sense about safety and take note of local customs and laws.

EUROPE

This is probably your most likely business destination particularly with the creation of the Single Market for trade. But do not make the mistake of assuming that customs and traditions are the same everywhere. Each country has its own way of life and way of doing business.

Belgium

Belgium is important as a business destination because its capital Brussels hosts the European Commission, the Council of the European Union and NATO, and is a centre of activity for the European Parliament.

Officially it is a bi-lingual country with Flemish spoken in Flanders, and French in Wallonia. The third official language is German which is spoken in the eastern corner. Brussels is in Flanders but is predominantly French-speaking. Most Walloons do not speak Flemish and most Flemish refuse to speak French, even to foreigners. In Flanders it is respectful to try a few words of another language first such as Dutch, English or German. Eventually you will invited to speak French if that is the only language you have in common.

Belgians as a whole hold very traditional views about women and there are few women professional managers except in family-owned companies.

In business Belgians prefer compromise and would rather find a solution than win an argument.

Flanders and Wallonia do differ in business manners. The Flemish are disciplined in applying systems and expect participatory decision-making, active consensus and delegation of responsibility. Wallonians consider themselves punctual, hard-working and practical. Distinctions of rank are important.

Meetings are more for exchanging information and discussing alternative proposals than for decision-making. Once a decision is taken, and confirmed in writing, it will not be questioned.

If you are thinking of starting a business in Belgium, you can contact *Focus*, a non-profit career services group (see 'Useful Addresses', p.217). A useful guide to living and working in Belgium is the bi-annual publication *Newcomer* (see 'Further Reading'. p.227).

France

Although women in France are increasingly represented in management there is still a bias against them in industry, especially outside Paris, so be prepared for some chauvinism.

The French prefer you to speak their own language so you should make the effort to do so. Even if you speak it badly they will appreciate the effort. Any written communications should be in a formal style with correct grammar.

Dress is important so opt for timeless chic. Choose quality over quantity and do not be worried about wearing the same outfit on many occasions; it can be varied with accessories.

Business etiquette is formal. Be punctual and shake hands briskly on meeting and parting. Good manners are important so say *'bonjour'* even when going into a shop or restaurant, or using a taxi.

Use last names in all formal situations and do not use first names unless invited to do so in private. In general, bosses do not usually socialise with subordinates at work or after hours.

Germany

On occasions, you may find that you have to overcome reservations held by German businessmen about your competence as a woman to talk serious business.

The German business world is dominated by banks and the style of working is controlled and conservative – there are rules for everything. Germans value conformity and dislike ostentatious displays of wealth. Women dress more formally than in the UK but you need only take a few outfits and interchange them. If in doubt, dress up.

Use the more formal *sie* most of the time until an older person invites you to use *du*. Address everyone by *Herr* or *Frau* then their title, if they have one, and their last name. If they have a title always use it. Greet people properly when you meet and always say 'good morning' and 'good-bye' in shops even if you don't buy anything. When answering or making a phone call begin with your last name followed by a greeting. Do not answer the phone with just 'hello'. Be prepared for Germans to be inhibited on the phone. Germans have a strong sense of privacy and prefer you to be friendly but reserved.

When conducting business make sure that you have all the facts at your fingertips and provide a translation of any documents. Meetings are usually scheduled weeks in advance. There may be a brief period for polite talk and tea or coffee but then meetings are strictly functional.

Expect to seat yourself in restaurants. During a business lunch important matters will be dealt with immediately after ordering.

Greece

The official working day starts early and ends at lunch-time although some larger companies keep north European hours. Bank employees tend to dress more formally than other workers. Formality on first acquaintance rapidly moves to informality and any attempt at Greek will be considered a compliment.

Formal meetings are arranged only for important issues. Frequent informal co-ordination and briefing meetings are preferred and are a valuable way of finding out what is going on. There will seldom be a formal agenda or minutes so make your own notes. Consensus is important and the meeting will be reconvended if none is reached.

There is a general distrust of written communication but any letter or memo should be formal. Personal contact is important for even the smallest matter and only if face-to-face contact is impossible will the phone be used, then at great length.

Italy

There are few women in top management positions in Italy except in family companies or professions, so management is male-dominated. Businesswomen are therefore expected to dress according to men's expectations. Wear the best quality clothes you can afford and dress formally for business.

Courtesy and good manners are important. Generally, use the formal third person. Professional titles, such as *Dottore* (used for any graduate), are often used. Be confident and dignified, but not overbearing or stiff, and be prepared for more formal behaviour the further north you go.

Be prepared to be flexible in business. Meetings are usually unstructured and formal presentations are uncommon. There is also an aversion to forecasting and planning so try to clear a proposal with a meeting's participants beforehand. Remember that a business association with Italians will only last as long as they find it consistently profitable.

It is rare to have a drink, except an aperitif in a café, without eating and dinner in a restaurant is the usual form of entertainment.

Luxembourg

The official language is Luxembourgisch which is mainly spoken in the home and on social occasions. Few foreigners bother to learn it so if you have mastered even a few words your relationships will be improved. Many Luxembourgers speak French and German fluently and a lot speak three or more foreign languages.

Business and social life is kept separate and there is a certain reserve but at work the atmosphere is collaborative and consensus oriented. It is unwise to assert a position unless you are very sure of your ground, and then only do so modestly. Assertiveness, strong criticism and personal remarks are considered aggressive and rude. In fact Luxembourgers themselves often seem over modest, and outside working hours you may have to take the initiative to establish social relationships.

The Netherlands

Dutch businessmen are generally chauvinistic but also adept at dealing with foreigners so you will find your usual etiquette acceptable. Business and social life in the Netherlands is less formal than in other parts of Europe so don't overdress. Take a simple, compact wardrobe of co-ordinated clothes. In many companies women wear trousers so you can be smart but understated.

Communciation should not be a problem because on average the Dutch are fluent in three additional languages (English, German and French) and many are reasonably proficient in several more.

Be businesslike and straightforward and honour commitments, however minor. Meetings are regular and serve as a time for decision-making after a thorough discussion. However, the Dutch are sometimes reluctant to give a straight yes or no.

There is no rigid barrier between home and work and socialising takes place over coffee rather than during meals.

Portugal

In Portugal business relationships are personal and informal and there is little distinction between dressing for work or for a social function. The amount of formality in dress varies with the seasons. There are familiar and polite forms of address. Generally use the formal *você*. *Doutor* is used indiscriminately to anyone who might have a university degree. It is most important not to use the informal *tu* with junior people and subordinates unless you have had a long business relationship with them. If you speak Spanish you will be understood but replies will probably be in Portugese.

Most appointments and meetings are unlikely to start on time. Meetings are for briefing and discussion, and are not meant to be implemental. If you need an agreement for a proposal at a meeting it is essential to have lobbied the participants in private beforehand. The business day includes long lunches and relaxed dinners at restaurants. Business and social life overlap so it is common to have evening meetings and phone calls.

Scandinavia

This consists of Denmark, Norway, Sweden, Finland and Iceland. There is well advanced equality of the sexes in Scandinavia but this does mean that women are expected to fend for themselves.

Dress depends on the climate. The long winters mean that for half the year warm and practical clothes are the norm rather than high style. Even in business most women wear trousers all the year round. Opt for comfort and practicality first otherwise you will seem overdressed. Take one striking jacket for the evening and layers of clothing which can be added or discarded.

In Denmark most people speak English. Everyone goes home at five and there is little social mixing among colleagues outside work. Entertaining is usually informal at home over an early dinner. The Danes prefer you to be frank and punctual.

In Sweden there is a high proportion of women in the workforce but jobs are still very sex segregated. If you are conducting business in a traditionally male-dominated industry expect to be dealing with men.

Finland was the first country in Europe to give universal and equal franchise to women and make them eligible for parliamentary elections. But there are still definite 'male' and 'female' jobs. The Finns dress formally for business meetings, at elegant restaurants and for some social functions, but otherwise dress is casual.

Spain

Women who are educationally qualified for professional and managerial positions are a recent phenomenon so expect to be dealing with men. Traditional Spanish organisations are built on the concept of a personal hierarchy and have a strong sense of order and discipline.

Business and social behaviour is very informal. You will be on first name terms quickly but manners are slightly more formal in the north of the country. Remember that modesty is valued over assertiveness.

With the exception of large companies there is a marked absence of correspondence, memos and other written communications. Communication is predominantly face-to-face. Procrastination and delay are endemic and the traditional function of meetings, if they occur at all, is to communicate instructions.

Lunches and dinners are a vital part of business life and are used to establish a personal working relationship. Discuss anything except business until coffee is served then wait for your host to bring up the specific subject of the meeting.

Eastern Europe and Russia

With the general decline in communism in Eastern Europe and Russia, the area has opened up more to Western business. However, there are still problems. A marked increase in crime makes it important to be more cautious about safety than usual. You would be sensible to go with a male colleague, if possible.

Ask about suitable hotels from the country's tourist board. Be careful about using private taxis and however tempting it seems, do not change money in the street. Dress smartly but casually and avoid wearing expensive jewellery or showing any other ostentatious form of wealth.

UNITED STATES OF AMERICA

Many UK companies have strong business links with the USA making it a common business destination.

Each geographic area has its own variations in culture, lifestyle and climate, resulting in wide variations in dress. Overall, the USA is fashion-conscious, especially in big cities. In the major cities female executives wear trainers for walking about town so you can do the same.

To do business in the USA you need to demonstrate competence and professionalism by taking a numerate, analytical approach to problem-solving. Modesty is not a virtue here – you will gain more respect by knowing your worth and showing motivation and commitment. Bluntness is preferred to subtelty. Companies operate a rigorously defined hierarchy. Status in the US business world is equated to power so be sure to use your business title.

Planning is detailed and taken very seriously; meetings are primarily for imparting and gathering information. A joke is obligatory as a warm-up to speeches and presentations. Long working hours are common in certain industries and cities, especially New York, and you should expect to be accessible in the evenings and at weekends.

Business relationships are tempered by a great deal of informal socialising and friendliness but at social events business is often the main topic of conversation. You will find that strangers at a cocktail party (including yourself) will be introduced by employer and business title as well as by name.

JAPAN

Japanese businesswomen have not been readily accepted by the business community in Japan. They are often an isolated class and are still rarely invited into the men's social circle. In Japan, you are most likely to be dealing with men. On-the-town business entertaining is an integral part of cementing business relationships but female executives and wives do not usually accompany men on business jaunts. When they do they remain on the sidelines and often other arrangements will be made for them. You should not expect to be invited to evening entertainments which often centre around drinking because these are regarded as men-only sessions. This can make it difficult for a woman to form the appropriate inter-personal relationships which are so important in Japanese business.

You should try to gain respect by showing an open interest in the language and culture. Dress in conservative, well-cut clothes and keep your gestures small.

Make appointments before arriving in Japan or there will be long delays. The company you are dealing with will require lots of information about your own organisation from the start and you must supply it in detail. You can respectfully ask for similar information from them and it may be considered negligent and inept not to do so. It is best to be introduced by a mutual contact such as a bank or other respectable business associate, otherwise you will need a letter of introduction.

Close attention should be paid to body language. Nodding the head means 'yes' but also 'I am paying attention' so it doesn't necesarily imply agreement. 'No' is only used with great reluctance and is usually implied rather than stated. The Japanese are extremely polite and deferential, and dislike confrontation. Relationships at all levels are built on exchange.

Use a person's last name followed by *San* or, with a senior person, their title then *San*. Always have plenty of business cards and present them to everyone in the business circle to avoid causing offence. When presenting a card to a superior do so with both hands. When presented with a card read it straightaway. Bowing the head is a mark of respect – on average two or three times. A subordinate bows slightly lower and longer.

Keep up a regular flow of letters and greetings cards otherwise Japanese businessmen will lose interest and consider the relationship arbitrary and short-term. Personal relationships are the key to business procedures.

THE ARAB WORLD

Some women are reluctant to travel to the Middle East on business (and their companies reluctant to send them) because the Arab business world is male-dominated and local customs unsympathetic to women. Recently, however, businesswomen have been more successful in the Arab world but in general businessmen will still be ill at ease with them. You may find it essential to employ a local agent or representative to accompany you throughout the business day.

Make sure that you are aware of the expectations of the particular country you are visiting. Islam influences every aspect of life in the Arab world but some places are much stricter than others. Saudi Arabia, for example, is probably the strictest whereas Dubai in the United Arab Emirates (UAE) takes a more lenient line.

Courtesy and hospitality to strangers are part of the Arab way of life and so you will be made to feel welcome. English is also widely used in business. Although a friendly approach to business is best, Arabs drive hard bargains despite their courtesy. Major business decisions are made at the very highest level and the need to pass decisions up can cause delays. But the end result can be quick rulings and fast implementation. Time is a weapon in negotiating. You will not succeed if you try to hurry. Integrity is vital and you will be expected to keep your word to the letter at all times.

In Muslim countries Friday is the holy day so no business is done. In some Middle East countries businesses are also closed on Sundays. Saturday is a normal working day.

Beware of over-familiarity and do not discuss politics, sex or religion. You should avoid pointing your foot at someone, or showing the sole of your shoe, so don't cross your legs and keep your feet on the floor. Always eat with your right hand. Don't be over-admiring of your host's possessions or he may feel obliged to give them to you!

Sometimes men will bring their wives to meet you. You may get invited by them to events, but these will be for women only. You are unlikely to be invited into someone's home because that honour is reserved for those who frequently visit and are real friends. It is the convention not to mention a man's wife, although he may talk about his children. Extend your greetings and respect to the family – this will imply the understanding that he is married and you are not 'available'. At a reception there is usually no alcohol.

Do not display much bare flesh. Revealing or figure-hugging clothing is offensive because of Islamic law. In some countries trousers are acceptable (if you keep them loose), however skirts or dresses reaching below the knee are advisable. Blouses and dresses must have long sleeves and high necks.

Beware of the heat. Loose cotton, washable clothes will protect from the heat and dust during the day. As you need to avoid dehydration in the high temperatures do make sure you keep your head shaded from the sun, drink enough fluids and keep a high salt intake.

Another reason for keeping covered up is to protect against malaria from mosquito bites. Use insect repellent creams and take anti-malaria tablets too.

Punctuality is not considered a major virtue; appointments are made to give a rough time of arrival. Some countries are very flexible about appointments. Although traditional Saudis keep an open office and anyone can arrive without an appointment, it would be discourteous for a foreigner to do so. Business is conducted at a leisurely pace and time will be taken to get to know you. Do not get impatient or try to hurry this process. The host may conduct several conversations at once.

Coffee is drunk a great deal; never leave before it is served – have one or two sips and then shake the cup and hand it back otherwise you will be kept supplied indefinitely. Try to learn a few simple Arabic phrases and greetings because they will be warmly received. Do not drink, eat or smoke in public during Ramadan and try not to make business visits during this time because Muslims will be tired.

CHAPTER

12

Sexual Harassment at Work

WOMEN are not immune from sexual harassment at work, in spite of the progress made towards equality of treatment. There are still men who feel the need to demonstrate their power over women in unpleasant ways. Sexual harassment, moreover, is not confined to any one age group, and nor does it take account of professional status.

WHAT IS SEXUAL HARASSMENT?

Sexual harassment is usually the harassment of women by men, although men can be harassed and women do harass other women. It can range from being called unpleasant names to groping or rape. In practice each woman differs about what she regards as harassment. One may find being called 'pet' endearing, while another may be upset and angry that it diminishes her status as a woman.

What is generally agreed is that sexual harassment is any *unwelcome* sexual attention. Now that organisations are beginning to take the subject seriously, many have produced their own definitions. For example the Transport and General Workers Union (TGWU) guidelines *Dealing with sexual harassment* say it is 'behaviour of a sexual nature, or other conduct based on sex, which is directed at someone who neither welcomes it nor returns it.' It can include unwelcome physical, verbal or non-verbal conduct.

Continuation of sexual harassment often occurs when advances have been rejected. The man may 'punish' the woman by complaining about her work, giving bad references, abuse or dismissal. The consequences of sexual harassment can last long after the original sexual advances, and cause as much if not more distress.

153

WHERE DOES IT HAPPEN?

The workplace is the most common stage for sexual harassment. If women have status and power this can make men nervous. The fact that many women are subservient to men in the work hierarchy, however high up they climb, is another reason for some men to want to demean them. Women working in male-dominated environments are particularly vulnerable to sexual harassment, but it is not confined to these places.

Many men assume that you will not report them because you risk losing your job or promotion. That is one of the reasons many women have put up with sexual abuse for years. But now women are deciding that fighting back is best.

WHO ARE THE CULPRITS?

There is no 'typical' man you can spot and avoid. A woman sharing a cab with a client after a business dinner may be attacked in the cab; she may have her knee fondled by the director at a meeting; she may be called sexually unpleasant names in front of clients by a colleague; she may be raped in an empty office by a member of staff – the list is endless, and there is no way of foretelling who will do what or when.

Most men would be horrified by the thought of such treatment of women, and go to great lengths to treat women with respect and consideration. But there are still men in all positions of business life who find women a threat.

There is no obvious pattern to harassment. One man may be an habitual harasser, another may be an opportunist, yet another may harass only when drunk, another may rape once when in a rage. Decide when you feel uncomfortable or unsafe with a man's attentions, and take action.

TYPES OF HARASSMENT

Name calling and other irritations

A common harassment is calling women by familiar names such as darling or dear. How you deal with this will depend on how seriously you take it. Many women simply dismiss it as a mild compliment and ignore it – others are upset by it. It is sensible to put it in perspective. Being called dear by the near-retirement stores manager who has called every woman that for his whole working life is not the same as being called darling by a male colleague. Being called pet by a Northerner, for whom it is a common form of greeting, is not the same as being called pet by the managing director.

If you really don't like it, simply say so politely. In most cases the man concerned will retire hurt and embarrassed and will not re-offend. If you continue to be on the receiving end, report it to your personnel manager or women's officer. If it is a client, send a male colleague or refuse to do business with them if you can.

Other harassments can range from staring at you to making unpleasant or untrue remarks about you to other people. It can be difficult to deal with, especially if your colleagues or staff are involved. If simply telling them to stop does not work then you may have to move or fire them – if you have the power – or report them to your union for further action. Sometimes merely the threat of reporting will do the trick. But do not be afraid to take it further if it does not cease. There are more details about dealing with harassment later in this chapter.

Benefit of the doubt

By no means all men who make mildly suggestive remarks or put a hand on your arm intend to intimidate or upset. They think they are being friendly and charming, and have no idea that they cause offence.

Don't immediately launch into an attack on any hapless male who happens to offend you by addressing you in the wrong way or by patting your hand. Simply say that you don't like it. Say with a smile, 'Calling me "pet" makes me feel like the office cat. I'd prefer you not to', will achieve the right effect with minimum aggro. In nine cases out of ten the man will back off immediately. It is in the tenth case that you need to take firmer action.

Telephone harassment

The telephone can be used for a nasty and insidious form of abuse, because the caller can remain anonymous while causing the maximum distress. A harassing call can be abusive, suggestive or pornographic. Many people do not take the idea of unpleasant telephone calls seriously. But the distress of the victim can be devastating, and affect home and emotional life and ability to do their job properly.

If you start receiving unpleasant calls at work, put the phone down immediately. Dial 1471 to use BT's new call return service to find the caller's number. If you have a phone with call display, the number will appear on the phone's screen. Report the calls to the police and BT (see Malicious calls helplines under 'Useful Addresses', p.219). BT can trace calls even if the caller dialled 141 to hide his number. If the call is internal then arrange for calls to be monitored until the caller is traced. Outside calls can be deterred by arranging for a male colleague to screen calls before passing them to you; an answering machine can also be used to screen callers.

Don't speak to anyone who refuses to identify himself, his place of work and reason for calling.

Women who work alone from home feel particularly vulnerable when such calls are made. Working late in an empty office creates the same effect.

BT has a system of tracing calls, and work with the police to trace callers so that they can be prosecuted under the 1984 Telecommunications Act. The Act makes it a criminal offence to make malicious phone calls. Section 3 states that:

(1)   A person who –

a) sends, by means of a public telecommunication system, a message or other matter that is grossly offensive or of an indecent, obscene or menacing character; or

b) sends by those means, for the purpose of causing annoyance, inconvenience or needless anxiety to another, a message that he knows to be false or persistently makes use of for that purpose of a public telecommunication system, shall be guilty of an offence and liable on summary conviction of a fine not exceeding level 3 on the standard scale.

The maximum penalty under the Act is a £1,000 fine. The new Criminal Justice Bill could raise this to three months in jail or a maximum fine of £2,500.

In 1994 the first phone pest was convicted for grievous bodily harm for causing his victim psychological suffering. A bank clerk bombarded a woman with over 500 obscene calls over a period of nine months, and he was jailed for 18 months.

In extreme cases you can ask to go ex-directory. This is only sensible if you work from home, and it can make life difficult in a world where the ability to be contacted by phone can mean business gain or loss.

Fear of the fax

Now that the fax is widespread in the business world it has also opened up the way for abuse. Dirty pictures and writing can be sent for you personally or for the whole office to see.

If you find the fax in your room is being used to attack you, then transfer it to the main office and arrange for your faxes to come through the main office rather than directly to you. Use a pseudonym or prearranged code to ensure that genuine faxes reach you and use the business name only in fax directories.

SERIOUS SEXUAL ASSAULT AND VIOLENCE

The worst kind of sexual harassment is physical contact which damages and abuses.

Any sort of physical assault should be reported immediately. But while you may be able to move away from a groper, getting away from a rapist may not be easy. If you are attacked violently try to get away fast. Do not be afraid of inflicting injury on your attacker by jabbing his eyes, twisting his balls, kicking his shin or biting. He is harming you. Scream as loudly as you can. In a workplace, even at night, there may be someone else in the building. At home a neighbour may hear.

If you can't get away and your life is threatened then you will have to give in. But try to remember as much about your attacker as possible.

Consider taking assertiveness and self-defence classes so that you can be trained to react in frightening situations. Sometimes the fact that you have reacted in a situation where the attacker was not expecting you to may deter him.

Choices

Your first duty is to yourself. Get to someone fast – a colleague, friend, neighbour. You need support. When reporting a serious sexual assault such as rape you may want to contact the Rape Crisis Centre (see 'Useful Addresses', p.219) or a close female friend or relative to accompany you to the police station. If you want to report the attack to the police then you must go to them without washing or changing your clothes.

Some police stations now have special rooms and trained female officers to make the physical examination and reporting of the incident as trauma-free as possible. A female doctor will do the examination if possible.

Many women still feel unable to go through with criminal proceedings, particularly as the trauma of court proceedings may not result in conviction for the attacker. But those who do help others by bringing attackers to justice.

If you decide not to report a serious incident to the police you may want to talk to someone at the Rape Crisis Centre or the Samaritans. Counselling is an important part of coming to terms with the attack and to expunging any feelings of guilt you may have. Get someone to take you to hospital.

How can you deal with them?

Do your best to avoid being alone with men who try to harass you. Report them immediately to your union representative, personnel manager and, if appropriate the police. If the person you are supposed to report such offences to is the person who attacked you or does not take you seriously, then report it to someone else in the organisation. Women working on their own should report it to a partner or the police.

Your company and union should have a policy statement on sexual harassment, and a standard grievance procedure to be followed in such cases. Few women use their company's grievance procedures because they fear that they will not be taken seriously, or that no action will be taken. Unions and other organisations, however, are now taking sexual harassment seriously, and are committed to action against it.

If you think you cannot approach them on your own, confide in sympathetic female colleagues and ask one of them to accompany you. Most of the main unions give similar advice:

- Tell your harasser that you do not want his attentions. If you cannot say so to his face, write him a letter and keep a copy.
- Keep a note of the date, place, time and name of any incidents of sexual harassment you experience.
- Tell female friends and colleagues and see if a joint represen-tation will halt the harassment.
- Report it to your personnel manager, union representative or other official.
- Report serious sexual assault to the police.

If you are denied promotion or forced to leave, or if you decide to leave because the harassment is too much, then you can claim constructive dismissal. Employers are responsible for the behaviour of their staff, and can be prosecuted for allowing you to be attacked.

Who else to turn to

The Rape Crisis Centre will help by listening to you, helping you and accompanying you to the police if you wish to report it to them. The chance to talk it through to a sympathetic listener should be taken.

Women Against Sexual Harassment supports and advises women who have been sexually harassed at work. Its activities include training, research and policy development work. It also takes men as clients, and works closely with employers, trade unions and other agencies to deal with harassment at work.

The Suzy Lamplugh Trust was started by Diana Lamplugh after the disappearance of her daughter Suzy in 1986. The Trust seeks through research, education and training to enable people to help themselves to go about their daily lives with increased confidence and without fear. It arranges conferences and seminars, campaigns for changes in the law and procedures and provides talks for organisations throughout the country. It also provides personal safety leaflets, books, videos, personal alarms, training manuals, education for children and training in the workplace.

The Samaritans will listen to anyone who phones them at times of distress and their phone number is in your local phone book. These and other useful organisations are listed in 'Useful Addresses', pp.218–219.

POLICY AND PROCEDURES

Most unions and organisations now have policy statements on sexual harassment and standard procedures for dealing with complaints of sexual harassment in the workplace. These stem from the knowledge that sexual harassment is an offence under the Sex Discrimination Act 1975. Most organisations follow certain general guidelines.

The first is that you are represented by people who are sympathetic to anyone who complains about sexual harassment – if possible a woman officer. The matter is treated in the strictest confidence, and any action is only carried out with your full consent.

Confirmation is sought that you did not want or welcome the sexual harassment and detailed notes are kept. The harasser is told about the complaint and an attempt is made to deal with it informally. If this has no result then formal procedures can be started, but only with the full consent of you and your union.

You are advised to keep full notes of what happened, times,

places, dates and any witnesses to the sexual harassment. These notes can be crucial if the case goes to an Industrial Tribunal. If you agree, other workers are asked if they have suffered similar harassment. If you report a serious sexual assault you are advised to go to the police.

If the case goes to an Industrial Tribunal it must do so within three months of the incident, or series of incidents, reported. If a formal procedure is instigated then your line manager must be told, and if possible a female manager with experience of dealing with sexual harassment cases is consulted.

To reduce possible distress to you, written reports are prepared as far as possible rather than asking you to repeat stories unnecessarily. The case is also dealt with within strict time limits.

You should not be made to agree to a transfer or suspension, nor should anyone dealing with cases of sexual harassment insist that you should continue to work with your harasser.

If the harasser is from your union then you and he should each have different representatives, and your representative should not be lower in rank than that of the accused.

If a member of the public has harassed you at work then your employer may be negligent for failing to provide a safe work environment.

You should be reminded of your right to take your case to an Industrial Tribunal under the Sex Discrimination Act and/or where appropriate the constructive dismissal provisions of the Employment Protection (Consolidation) Act.

Taking a case of sexual harassment to an Industrial Tribunal is seen as a last resort, because they have not had a high success rate. There are now pressures on Tribunals to take the European Recommendations and Directives into account, however.

The harasser's rights

The accused has rights too, and these must be adhered to for justice's sake. However a woman who has been a victim of sexual harassment feels about it, her harasser is entitled to a fair hearing.

People accused of sexual harassment and subject to disciplinary action must be told what the charges are against them and should be allowed to state their case. The enquiry should be conducted by impartial people, and be seen to be free from bias.

If someone appeals then a time limit should be specified within which the appeal should be lodged. It should be dealt with speedily, should be held by a higher authority than the person taking disciplinary action, should say what action may be taken, and allow the employee or his representative to comment on new evidence.

This all sounds fair. Unfortunately, the reality for the victim is that the case becomes drawn out and the embarrassment and misery of the original action can mean that it is the victim who suffers more than the offender.

The ordeal of sexual harassment is harrowing enough. But women who are driven to take legal proceedings to claim compensation, to protect their professional and personal reputations, and to restore their self-esteem, often find that the proceedings themselves are extremely difficult It is hardly surprising that many women who start such proceedings end up by settling out of court with a 'no publicity' clause, or give up.

Whatever the outcome of the case, it is often the victim who is left without a job or promotion prospects, and the perpetrator who remains in his job or is sacked with a decent monetary package.

THE LAW

A MORI poll commissioned by the BBC in 1993 found that nearly a third of working women had been harassed at work. An Industrial Society survey put the figure even higher, at one in two. The Equal Opportunities Commission (EOC) noted that complaints about sexual harassment had increased by 50 per cent per annum since 1991. A survey by the *Independent on Sunday* in 1991 concluded that almost 2 million women in the UK had experienced this.

With such overwhelming evidence of sexual harassment of women in the workplace, it is alarming to learn that there is no legislation which specifically refers to it. Although many more women are taking legal action against sexual harassment, redress is usually sought under the Sex Discrimination Act of 1975. The Act states that (section 1(1)(a)):

A person discriminates against a woman in any circumstances relevant for the purposes of any provisions of this Act if:

a) On the grounds of her sex he treats her less favourably than he treats or would treat a man . . .

and (section 6(2)(b):

It is unlawful for a person, in the case of a woman employed by him at an establishment in Great Britain, to discriminate against her:-

a) In the way he affords her access to opportunities for promotion, transfer or training, or to any other benefits, facilities or services, or by refusing or deliberately omitting to afford her access to them, or

b) by dismissing her, or subjecting her to any other detriment.

Successful claims against sexual harassment have also been achieved in the courts under other forms of legislation, where employers have been found negligent in their duty to protect the claimant at work, and also in the light of assault and battery charges against the sufferers.

Since the mid-1980s, the EAT (Employment Appeal Tribunal) has recognised that if any part of the treatment of a woman by another person includes elements of a sexual nature to which a woman is vulnerable but a man is not, then clearly the woman is being treated less favourably on account of her sex. One single act of a 'serious nature' can support a claim of sexual harassment under the Act.

Employer's negligence

Employers who fail to stem sexual harassment on the part of their employees who are 'acting within the course of their employment' can be sued along with the harasser. If the employer fails to take appropriate action – such as by mounting a serious investigation into the complaint – then the complainant may be able to claim constructive dismissal. Many victims of sexual harassment who resist sexual advances suffer by losing out in promotion chances or by being dismissed. If a victim cannot bear to remain in her workplace she may resign or ask for a transfer.

Employees who have worked for the same employer for two years may also be able to make a complaint of constructive dismissal under the Employment Protection (Consolidation) Act 1978.

If the victim remains at work and complains to an Industrial Tribunal she can satisfy the need for the Act to show 'detriment' if she has suffered sexual harassment which causes her legitimately to complain of her working conditions or environment. She does not have to have been dismissed or suffered some other adverse career decision on her employer's part to claim this.

If an employer can prove that he or she took all reasonably practicable steps to prevent the conduct in question, then they can avoid prosecution.

EUROPEAN COMMISSION

The European Commission adopted a Recommendation and Code of Practice in November 1991 on the protection and dignity of men and women at work. Although Recommendations are not binding on Member States, the ECJ (European Court of Justice) ruled that national courts must take them into account when deciding disputes submitted to them. As a result, a woman who claims sexual harassment will be able to refer to this Recommendation and Code of Practice to support her case. All workers have an equal right to work in an environment free from sexual harassment.

The Code recommends that senior management should formulate a policy statement which should be communicated to all staff. It should:

- state that sexual harassment will not be permitted or condoned;
- make it clear that managers and supervisors have a clear duty to implement the policy and to take corrective action to ensure that it is complied with;
- explain what procedures should be followed by employees who are victims of sexual harassment at work in order to get help;
- contain an undertaking that any complaint of sexual harassment will be dealt with seriously, quickly and in confidence, and that complainants will not be victimised;
- state the disciplinary measures which will be taken against employees who are guilty of sexual harassment.

A European Court ruling in 1993 removed the £11,000 upper limit on damages that can be awarded in cases of sexual discrimination.

While Europe has clearly got the measure of sexual harassment rulings we still wait for such an equally clear understanding of it in British law.

WILL YOU GET ANOTHER JOB?

Whether or not you are dismissed or resign because of the pressure you need to look for a new job. You may be concerned that a new employer may not look kindly on someone who has no references, or misleading references from a disgruntled boss or firm.

Be honest in your applications. If you have won a dismissal case then you should have no trouble in eventually finding employment again. But some organisations may consider even a successful complainant a potential embarrassment or troublemaker. If you failed to win even though harassment occurred, you may be in a more difficult position. Be as honest as possible. Try to find two or more colleagues who are on your side to put as referees to bypass inaccurate reports from a previous boss. If it comes to the worst, consider starting a business on your own.

Women who work for themselves have no such problem. Their difficulty will lie in deciding whether a client or colleague who sexually harasses them is so valuable that they cannot afford to lose them. You may well suffer a loss of income if you stop doing business with him, but you will suffer more if you take no action.

WORKING FROM HOME – HOW
TO KEEP SAFE

If you work from home at your own business you will not be immune from sexual harassment. You still have to meet clients, open the door to strangers and answer the phone. Much of how to deal with sexual harassment in the workplace will apply to you. But you have some added problems. If you are the victim of sexual harassment there are unlikely to be any witnesses.

Play safe by refusing to meet anyone alone if possible. Why not come to a reciprocal arrangement with another lone business-woman in your area that you have certain times when you meet each other's clients together?

Always find out the name, address and phone number of anyone who phones, and then make an excuse to phone back to check on them. Write the details of who and where you are to meet and the time in a large desk diary and leave it open to view on your desk. Try and let someone else know where you are going to meet a client. If this is not possible, leave a message on your answering machine to that effect.

Never open your door to anyone you don't know or haven't arranged to call. Invest in good locks and a door chain. Check IDs by phoning the company named on the card, not the number on the card.

Always wear clothes you can move easily in, and carry a personal alarm and a few coins for the phone or a phone card. Keep car doors locked and do not stop for accidents (unless you are involved) – report them to the police.

Women who work late in offices are also subject to danger.

Always make sure someone you trust knows you are there, and arrange for a cab or someone to collect you. Make sure there is good phone contact with security staff.

HOW CAN BUSINESSWOMEN
HELP EACH OTHER?

There are a number of practical steps you can take to improve the climate for women in your workplace and to improve procedures in your organisation for preventing and dealing with cases of sexual harassment. You can try to change unacceptable attitudes and bad practices in your workplace. Take time to listen to other women who report sexual harassment to you, and advise them how to deal with it. Tell them what grievance procedures they can use, and how to instigate legal action or report incidents to the police. Advise victims of serious assault to go to the police, and support them if necessary.

Check whether your organisation has an equal opportunities policy which includes a statement that sexual harassment will not be tolerated, and let other workers know. Ask for grievance procedures which deal specifically with sexual harassment cases to be adopted.

Ask your management to nominate a woman from the management team to be responsible for sexual harassment cases. If you are suitable why not volunteer? Arrange for your staff and workplace representatives to have training in dealing with sexual harassment cases.

Raise the subject of sexual harassment at management and union meetings, and try to promote discussion about removing pin-ups and 'girlie' calendars.

Report all incidents of sexual harassment to your women's representative and your line manager. By making a positive contribution to sexual harassment awareness you will be making life easier for the next generation of businesswomen.

Summary points for dealing with sexual harassment at work

- Avoid working alone late at night.
- Keep a personal alarm on you.
- Tell the harasser orally and in writing that you don't want his attentions.

- Keep a diary of the harassment.
- Get support from female colleagues.
- Report the harassment to your personnel manager and union representative.
- If you suffer a serious sexual assault report it to the police.
- Don't be afraid to fight back if attacked.

13

Losing Your Job

THE THREAT of losing a job is one of the fears that haunts everyone in today's recession-led society. Nobody from the director down can be sure that the next time staff are surplus to requirements their name will not be on the list.

For women who are the main breadwinners or whose salary makes a vital contribution to the household budget, losing their job clearly means a great deal more than the misery of rejection.

This chapter will explain what redundancy is, how it affects women in particular, what your rights are, and how you can cope with it. It will also discuss the problem of unfair dismissal.

WHAT IS REDUNDANCY?

Redundancy occurs when an employer's need for work of a particular kind done by an employee has come to an end, or is reduced either on a temporary or permanent basis. It is not simply cutting back on production when the employees are retained, even if hours are reduced. An employee cannot refuse to accept this situation and claim redundancy.

WHY MIGHT YOU BE MADE REDUNDANT?

There are many reasons why you might be made redundant. You might:

- be surplus to staff requirements because the work you do is no longer needed by the company;
- be part of an entire department which is to be axed;
- be the victim of firm closure or bankruptcy;
- be with a firm which has been taken over by another company.

Whatever the reason, the result is a feeling of failure. It can even be severe enough to cause physical symptoms.

The immediate result can also be anger, but then a lassitude can set in, with the effort of applying for new jobs debilitating and dispiriting.

There may be hostility from partners or families, which may be overt or unintentional. If your income was vital to the household budget, then the strain a redundancy puts on a working partner can be considerable. It can lead to the break-up of an otherwise healthy relationship.

REDUNDANCY RIGHTS

You do have certain rights when you are made redundant, as a member of a union and as an individual. All workers are protected from redundancy on grounds of race or sex, however short their service. Your union rights apply however long you have worked for the firm, even if you have less than two years service. Part-time workers now also have the same redundancy rights as full-time employees. These rights do not, however, apply to Crown employees or short-term workers.

Part-time workers

Women make up 87 per cent of part-time workers. Discrimination against part-time workers can therefore be considered sex discrimination.

Until recently part-time workers did not have the same rights of employment protection as their full-time colleagues. Until recently part-timers working between eight and sixteen hours a week had to wait for three years longer than their full-time counterparts – that is five years – before they were entitled to statutory redundancy pay and the right to claim unfair dismissal.

The government was not keen to introduce the necessary legislation to improve rights for part-time workers, but was challenged in court by the Equal Opportunities Commission who brought the case on the grounds of sex discrimination. The House of Lords ruled in 1994 that part-timers who work more than eight hours a week are to have the same employment protection as full-timers.

The new ruling finally became law in January 1995 despite government opposition. As forecasts indicate that most jobs created in the future will be part-time, this is an important victory for the rights of women and part-timers in general.

Until now women risked dismissal because of pregnancy. However, a legal judgement in October 1995 confirmed that employers who sack women for becoming pregnant are automatically guilty of sex discrimination. Employers who ignore the law in such cases could face claims for unlimited compensation.

Union rights

Under Section 99 of the Employment Act 1975, employers must consult the relevant trade union about redundancies concerning all workers. This means that:

- the employer must tell the union the reasons for any proposed redundancies, the number of redundancies proposed, the methods proposed for choosing whom to make redundant and how redundancies are going to be carried out;
- the consultation must start as soon as possible. If the employer doesn't abide by the rules, workers may be entitled to compensation.

Your individual redundancy rights

You are entitled to be treated fairly in matters concerning your redundancy. What constitutes 'fairness' will depend on the circumstances of each case. The following conditions should apply:

- *Proper notice.* Where there is no written contract of employment you must get the statutory minimum, which is one week's notice if you have worked from one month to two years for your employer; one week for each full year of employment where you have worked for two to twelve years; and twelve weeks notice if you have worked for your employer for over twelve years. Anyone who has worked for less than one month is not entitled to notice. You may be able to show that a certain length of notice was implied in the terms of employment. So if you have been employed on a monthly basis you can argue that you are entitled to a month's notice even if the statutory minimum is less. The more highly paid the profession and the more senior you are the more notice you will be given. Your employer can give you notice to leave and ask you to do so immediately but must pay you for the period of notice you are entitled to. This is 'wages in lieu of notice'.

- *As much warning as possible to your trade union and fellow workers.* Your employer must consult your trade union about how the reduction in employee numbers can be met with as little hardship as possible. Part of the consultation should aim at setting criteria for how individuals are selected for redundancy.
- *Criteria for making people redundant should be applied in an objective way, and it should not rely on the sole discretion of one person.*
- *Your employer should ensure that selections for redundancy are made according to the agreed criteria, and should consider any representations from your union.*
- *Your employer should closely investigate any opportunity for offering alternative employment.*

In short your employer must act reasonably towards you in the matter of redundancy.

Giving your notice

If you want to leave your job you must give a week's notice if you have worked for your employer for four weeks or more. You may have a written contract of employment which specifies a longer length of time. If you resign without giving notice you can be sued by your employer for breach of contract. As an employer is unlikely to sue because of the effect on workplace morale and courts tend to be sympathetic to employees, the most he or she will usually do is refuse to give you a reference.

WHEN A BUSINESS IS TRANSFERRED

If your company is taken over and employees are transferred to a new company, the new owners may want to reduce overheads and labour costs. Fortunately, when a business is sold or employees transferred, the rights and duties of your employers and their employees are transferred too. If dismissals occur as a result of a transfer these are usually regarded as unfair. This is a complicated area of law, however, and if you are affected in this way you should get professional help.

OFFER OF NEW EMPLOYMENT

If you qualify for redundancy payment then you may be offered other employment. If you unreasonably refuse an offer of other employment then you might lose your entitlement to payment. An offer of work could be re-employment on the same terms, or suitable employment where the terms differ.

If you are offered an appropriate new job on different terms to your old one you are entitled to a trial period in the new position. When an employer imposes new terms of employment which technically amount to a breach of contract, you must be given a reasonable period to consider your response to the new arrangement. If before this reasonable time is up you decide that you don't like the new job you can then claim redundancy payment.

GUARANTEED PAYMENTS

If there is a layoff caused by reduction in your workload you may be entitled to guaranteed payments. To qualify for such payments you should have lost a complete day or day's work and have complied with reasonable requests to ensure that your services are available.

You should not have unreasonably refused any offer of suitable work and there must not have been any industrial action.

How much redundancy payment?

The amount of redundancy pay will depend on your age, what you earn each week and how long you have been continuously employed by your employer. Statutory redundancy pay is calculated on a week's pay, that is the money which is payable for a week's work while under contract of employment. It may be more difficult to calculate this sum if you work overtime, varied shifts or piecework.

This weekly sum is multiplied by certain numbers depending on your age. For each year of employment you will get one-and-a-half times your weekly pay for each year of your age between 41 and 65; one times your weekly pay for each year of your age between 22 and 40; and a half of your weekly pay for each year you were employed between the ages of 18 and 21. No more than 20 years service can be taken into account, and earnings more than a certain amount will be disregarded. Therefore the maximum redundancy is 20 x $1\frac{1}{2}$ x the upper weekly pay limit. This amount is reduced if you are made redundant after your 64th birthday. To qualify for this payment you must have had an approved period of continuous employment. Some employers have a more generous severance scheme.

Unemployment benefit is not means tested and is not affected by any redundancy payment. However, redundancy pay is taken into account for anyone claiming income support.

If your employer can't pay

If your employer cannot pay redundancy payments because he is insolvent – that is his liabilities exceed his assets – arrangements can be made for the payments to be made directly from the Redundancy Fund of the Department of Employment (DoE). The DoE will then try to recover the money from the assets of the business. Certain employees can make preferential claims, including people who are owed wage arrears up to four months, holiday pay or pension contributions up to four months. There is a limit on these payments, and you will not get them if your employer simply disappears.

EMPLOYMENT PROTECTION (CONSOLIDATION) ACT 1978

The redundancy provisions in this Act provide for a lump sum payment to an employee who is made redundant or is laid off or kept on short time for a substantial period.

The Act says that an employee has 'accrued right in his job' and is therefore entitled to monetary compensation for loss. There are some exceptions, but in general it applies to employees under 65 who were employed after the age of 18 and have been under contract of employment for two years.

You have been dismissed because of redundancy if:

1. your contract of employment is terminated by your employer with or without notice;
2. your fixed term contract has expired and you are told it cannot be renewed;
3. you terminate your contract, with or without notice, in circumstances such that you are entitled to do so without reason because of your employer's conduct.

The latter includes such things as leaving because of sexual harassment or discrimination by your employer. Dismissal can also occur on dissolution of a partnership, the death of an employer or the winding up of a company.

If you decide to go before an Industrial Tribunal to claim your entitlement to redundancy compensation it is presumed that the dismissal was for redundancy. This may be rebutted by your employer who may show evidence that redundancy was not the cause of dismissal.

Dismissal is due to redundancy if:

- your employer has ceased, or intends to cease, to carry on business for the purposes you were employed for by him;
- your employer carries on or intends to carry on the business in the place where you were employed;
- the requirements of the business for employees to carry out work of a particular kind where you have been employed has ceased, diminished or is expected to diminish. Even the temporary cessation of the business may mean redundancy.

If a company moves and a woman is made redundant she is often more vulnerable than a man would be. Women often have more constraints against moving to follow a job, and are therefore more likely to be made redundant if a company moves.

You are not justified in refusing to move to another location if your contract, collective agreement or custom permits such a move. The majority of employees' contracts do not contain such provisions, however. Each case must be judged on merit. If the company moves to a nearby location, that is not dismissal.

The volume of traditional work in your company may have decreased, or new technology has been introduced so that fewer employees are needed. If you are dismissed for these reasons then you have been made redundant. Redundancy is not the failure of employees to adapt to new methods and techniques. If they fail to do this and are dismissed, they have not been made redundant.

If you are replaced by an independent contractor it is presumed that the requirements of the business for employees of a particular kind has ceased.

If there is a change of owner at your company and the new employer offers to employ you on the same terms as your old contract, or re-engage you with a new contract, this equals an offer of renewal. You cannot claim redundancy pay if you refuse this offer, unless you can show reasonable grounds for doing so.

If you stay at work but do not claim redundancy from your old employer you can substitute a claim from your new employer, but cannot count the time in your old job towards the claim.

If your contract is renewed with new terms and conditions you are entitled to a trial period of four weeks, or longer if agreed with the employer. The new agreement must be made to you in writing by the time you start work, and it should specify the end date of the trial period and the terms and conditions which will apply after that period.

During the trial period both parties are free to terminate the arrangement, in which case the employee is considered dismissed at the termination date of the original contract.

If before or during the trial period the employee decides that the terms and conditions are unreasonable she will not get redundancy pay. The burden of proof is on the employer to prove the employee's conduct was unreasonable in refusing an offer of employment.

If the employee leaves before the notice of redundancy dismissal expires she must give notice in writing. If the employer raises no objections, then redundancy pay is given. If the employer does object, he or she must give written notice stating the objection and ask the employee to withdraw her notice. It must say that if this is not done the employer will contest liability to pay redundancy pay, and if he or she does the employee can appeal to a tribunal to examine the case on its merits.

If you leave without being dismissed when told of possible redundancy then you will not get any redundancy pay.

There are different circumstances for short-term lay-offs, or short-term working where this means that you earn less than half a week's pay due to shortage of work. If there is simply not enough work and you are laid off for a short period, you will not get redundancy pay because your employer is still providing you with work when it is available. Unless your employer has reserved the right to do so in the contract of employment this equals constructive dismissal. Even so, you may be entitled to redundancy pay in certain circumstances. You can claim it if you are laid off or on short-term working for more than four consecutive weeks or at least six weeks in any 13. The employee must give the employer notice no later than four weeks after being laid off that she intends to claim redundancy pay.

Before an employer makes employees redundant he or she must consult the appropriate trade union. The employer should consult the union even if the employees take voluntary redundancy.

For further information on redundancy procedures and implications speak to your union representative or professional association, and see 'Further Reading', p.228 for helpful books on the subject.

UNFAIR DISMISSAL

If you are caught stealing at work or attacking a colleague you will deserve to be dismissed. If, however, you are dismissed for reasons you consider unfair such as sex discrimination or pregnancy, then you can take your case to an Industrial Tribunal.

If your employer admits to dismissing you, he has to show that this was for one of the following reasons:

1. Your misconduct.
2. Your inability to do the job or unacceptable qualifications.
3. Redundancy.
4. You have done something illegal which stops you doing your job.
5. Another substantial reason.

A tribunal will then decide whether the dismissal was unfair, judging each case according to the circumstances.

If you decide that your dismissal was unfair and want to take it to a tribunal your circumstances must satisfy certain conditions.

- *Constructive dismissal.* This occurs when your employer has behaved in such a way that you are entitled to leave without giving notice. For example, sexual harassment.
- *Qualifying period.* You must have worked for your employer for a minimum period of two years to be able to bring a case of unfair dismissal. There is no qualifying period for cases of sex or race discrimination or those which involve trade union activities. You must show that you have worked for your employer continuously during this period. Only short temporary breaks are acceptable, as is absence due to sickness, injury or pregnancy up to 26 weeks. Failure to prove continuous employment may affect the amount of compensation you are entitled to. Continuity of employment is not affected if your company is taken over or transferred to an associated employer.
- *Hours of work.* All employees, whether full or part-time who have worked eight hours or more a week for two years for the same employer can bring a case of unfair dismissal.
- *Time limit.* You must make your claim within three months of dismissal. You may be able to persuade a tribunal to allow your claim out of time, but this is very rare.
- *Excluded categories.* If you are over the age of retirement or usually work abroad you cannot claim for unfair dismissal.

- **Reasons for dismissal**. If you request your employer to do so in writing he must give you written reasons why you have been dismissed.

The Advisory, Conciliation and Arbitration Service (ACAS) (see 'Useful Addresses', p.219) can act on the request of either an employer or trade union to help settle a trade dispute between them. ACAS conciliation officers must also try to settle complaints made by individuals who allege infringement of certain employment rights. A copy of the complaint presented to an industrial tribunal must be sent to a conciliation officer who must try to resolve the complaint without recourse to a tribunal hearing.

For information about industrial tribunals look in your phone book for the address of your regional office.

Compensation for unfair dismissal

If a tribunal accepts your claim of unfair dismissal, you will be awarded whatever your redundancy pay would have been.

In addition the tribunal can make a compensatory award based on loss of earnings from the date of dismissal to the date of the hearing, with extra time for reasonable unemployment; loss of statutory protection – that is, the need to work for two or more years to gain redundancy rights; loss of pension rights; expenses incurred in seeking new employment; loss of the right to long notice; and the loss of National Insurance (NI) contributions.

If your behaviour contributed to your dismissal, you fail to seek new employment, or have received an ex gratia payment from your employer, the award may be decreased. It may be increased if your employer fails to comply with a reinstatement or re-engagement order.

FAIR DISMISSAL

Your employer is entitled to dismiss you for misconduct or poor job performance. If you decide to take your case of dismissal for misconduct to a tribunal then the tribunal will decide whether what you did or didn't do amounted to misconduct.

Dismissal for poor job performance is common. In this case you are entitled to:

- a written warning that you will be dismissed if your work performance does not improve. You should ask your employer

for a written statement of what constitutes adequate job performance.
- proper training and information to enable you to do your work adequately.
- a chance to explain why you are not working as well as you should be.

If you receive a written warning – or indeed a verbal one – discuss it straightaway with your union rep, if you have one.

WHAT CAN YOU DO NOW?

After the initial period of shock and distress try to get yourself back into a routine and applying for jobs as quickly as possible. The skills and determination you will need to search for suitable employment should be treated as a full-time job in itself. This will give discipline to your days and encourage you to get up in the morning and get going. Staying at home and doing less and less may lead to depression, and also put a strain on your partner and family.

Be methodical. Apart from the standard searching in papers and at the employment exchange for work, attend your local job centre (see your local phone directory for your nearest centre) to find out how to update your CV and produce a good one. These centres also have phones, faxes, computers, paper, etc., so that you can save money. They also run counselling sessions and give support and help to the long-term unemployed.

You will need to sign on at your local Department of Social Security (DSS) office and be available for work – even if it is not the kind you would like. The government has now given quite extensive powers to DSS officers, who can refuse payment for up to two weeks at a time to people whom they believe are not taking job-seeking seriously.

Keep your appearance smart and make the most of any courses on interview, assertiveness, and communications skills. You might consider retraining if you think your chances will be improved in this way, and you can get government help to do this. You may also consider self-employment, which is discussed in Chapter Fourteen.

Be prepared to take work which is below your previous level or at less pay if it will get you back into the job market in an appropriate area.

Older women may have a harder time finding a new job. Fortunately, there are employers who appreciate the skills that older women have to offer but they can take some tracking down.

You may want to consider taking temporary work and waiting until a full-time placement becomes available. It is easier to make progress once you are in employment where you can demonstrate your capabilities. The Department of Employment issues a useful booklet called *Too old, who says?* which gives advice for older people wanting employment. Agencies which help older people to obtain work include Ageworks, Forties People (London only), Careers Continued and Recruit. Most of these deal mainly with office work. You might also like to contact the Campaign Against Age Discrimination (CAADE) or the Retired Executives Action Clearing House. (See 'Useful Addresses', pp.219–220). For the address of your local Employment Service office, look in the telephone directory.

Ask for help

This is not a time to stand on your pride. Use your networking skills as described in Chapter Six to find out about jobs which may not get advertised, and to keep your name in front of prospective employers. Ask your friends for support and practical help, and take up any official offers of help or training. Register with a head-hunting agency if you were in a senior position.

Do not try to do everything on your own. Once you are back in work you can help others by giving them the support that you needed.

CHAPTER 14

Self-Employment

MORE women are setting up in their own businesses now than ever before. Some dislike the stress of a traditional working day, others need to fit work around family commitments, but for many it is the challenge of running their own business which attracts them. Although the trend towards self-employment is generally increasing, however, only 25 per cent of self-employed people in Britain are women.

Self-employment gives women the chance to work either in their own homes or to set up their business in an office or shop outside the home with the status and interest that brings. Many women find it a strain trying to fit care of children, elderly relatives or other dependants into a traditional working day. Being self-employed gives them control over their working hours as well as their work environment. Whether working from home or in an office away from the home, it gives them independence and a chance to shape their own work.

Self-employment gives women the chance to show what they can do without being beaten by the glass ceiling or sexism in the workplace. Ideas and initiatives which might have been blocked or dismissed by male colleagues can be tried out without these constraints.

CAN YOU DO IT?

Before you take the step of becoming self-employed you need to take a good look at yourself and your circumstances and decide whether it is practicable. Self-employment may seem a sensible option for many women, but it can be a shock when you discover the amount of time, work and worry that it can entail. Without the set routine of a traditional working day and the company of fellow employees it can be a lonely way to work. Ask yourself some searching questions, and be honest with yourself.

179

- Can you work on your own?
- Are you self-disciplined?
- Have you got the stamina necessary to do the work?
- Are you prepared to work long hours for small returns at first?
- Are you willing to go out and promote your business and talk to prospective customers?
- Can you fit the work in with your other commitments?

Next consider the practical arrangements necessary.

- Do you want to work at home or elsewhere?
- If you want to work from home have you space to do so?
- If you want to work outside your home do you have, or can you raise, enough capital?
- Can you afford the rent/rates/taxes?
- Can you afford to employ other people?
- Is there safe storage for your tools/stock/paper/computer?
- Can you fit your work into your daily routine?
- Have you got or can you afford to buy or hire the necessary equipment, including computer, phone, fax, answering machine?

There is no point in trying to become self-employed unless you are temperamentally suited to the life, and can deal with the practicalities of the arrangements. If you are unsure about whether you can do this you could become self-employed on a part-time basis to see whether it would suit you. You would then have a regular income coming in from your normal work, and would be able to find out whether it suits you, or if you are likely to find enough customers to go self-employed full-time.

FIRST STEPS

A woman setting up on her own needs to take a number of things into account:

- market;
- finance;
- location;
- competition;
- stock;
- safety.

Market

Market research is vital, but often overlooked or skimped on. You may make the most wonderful painted boxes for example, but unless there is a market for them you will fail.

To decide whether your business will be viable, put questionnaires through people's doors; write to the local papers asking for opinions; ask your friends, neighbours, strangers in the street; knock on people's doors; consult your local trade council; ask local firms. Contact the appropriate trade or professional organisation for their views on the market. You may also be able to get work from the company where you were previously employed.

Finance

Unless you are starting your business with a service needing very little equipment you will need to borrow some start-up money. You can approach the bank, in which case you will need to show your manager that you have done adequate research into the market and have prepared a business plan. It shows who you expect your customers to be, the anticipated costs and turnover, etc.

Barclays and other major banks provide useful help for small businesses. They produce brochures on setting up a business, which include forms for a business plan. You can also arrange a meeting with the small business financial adviser where you are presently banking, or with another bank.

According to Barclays Economics Department 20 per cent of small businesses fail in the first 12 months rising to a 54 per cent failure rate after 36 months. You should therefore ensure that your preparation is adequate, because it is this initial work which will give you a fighting chance. The fewer surprises there are and the more realistic your expectations, the better chance you have of surviving.

Location

Whether you are setting up in your own home or business premises you will need to find out whether it is in a good location, if you need clients or customers to come to you. Is it accessible for cars, delivery vehicles, disabled people? Is it off the beaten track or near the main shopping centre? Are there similar shops – or any shops nearby? If it is a supply business and you do not need to see your customers, is it near a post office? Does it have phone lines, heating, electricity, or must you install them?

Competition

When you have found out whether people want what you are offering you will need to find out who your rivals are. Remember that they will not always be in the same town. If they are supplying or providing what you intend to, but from outside your area, can you do it cheaper and better? Are there nationwide firms competing with you or are your only other competitors local firms? Is there a section of the business under-catered for by them?

Stock

Good communication systems are particularly important if you want to supply a service. Can you afford all the necessary equipment? If possible you should have a dedicated phone line for your business. If your business involves a product you need to find out if you can get adequate supplies at reasonable cost. Can they be delivered easily or can you fetch them without trouble? Would your stock cost more than would make your product saleable? Have you adequate and safe storage space?

Safety

Whether you set up on your own in other premises or work from home, you must be aware of personal safety requirements. You will, for example, need to visit customers to present your produce and sell your services. Even if you do most of your selling by post you will still occasionally expect to meet customers.

Take sensible precautions. Always let someone know where you are going and whom you are going to see. If you work alone then tell your partner or a neighbour, and ask someone to phone you at the meeting if you have not returned by a particular time. Travel by a well-marked route and leave a message about which way you will be going. Invest in a car phone as soon as you can afford to, and carry a personal alarm. Take a self-defence course in your area, and ask the police for advice.

On the premises, whether at home or in an office, do not leave a message on your answerphone which would let anyone know whether you are in or out. Keep the curtains or blinds drawn after dark. Do not let anyone into your home unless you know who they are and are expecting them. Do not be afraid to ask for ID cards from utilities reps, and check with their companies.

If you are running a shop then try to have an assistant even if their wages do keep your profits down. Keep the back of the shop locked until you need to go out that way, and travel home together by taxi if you can afford it and do not have a car.

Health and safety regulations

You need to be aware of the health and safety regulations affecting your business and premises. This is particularly important if you employ other people in your home or elsewhere.

You can get advice about this from your local authority health and safety officer, and see Chapter Nine for more on this subject. The Health and Safety Executive (see 'Useful Addresses', p.215) publishes useful books and brochures which will help you.

TYPES OF SELF-EMPLOYMENT

Financial and domestic considerations will largely dictate whether you set up at home or elsewhere. If you are operating a mail order service then working from home is possible. If you need to meet your customers, then a separate workplace may be a better choice. If you do decide to work from home you must check with your local council that you do not need permission or planning consent for change of use. Also check with your mortgage company or landlord to see whether working from home will break your agreement. Whatever you decide to do there are various kinds of self-employment situations which you can set up.

You have three choices about running your own business. You can be self-employed, operating as a sole trader; set up in a partnership; or form a limited company. There are also variants within these, such as franchising.

Self-employed sole trader

There are no legal formalities if you wish to be a sole trader. You don't even have to have your accounts audited, and if your earnings are less than £15,000 (1994 figures) per year then you need only supply a three-line profit-and-loss statement to the Inland Revenue.

You need to tell the DSS, Inland Revenue and your local authority that you are starting a business. Once your turnover is over £46,000 then you must register for VAT and you would be wise to employ an accountant. An accountant can also advise you about the tax situation when you use a portion of your house as business premises.

Although it is simple to set up, and you get all the profits, you also are liable for all the debts.

Partnership

Again there are no legal formalities – you can simply decide to work with one or more people. It is safer, however, to get a solicitor to produce a simple agreement for you and your partners to sign. This will mean that you all know your rights, such as what proportion of the profits each is entitled to, what should happen if one partner wishes to leave and what will happen if the business closes.

Each partner is responsible for all the debts of the partnership, so your home could be at risk in extreme cases.

Limited company

A limited company has a legal existence separate from the people who own or run it, so you have some protection if the business gets into difficulty. You will have to pay a lawyer and accountant, and there will be costs for registering the company with the Companies Registration Office at the Department of Trade and Industry (DTI) and auditing and filing the company's annual accounts. The most popular method of acquiring a company is to buy one 'off the shelf', which you can arrange through your accountant or solicitor.

Franchising

This is a popular form of business enterprise, and can be anything from running a branch of McDonald's to having a travel agency in your front room. There are two kinds of franchise – a business franchise or a licence.

Business franchise

A franchise is usually a business franchise. This is a package which includes the entire business concept – everything from the use of the company name, how the goods are presented, what any uniform must look like, the shop sign and so on. It also includes training and continued help. The package is designed so that anyone can be taught how to set up and run it. The franchisee (you) invests in the business and owns it, but continues to pay the franchiser (the company owner) for continuing rights to use the concept.

The franchiser decides what goods or services will be offered, the standards of service, price structures, the design of premises and stationery, and any other ways the business is presented to the public. The result is a business with an immediately recognisable company identity. The Body Shop is good example of this kind of franchise.

Licence

Another common use of the word franchise nowadays includes any transaction where one person licenses another with the rights to do something. It may not include all the help given in a business format franchise. When taking out a franchise it is important to find out exactly what you will be getting. A full business franchise may cost more initially, but may prove to be more reliable.

How to get a franchise

There are two stages to obtaining a franchise. First you pay for the services that you need before you can start the business, which should include the necessary training. Then you should have continuing help and advice from the franchiser after that.

The advantages of a franchise is that most of the problems of running the business should already have been sorted out. You will, however, have limited opportunities for making your personal mark on the business. A disadvantage is that you risk being deserted after the initial stage – more common with a licensing franchise. If you are asked for a great deal of money at the first stage be wary. Get any contract checked by a solicitor, and make sure that there are safeguards against unfulfilled promises. Ask to talk to other franchisees with the same company.

For information and advice about franchising contact the British Franchise Association (see 'Useful Addresses', p.220) which is a non-profit-making association responsible for the promotion and enforcing of fair and ethical franchising through its Member Franchiser Companies. You can buy its Franchise Information Pack, which will help you decide whether franchising is for you and where to start looking. The magazine *Business Franchise* gives advice to prospective franchisees and lists available franchises.

Multi-Level Marketing (MLM)

Multi-level marketing works on a network marketing principle. One person sells the product on to several other people, and also sells the distribution rights to the product. Each person who starts selling the product gets commission, but also pays a fee to the person who recruited them. With some products selling the distribution rights is more important than selling the actual product, and these schemes should be avoided.

The schemes may work well for those at the top of the network, but demand unlimited hard work for little reward for those further along. MLM schemes have to operate within the strict guidelines of the Fair Trading Act of 1973 or else risk being labelled illegal as 'pyramid' schemes. Check on any MLM schemes by contacting the Office of Fair Trading or the Direct Selling Association (see 'Useful Addresses', p.221). Beware of any advertisement which says it is not MLM, but which does not tell you exactly what it *really* is.

Co-operatives

Everyone works for the business in co-operative arrangements, sharing the decision-making as well as getting a share of the profits and problems. For expert advice on forming a workers' co-operative or a small-enterprise co-operative, contact the Industrial Common Ownership Movement Ltd (ICOM) (see 'Useful Addresses', p.221). ICOM can advise you on all aspects of forming a co-operative and tell you whether your particular co-operative should register at Companies House or with the Registrar of Friendly Societies. ICOM provides a wide range of model rules and can give tailor-made help for co-operatives which do not fit the usual models.

YOUR BUSINESS PLAN

In order to see if your business is viable, keep you on track, and impress your bank manager enough to give you a loan, you must have a business plan. By writing the plan you can see its weak points and get an overall feel for how the business will operate.

A business plan should contain:

- the definition of the business;
- its objectives;
- the plan of operation;
- the financial plan;
- personal profile and relevant work experience;
- plans for the future.

You will also need a 'unique selling proposition' – what makes your business different from similar ones?

Definition of the business

Your business plan needs a basic objective, for example: 'to provide top quality desk-top publishing services for local businesses in Dunchester'. You should also identify some early objectives. You could aim, perhaps, to identify what services are on offer; underline the cost effectiveness of your services compared to others in the area; identify the unique selling proposition; to underline that it is a family business.

Objectives

This will need to say how you will achieve your objectives. You should set out in detail your marketing and publicity plans, explain how you will identify and deal with the competition, and what resources you will need.

Plan of operation

This covers in detail much of the above. It should give details of the business, the market and a survey of the competition. It will say why your business is unique, how it will work and be managed, selling and publicity plans, costs of staff and resources, what premises will be needed, what equipment etc.

Financial plan

This should be as detailed as possible, and include:

- sales and costs forecasts;
- resources needed and how they will be paid for;
- at least 12 months of monthly cash flow forecasts;
- at least 12 months of profit and loss forecasts;
- yearly profit forecasts for the next five years;
- assumptions behind the forecasts;
- information on risks affecting the business, how you will avoid them, and how you will deal with failure.

Plans for the future

Again, give as much information as you can. Such things as your objectives for the next five years, whether you will need more capital, your prospects with customer suppliers and employers, your needs later in life such as at retirement.

WHO CAN HELP YOU?

You should talk to as many people as possible about your plans. Talk to:

- friends;
- local people who may become customers;
- other people running their own business;
- suppliers;
- bank manager;
- Training Enterprise Councils (TECs);
- Women's Enterprise Centres (WECs);
- librarian;
- local shopkeepers.

Fortunately there is a lot of help available. The Department of Trade and Industry (DTI) produces information for small firms, (see 'Useful Addresses', p.221) giving details about what help the government gives small businesses as well as guides to the regulations for setting up a small business.

Barclays Bank plc provides specific advice on setting up a small business in the form of three packs – *Thinking of starting up a business?*, *Setting up and running your business*, *Managing your business*. These contain booklets full of useful information as well as a business plan form and forms for a profit and loss forecast and a cashflow forecast. The other main banks provide a similar service.

Your local Inland Revenue office can give you a booklet called *Starting a Business*. Also contact your local Training Enterprise Council (TEC) and Chamber of Commerce (see your phone book or ask your local council). Small businesses can also attract help from the government Enterprise Allowance or business start-up schemes. You used to be paid a fixed amount from the scheme, but privatisation of the national scheme has broken up into over 80 local TECs, each with different criteria for giving financial assistance. This system may also be undergoing further changes at the time of going to press.

See 'Further Reading', pp.228–229 for helpful guides to running a small business.

WOMEN'S ENTERPRISE CENTRES (WECS)

These are an initiative of the Women's Enterprise Forum (WEF) and Business in the Community, and they aim to help women explore their ideas for business as well as to provide a support network for women running their own business. The WEF is sponsored by six major companies – British Gas, Barclays Bank plc, BT, Legal & General, British Rail (Network SE) and National Westminster Bank plc.

There are 55 WECs throughout the country, all of which are part of a national network with access to information on what is available nationally. Women benefit from WECs because they provide promotional literature which does not promote business as a men-only activity, counselling, training courses, confidence building, child-friendly premises, information and business networks, monitoring and aftercare programmes, events targeted at women, and services responsive to local needs. Being part of the national network provides WECs with opportunities to increase their profile and they benefit from:

- being part of a nationally recognised network;
- excellent PR opportunities resulting in increased sponsorship and funding;
- free copy of *Centre Focus*, a newsletter giving details of what is happening nationally and an opportunity to promote and exchange news of events and initiatives;
- biannual conference with opportunity to meet women from other WECs to exchange ideas;
- access to national Women's Enterprise Forum for support and assistance.

For more information contact the Women's Enterprise Forum – see 'Useful Addresses', p.222.

TRAINING ENTERPRISE COUNCILS (TECS)

Unlike WECs these do not offer advice specifically for women, but they can give general help and advice and suggest where else you can get help.

There are 82 TECs in England and Wales and 22 Local Enterprise Councils (LECs) in Scotland. They are responsible for providing information, advice, counselling and training services to small businesses across the country to meet local needs and circumstances.

Help from TECs and LECs includes business information; advice and counselling; financial assistance for unemployed people to start a business; courses in business skills; help with the cost of accountancy to develop staff and meet future needs; help for firms wishing to train young people or adults.

LECs

LECs (Local Enterprise Councils) can provide help to business in Scotland. It also has the Scottish Business Shop (see 'Useful Addresses', p.222) which provides a range of integrated business services to small businesses, access to government departments, company information and a franchise desk.

Wales

In Wales there is the Welsh Development Agency and, in mid-Wales, the Development Board for Rural Wales.

Northern Ireland

This area has the Local Enterprise Development Unit (LEDU) which provides comprehensive information, advisory services and financial help to small firms employing up to 50 people.

ACCOUNTS

If you can afford to, employ an accountant. The few hundred pounds it will cost each year will be amply repaid by your financial affairs kept in order. If you become liable for VAT, have a turnover of over £15,000 or employ others an accountant is vital. Ask firms whether they have expertise in or specialise in self-employment accounting.

Keep detailed financial records. Self-employment account books can be bought from any office stationers. If you are reasonably computer literate there are a variety of computer software packages available for your accounts. Keep all receipts, bills and copies of invoices. Record all financial transactions regarding your business, however small, and be prepared to show them to the Inland Revenue and Customs and Excise (who collect VAT) if required. You may want to take an evening class in simple book-keeping if doing your own accounts, or you could employ a book-keeper on a freelance basis.

Fully self-employed workers are taxed under schedule D. If you are self-employed and have an additional source of income to your main employment you will be taxed at source, as well as under schedule D for the part of your income earned from self-employment. As a self-employed person you can claim expenses against tax for things necessary for your work such as equipment, travel, part of heat and light bill for a room used partly for your work, subscriptions to professional journals, etc. There are a number of helpful leaflets on tax and the self-employed which you can get from your local tax office.

You can also set off the loss made in one accounting year against other income in the tax year in which the loss occurred. Because it is open to interpretation and abuse, you should consult an accountant about this. This is especially important because soon everyone will be responsible for assessing their own tax. This means that you will have to make sure you have all the correct figures, work out how much you owe, and send in a cheque to the tax office for the right amount.

You can claim a percentage of capital items against tax. You claim 25 per cent of the cost against income for the first year, 25 per cent of the remainder the second year, and so on. This is called a writing down allowance, and again is best left to an accountant to calculate. If you give the details to the tax office, they will do the calculations for you.

NI

If you are self-employed you will have to pay National Insurance under Class 2. This is a weekly flat fee which you can pay to the DSS by direct debit, either monthly or quarterly, or by receiving a quarterly bill. Once your income reaches a certain level you will also have to pay Class 4 contributions, which have an upper limit. This is collected by the Inland Revenue and is assessed at the same time as your tax.

Insurance

When working from home get insurance for any equipment and stock. Your own house insurance may not cover you for business equipment, but two insurers specialise in insurance for the self-employed. Both Tolsen Messenger and the London and Edinburgh Insurance Group can provide affordable policies specifically for home-based businesses. If you work by phone

(teleworking) then Daved Sanders Associates provides a teleworkers insurance (see 'Useful Addresses', p.222).

BUSINESS LINK

Business Links are formed by local partnerships of business
support providers, giving one-stop access to the full range of
business support services available, including those from the
DTI services. It aims to boost the help available to small businesses and to decrease the casualty rate by making them more
competitive. Once your business has taken off then these are
the people to contact.

Contact your nearest DTI Regional office, TEC or Chamber of
Commerce to find out when and where a Business Link will be
opening near you.

The Rural Development Commission

This provides businesses in rural England with free general advice
and in-depth technical support, including skills training, for which
a charge is usually made.

It also provides help in converting and acquiring business
premises, including financial assistance in designated development
areas, limited loan facilities, and grants for exhibition participation
and marketing consultancy. Grants, however, often have conditions
attatched which limit you to using local suppliers. Before accepting
a grant make sure that the stipulated suppliers are suitable for your
business.

Inner cities

In these areas special help is available as part of the government's
Action for Cities programme. Also at the time of writing Inner City
Task Forces in urban areas help small businesses with grants and
loans through their Task Force Development Funds.

City Action teams co-ordinate government programmes in inner
cities, and can offer extra support to individual projects which are
not available for main programme funding.

In certain urban areas small firms can get help from Urban
Development Corporations through the government's Urban
Development Programmes, which are run through local authorities.
The programme can provide help with renting premises and training.

Europe

The DTI's Europe Open for Business information service provides a hotline, an on-line database of single market measures, fact-sheets, booklets and guidance on courses or more specific information and advice. European Information Centres (EICs) also provide information on the single European Market, and can connect enquirers to the EC Business Co-operation Network (BC Net) so you can liaise with other companies across Europe to establish partnerships or other contacts (see DTI, 'Useful Addresses', p.221).

The Enterprise Initiative

This provides, through the DTI, practical help and guidance for small firms, including financial assistance for consultancy projects, practical information and advice through the 'Management in the '90s programme'; Regional Selective Assistance which can help with discretionary grants and a simplified small grants procedure; regional Enterprise Grants; assistance for innovation.

In Scotland some areas can get help with consultancy recruitment through the Better Business Services (BBS) by contacting Scottish Enterprise (see 'Useful Addresses', p.222).

FINANCIAL HELP

There are a number of schemes to help small businesses financially. These include:

- *Loan Guarantee Scheme.* A government guarantee for loans by banks and other financial institutions for firms unable to obtain conventional loans because of lack of security or track record.
- *Business Expansion Scheme.* Makes shares in small companies attractive to outside investors.
- *Share buy-back.* Small businesses can sell shares to outside investors and agree that the company will buy them back after a certain time.
- *Enterprise Allowance.* To assist eligible unemployed people to start new businesses. Discuss your idea with your TEC or LEC.
- *British Coal Enterprise Ltd.* To help businesses start up, expand or relocate in a coal-mining area.

- ***British Steel Industry Ltd.*** To help businesses start up, expand or relocate in traditional steel areas.

TELEPHONE HELP

There are a number of helplines using Mercury FreeCall numbers. Each line has an individual sponsor and your call is free. The calls are recorded, and the sponsor or co-sponsor responds in writing. (See under Helplines in 'Useful Addresses'.)

OTHER CONSIDERATIONS

If your job will involve keeping lists of names and addresses on a computer, you should contact the Data Protection Registry (see 'Useful Addresses', p.220) and find out whether you need to register. If you do you will have to pay an annual flat fee and obey certain rules concerning the data, including providing information to individuals on your list if asked to do so.

You should take steps to secure your home if you work from home, and be aware of the Trade Descriptions Act 1968 and the Sale of Goods Act 1979. Other Acts may be relevant, and you can read them up at your local library. Your professional or trade organisation may have its own rules and code of conduct which you should follow.

15

Taking a Break

NOT ONLY do women have to work hard to compete within a work environment which is male-dominated, but the majority still take on most of the domestic tasks at home. So a woman with a job is doubly in need of the relaxation that a holiday provides.

Many women believe that they need to work twice as hard as men to get the same opportunities at work. So they often skip holidays and work long hours in order to do well. In the 1980s more women aimed high at work, and copied the male work ethic. This meant long hours and taking work home at weekends in order to keep up with their male colleagues.

In the 1990s we see the start of a trend away from high-powered work. Some women in good positions are starting to turn their backs on the male work ethic. They do this in many ways, such as by refusing to take promotion when offered or by taking a sideways move to a less stressful job. They may take a step down and the loss of pay that goes with it, start their own business where they can control the workload, or do part-time work from home.

By voting with their feet women are saying that it is the quality of life that matters, not the amount of money or prestige you earn. In this they differ from most men, who overwork continuously to get to the top.

One way that women can make their working life a better experience is by taking their holidays in full, and making the most of free time at weekends and evenings. This of course depends on the kind of work you do, and whether you have to work during unsocial hours.

ALL-WOMEN LEISURE ACTIVITIES

If you want to involve yourself in a leisure activity regularly on a women-only basis, many places now provide these. Some activities have swung full circle in favour of segregation. Public bathing was a segregated activity until the mid-twentieth century in many areas in the UK. Men and women had separate swimming times and attendants of the same sex. Now that mixed bathing has become the norm, there has been a return to women-only bathing sessions. A large part of the demand has stemmed from women from ethnic minorities whose culture and religion forbid them to dress immodestly in front of men. Other women feel more comfortable at an all-female session.

Other sports offer similar sessions. Some are typically women's sports (so-called) such as netball. Others such as football, rugby and cricket give women a chance to try 'male' sports.

Adult education classes often provide all-women classes in a variety of subjects ranging from photography to car maintenance. These are different from classes where students tend to be predominantly female, such as flower arranging. Women-only classes may also be held for women from particular ethnic groups.

All-women sections of societies

Large societies such as political parties or special interest groups often have women's sections. These, like black or gay sections, aim to encourage and support a particular sub-group (in this case women) within the main organisation and encourage them to take part in the society as a whole. Whether you feel like joining one of these sections will depend on whether you consider the idea patronising.

These sections are different from networking women's groups, which are quite separate organisations. They are designed to build up work and social relationships between like-minded women and are discussed in more detail in Chapter Six.

HOLIDAY PAY

If someone else employs you then you will be entitled to a specified number of weeks of paid holiday, the amount depending on the nature of your job and your seniority within the company. You are entitled to have the terms of your holiday entitlement set out when you join the company. Holidays will have been negotiated by your union where there is one.

If you are self-employed then you will not receive holiday pay from anyone, so you need to have saved enough during the previous months. When you set out your yearly financial plan make sure that you include holidays in the calculations.

BOOKING TIME OFF WORK

You may be senior enough to dictate when you can take your holidays but in most cases you will have to fit in with colleagues and bosses. Bear in mind that although you may get time off at Christmas or New Year it is not fair to others to insist on it every year. Some people actually like being in the office over this period as it gives them something purposeful to do. They can escape family responsibilities (or fights!) or they like the peaceful atmosphere and can get some extra work done.

If you have a particular holiday in mind that you can only take at a certain time then you must book time off well in advance, if necessary negotiating a swap of responsibilities with other people.

ORGANISING WORK FOR HOLIDAYS

To take advantage of your holidays and free time you need to organise your work so that you feel free to take the time off. If you are taking a lot of work home you either need an assistant or you are not organising your work properly.

Try not to let your work pile up so that you have to rush to finish it in the last few days before your holiday. If you do, you will go on holiday stressed, perhaps even taking work with you.

Delegate as much as possible in the fortnight before you leave and arrange for your secretary or a colleague to open all non-personal post and deal with standard enquiries. Leave your holiday phone number – if you have one – but make clear that it is to be used in emergencies only. Tell colleagues when you will be away so that work does not pile up in your absence.

WOMEN-ONLY HOLIDAYS

There has in recent years been an increase in the number of holidays that are run by and cater only for women. This upsurge in all-women holidays owes something to the times, where women can feel overwhelmed by male-oriented pursuits and the inter-sex by-play that can be emotionally draining.

Many individuals are meeting the need for this kind of holiday, and they can range from a retreat in a nunnery in Italy to cycling in England. The following are a few examples of women's holiday companies. You are sure to come across others. See 'Useful Addresses', pp.222–223 for details.

The Women's Travel Advisory Bureau

This is an advisory service for women travellers, run by Lee Ronald. It aims to tackle the particular problems women face which are not fully addressed by traditional travel companies or guidebooks. The Bureau aims to make modern women more aware of the facilities available to them, from books to holidays, as well as alert them to their own resources. The Bureau provides, for a few pounds each, travel packs that focus on areas specific to women travellers. The packs contain details about some holidays specifically for women. Together with the tour company for women, Tiger Travel, they arrange a series of Women and Travel seminars. Contact them for details of the latest courses.

Tiger Travel

Tiger Travel specialises in tours for women, mainly in India, although they are extending their programme all the time. This company offers tours based on particular itineraries, but will also tailor-make tours on request, including a guide, driver, etc. The service is flexible, and the aim is to enhance the individual's experience.

The tours range from two weeks for the adventurous, including cycling, trekking and rafting to two weeks' camel trekking or three weeks touring Southern India. For an up-to-date brochure contact Tiger Travel yourself.

Talbontdrain Guest House

This centre is run by Hilary Matthews and Jenny Dingle. In their Welsh farmhouse they run courses for women to help them increase their skills and confidence in the outdoors. Group numbers are kept small so that the programme can cater for individual women's particular needs.

The courses appeal to women from a wide range of ages and backgrounds. Courses include Map Reading, Family Holiday, and Women's Wilderness. This latter course is very popular. During it a woman can spend time on her own in remote countryside with preparation and support from the Talbontdrain team. Jenny Dingle is a qualified teacher and holds a mountain leadership certificate. Hilary Matthews provides home-made food.

Travel Companions

Vera Coppard started Travel Companions in 1986 as a service to people, mainly women, who are on their own. The company caters for single travellers who often do not enjoy travelling alone, have difficulty getting a single room and have to pay extra for what can be the worst room in the hotel. With a travel partner they have the option of sharing a room if they wish to save the single room supplements. Like-minded individuals are put in touch with each other so that they can get to know each other and share holidays, whether they travel together, do their own thing or travel with a tour operator.

Although men can join, the membership is mostly women – and it is not a dating agency. Most members prefer to travel with somebody of their own sex. For £40 you are given three introductions; any more are free, if your haven't found a suitable companion.

Canopy Training

Canopy Training specialises in outdoor activity courses run by women for women. It caters for women of all ages and levels of fitness. It is based on the edge of the Peak District, and runs weekend and day courses. The weekend courses include food, dormitory accommodation and transport in the price. For single day courses participants bring their own lunch and refreshments.

Courses include caving, canoeing, rock-climbing and abseiling, kayaking, sailing, mountain biking, map and compass work, caving and walking, and general activity weekends. Canopy Training can tailor courses to a particular group and can arrange individual tuition.

BOSS (British Offshore Sailing School)

This is Britain's leading sail training school, and has Royal Yachting Association (RYA) recognition. It offers a range of RYA practical and shore-based cruising courses, from introductory weekends for complete beginners to training courses for RYA instructors. There are also a wide range of special one-day and weekend courses for all levels.

BOSS also specialises in women-only courses, run by RYA qualified female skippers. These are five-day or weekend courses, and have the same format as the mixed courses. While you cruise you learn about safety at sea and get a chance to master the skills of steering, changing sails, reefing and tying knots. You will also

learn what to do in an emergency situation such as when somebody
falls overboard. You live on board during the course and each night
is spent in a new place. Everybody takes a turn at cooking.

New women weekend courses on boat handling have been introduced. These focus on skills needed to manoeuvre a yacht in and
out of marinas under power and other mooring situations. The
women-only courses take place from June to September.

Wild Rose

Wild Rose is a holiday house for women run by Sheila Gwyn. It is
situated in south east Cornwall, and provides a small-scale peaceful
retreat where women can come together to have interesting, inspir-
ing and relaxing holidays. The holidays are run on specific dates
throughout the year, and are usually based on an activity or special
interest. The majority of women who go to Wild Rose do so on
their own, and the group size is small. Bedrooms are shared, with
single beds. The price of a holiday includes the activity of the week
and full board. Examples of holidays for 1995 include drumming,
walking, looking at wildlife, writing, massage and singing as well
as special breaks at Christmas and New Year.

Fawcett Mill Fields

Fawcett Mill Fields runs holidays for women in converted mill
buildings in Cumbria. It offers catered and self-catering accommodation for up to 16 people, and also arranges activities in the area
on request. Theme-based holidays for 1994 included such things as
yoga, walking & healing, circle dancing, house parties, lesbian-
only events, and workshops.

Island Horizons

Island Horizons, formerly Ladytrek, is based in the Highlands and
Islands of Scotland, and can offer Ladies Only weeks or a bias
towards women's preferences. Jean Stewart, mountain leader and
ecologist, and her team provide walking holidays, most of which
are based at Lochcarron. The emphasis is on relaxed walking in a
wild and remote setting whilst enjoying the company of a small
group and an experienced guide.

Accommodation is in two adjacent cottages which have five
bedrooms between them, three of which are singles. Other holidays
are based on islands. The catering is to a high standard.

Ten Tips For Making The Most Of Holidays As Preparation For Work

1. Try not to take your work away with you.

2. Do not pack too much into your holiday.

3. Relax and get enough sleep.

4. Finish as much work as possible beforehand then forget about it.

5. Make sure that at least one part of the holiday is something that *you* want to do.

6. If you want to be alone do not be afraid to leave your family behind.

7. Several short breaks may be more relaxing than one long one.

8. Get out in the fresh air.

9. Do something completely unrelated to work.

10. Take some physical exercise.

Useful Addresses

Where the telephone number or address only is given, this is usually because the organiser prefers initial contact in this way.

Chapter 1
Equal opportunities

Commission of the European Communities
Rue de la Loi 200
B-1049 Brussels
Belgium
Tel: 32 2 295 9772/2860

Representative Offices:
Jean Monnet House
8 Storey's Gate
London SW1P 3AT
Tel: 0171 973 1992

Windsor House
9/15 Bedford Street
Belfast BT2 7EG

4 Cathedral Road
Cardiff CF1 9SG

7 Alva Street
Edinburgh
EH2 4PH

Jean Monnet Centre
39 Molesworth Street
Dublin 2
Eire

Commission for Racial Equality (CRE)
Elliot House
10/12 Allington Street
London SW1E 5EH
Tel: 0171 828 7022

Alpha Tower
(11th floor)
Suffolk Street
Queensway
Birmingham
B1 1TT
Tel: 0121 632 4544

100 Princes Street
Edinburgh EH2 3AA
Tel: 0131 226 5186

Yorkshire Bank
Chambers (1st floor)
Infirmary Street
Leeds LS1 2JP
Tel: 0113 2434413

Haymarket House
(4th floor)
Haymarket Shopping
Centre
Leicester LE1 3YG
Tel: 0116 2517852

Maybrook House
(5th floor)
40 Blackfriars Street
Manchester M3 2EG
Tel: 0161 831 7782

CRE publications can
be obtained from
Lavis Marketing
73 Lime Walk
Headington
Oxford OX3 7AD
Tel: 01865 67575

Committee on Women's Rights
Centre Européen
Plateau du Kirchberg
Luxembourg
or Rue Belliard 97 113
B1049 Brussels
Belgium

Council for the Status of Women
64 Lower Mount Street
Dublin 2
Eire
*Tel: 353 1
615268/611791
Fax: 353 1 760860*

Equal Opportunities Commission (EOC)
Overseas House
Quay Street
Manchester M3 3HN
*Tel: 0161 833 9244
Fax: 0161 835 1657*

Caerwys House
Windsor Lane
Cardiff CF1 1LB
*Tel: 01222 343552
Fax: 01222 641079*

St Andrew House
141 West Nile Street
Glasgow G1 2RN
*Tel: 0141 332 8018
Fax: 0141 353 1892*

39 Molesworth Street
Dublin 2 Eire
Tel: 3531 71 22 44

**The European
Parliament**
L-2929 Luxembourg
UK contact
Tel: 0171 222 0411

The Fawcett Society
40/46 Harleyford Road
Vauxhall
London SE11 5AY
Tel: 0171 587 1287
Fax: 0171 793 0451

**Institute of Race
Relations**
2-6 Leeke Street
Kings Cross Road
London WC1X 9HS
Tel: 0171 837 0041

**Joint Council for the
Welfare of Immigrants**
115 Old Street
London EC1V 9JR
Tel: 0171 251 8706/8

**Liberty (National
Council for Civil
Liberties)**
21 Tabard Street
London SE1 4LA
Tel: 0171 403 3888

**National Association
of Racial Equality
Councils**
8-16 Coronet Street
London N1 6HD
Tel: 0171 739 6658

**New Opportunities for
Women (NOW)**
200 Rue de la Loi
B-1049 Brussels
Belgium
*Tel: 32 2/295 01 01 or
32 2/295 42 95*
Fax: 32 2/295 62 80

32 Upper Fitzwilliam
Street
Dublin 2
Eire
*Tel: 353 1 661 52
68/661 17 91*
Fax: 353 1 76 08 60

EC Unit
Training and
Employment Agency
Clarendon House
Adelaide Street
Belfast BT2
Tel: 232 23 99 44
Fax: 232 89 56 75

Department of the
Environment
European Social Fund
Unit
Level 1
236 Gray's Inn Road
London WC1X 8HL
*Tel: 0171 211 30 00
X4710*
Fax: 0171 211 47 49

**The Race Relations
Employment Advisory
Service (RREAS),
Department of
Employment**
(SE & SW England)
11 Belgrave Road
London SW1V 1RB
*Tel: 0171 834 6644
X3432*

(W Midlands & Wales)
14th floor
Cumberland House
200 Broad Street
Birmingham B15 1TA
Tel: 0121 643 8144

(E Midlands)
Cranbrook House
Cranbrook Street
Nottingham
NG1 1EY
Tel: 0115 9581224

(Yorkshire &
Humberside,
N England)
City House
New Station Street
Leeds LS1 4JH
*Tel: 0113 2438232
X2344*

(NW & Scotland)
Washington House
New Bailey Street
Manchester M3 5ER
Tel: 0161 837 7114

**Racial Discrimination
Legal Defence Fund**
Unit 133
Brixton Small Business
Centre
444 Brixton Road
London SW9 8EJ
Tel: 0171 274 4000 X278

**Research Institute for
the Development of
the European Cultural
Area**
International Women's
Addresses
50 Rue de Roumanie
B-1060 Brussels
Belgium
Tel: 32 2 537 9760

Rights of Women
52–54 Featherstone
Street
London EC1Y 8RT
Tel: 0171 251 6577

**Trades Union
Congress (Women's
Committee)**
Congress House
Great Russell Street
London WC1B 3LS
Tel: 0171 636 4030
Fax: 0171 636 0632

Chapter 2
The working woman's lifestyle

Lifestyle Management Consultants
13 Merton Hall Road
London SW19 3PP
Tel: 0181 543 2086

Chapter 3
Pay and promotion

Federation of Recruitment & Employment Services
36 Mortimer Street
London W1N 7RB
Tel: 0171 928 9272

Chapter 4
Training for the top

Association of MBAs (AMBA)
15 Duncan Terrace
London N1 8BZ
Tel: 0171 837 3375

Birkbeck College (Extra-Mural Programme)
Information Bureau
26 Russell Square
London WC1B 5DQ
Tel: 0171 631 6633
Fax: 0171 631 6688

Prospectus requests
Tel: 0171 631 6687
(24hr answerphone)

Birkbeck College
(Degree Admission Enquiries)
The Registry
Birkbeck College
Malet Street
London WC1E 7HX
Tel: 0171 631 6561

Careers for Women (CFW)
2 Valentine Place
London SE1 8QH
Tel: 0171 401 2280
Fax: 0171 401 2938

Chartered Association of Certified Accountants
29 Lincoln's Inn Fields
London WC2A 2EG
Tel: 0171 242 6855

Chartered Association of Management Accountants
63 Portland Place
London W1N 4AB
Tel: 0171 637 2311

Chartered Institute of Public Finance and Accountancy
3 Robert Street
London WC2N 6BH
Tel: 0171 895 8823

The Council of Legal Education
39 Eagle Street
London
WC1R 4AJ
Tel: 0171 404 5787
Fax: 0171 831 4188

The European Women's Lobby
Rue du Méridien
22 B-1030 Brussels
Belgium
Tel: 32 2 217 90 20
Fax: 32 2 219 84 51

The General Council of the Bar
3 Bedford Row
London
WC1R 4DB
Tel: 0171 242 0082

Graduate School of International Business
The Business Team
The MBA Programme
West Midlands House
Gypsy Lane
Willenhall
West Midlands
WV13 2HA
Tel: 0121 609 7100
Fax: 0121 609 7103

Henley Management College
MBA Information
Greenlands
Henley-on-Thames
Oxfordshire
RG9 3AU
Tel: 01491 571454
Fax: 01491 410184

Institute for Financial Management
(distance learning MBA)
University of Wales
Bangor LL57 2DG
Tel: 01248 371408
Fax: 01248 370408

Institute of Chartered Accountants in England and Wales
PO Box 433
Moorgate Place
London EC2P 2BJ
Tel: 0171 920 8100

Institute of Chartered Accountants in Ireland
Chartered Accountants House
87–89 Pembroke Road
Dublin 4
Tel: 353 1 680400

Institute of Chartered Accountants of Scotland
27 Queen Street

Edinburgh EH2 1LA
Tel: 0131 225 5673

The Institute of Legal
Executives (ILEX)
Kempston Manor
Kempston
Bedford MK42 7AB
Tel: 01234 841000

Institute of
Management
(Publications)
Burston Distribution
Services
Unit 2A
Newbridge Trading
Estate
Newbridge Close
Bristol BS4 4AX
Tel: 0117 9724428
Fax: 0117 9711056

Institute of Manpower
Studies
Mantell Building
University of Sussex
Falmer
Brighton BN1 9RF
Tel: 01273 686751
Fax: 01273 690430

Institute of Personnel
Management
IPM House
Camp Road
Wimbledon
London SW19 4UX
Tel: 0181 946 9100
Fax: 0181 947 2570

The Institute of
Training and
Development
Marlow House
Institute Road
Marlow
Buckinghamshire
SL7 1BD
Tel: 01628 890123

The International Co-
Operative College
Tel: 01509 852333
Fax: 01509 856500

Invicta Training
Limited
240 Green Lane
New Eltham
London SE9 3TL
Tel: 0181 851 4044

Keele University
Department of
Management (MBA)
Staffs ST5 5BG
Tel: 01782 583425
Fax: 01782 715859

Law Society of
England and Wales
113 Chancery Lane
London WC2A 1PL
Tel: 0171 242 1222

London Business
School
Sussex Place
Regent's Park
London NW1 4SA
Tel: 0171 262 5050
Fax: 0171 724 7875

Loughborough
University of
Technology
Management
Development Centre
(part-time MBA)
Rutland Hall
Loughborough
Leicestershire LE11 3TU
Tel: 01509 223140

Manchester Business
School
Tel: 0161 275 6333

Middlesex University
(MBA)
London NW4 4BT
Freephone 0800 181170

The National Council
for the Training of
Journalists
Carlton House
Hemnall
Epping
Essex
CM16 4NL
Tel: 01378 72395

National Extension
College
18 Brooklands Avenue
Cambridge
CB2 2HN
Tel: 01223 316644

Newport University
UK Campus
67–83 Seven Sisters
Road
Holloway
London
N7 6BU
Tel: 0171 272 3882
Fax: 0171 281 9298

The Open Business
School
Walton Hall
Milton Keynes
MK7 6AA
Tel: 01908 653028

Open College of the
Arts
Enquiries Office
(Dept/OU/SWOU)
Houndhill
Barnsley
South Yorkshire
S70 6TU
Tel: 01226 730495

The Open University
Central Enquiry
Service
PO Box 200
Walton Hall
Milton Keynes
MK7 6YZ
Tel: 01908 653231

The Open University
Learning Materials
Sales Office
PO Box 188
Milton Keynes
MK7 6DH
Tel: 01908 652185
Fax: 01908 654320

**Oxford Brookes
University**
Course Administration
Centre
The Institute of
Management
Management House
Cottingham Road
Corby
Northants NN17 1TT
Tel: 01536 204222
Fax: 01536 201651

**The Telecottage
Association**
The Other Cottage
Shortwood Nailsworth
Gloucestershire
GL6 0SH
Tel: 01453 834874
Fax: 01453 836174

**The University of
Bristol**
Bristol BS8 1UQ
Tel: 0117 9737683
Fax: 0117 9737687

University of Leicester
The Admissions
Officer (MBA)
Management Centre
Leicester LE1 7RH
Tel: 0116 2523952
Fax: 0116 2523949

University of London
Senate House
Malet Street
London
WC1E 7HU
Tel: 0171 636 8000
Fax: 0171 636 5841

University of Surrey
SEMS (MBA)
Guildford
Surrey
GU2 5XH
Tel: 01483 259347
Fax: 01483 259511

Wolsey Hall
66 Banbury Road
Oxford OX2 6PR
Tel: 01865 310310

**Women in
Accountancy**
c/o Anne Bryce
ICAS
27 Queen Street
Edinburgh
EH2 1LA
Tel: 0131 225 5673

Women and Training
Hewmar House
120 London Road
Gloucester GL1 3PL
Tel: 01452 309330

**Chapter 5
The working
woman's finances**

Abbey Life
Abbey Life House
PO Box 33
Holdenhurst Road
Bournemouth BH8
8AL
Tel: 01202 292373

Abbey National
Abbey House
Baker Street
London NW1 6XL
Tel: 0171 612 4000
*Fax: 0171 612 4000
X4230*

**Alliance & Leicester
Building Society**
49 Park Lane

London W1Y 4EQ
Tel: 0800 777 070

**Association of British
Insurers**
51 Gresham Street
London EC2V 7HQ
Tel: 0171 600 3333
Fax: 0171 696 8999

Bank of Scotland
Uberior House
61 Grass Market
Edinburgh EH1 2JF
Tel: 0131 243 5908
Fax: 0131 243 5738

Banking Ombudsman
70 Gray's Inn Road
London WC1X 8NB
Tel: 0171 404 9944

Barclays Bank
PO Box 120
Longwood Close
Westwood Business
Park
Coventry CV4 8JN
Tel: 01203 694242
Fax: 01203 532233

Benefits Agency
Tel: 0800 666 555

**Black Horse Financial
Services Group Ltd**
Mountbatten House
Chatham
Kent ME4 4JF
Tel: 01634 834000
Fax: 01634 815248

**Building Societies
Ombudsman**
35 Grosvenor Gardens
London SW1X 7AW
Tel: 0171 931 0044

**The Business
Administration Centre**
Freepost MR 9607
Olympic House
6 Olympic Court

off Montford Street
Salford M5 3GL
Tel: 01345 213 213
(8.30am–5.30pm M–F)

Citizens' Advice
Bureaux
Your local branch will
be listed in your phone
book

Co-Operative Bank
City Office
78 Cornhill
London EC3V 3NJ
Tel: 0171 626 4953

Financial Forum for
Women
Tel: 0800 590 682
(8am – 8pm seven days
a week, free)

Financial Services for
Women
National and Provincial
Building Society
FREEPOST
Bradford BD1 1BR

Fiona Price &
Partners
33 Queen Street
London WC2B 5AA
Tel: 0171 430 0366

First Direct
Freepost HK16
Leeds LS11 0YF
Tel: 0800 222 000

IMRO (The Investment
Management
Regulatory
Organisation Ltd)
Broadwalk House
Appold Street
London
EC2A 2LL
Tel: 0171 628 6022

Insurance
Ombudsman
City Gate One
135 Park Street
London SE1 9EA
Tel: 0171 928 7600

Legal & General
Head Office
Temple Court
11 Queen Street
London EC4N 4TP
Tel: 0171 528 6200

Legal Services
Ombudsman
22 Oxford Court
Oxford Street
Manchester M2 3WQ
Tel: 0161 236 9532

Lloyds Bank
Head Office
71 Lombard Street
London EC3P 3BS
Tel: 0171 626 1500

Maternity Alliance
15 Britannia Street
London WC1X 9JN
Tel: 0171 837 1265
Fax: 0171 837 1273

Midland Bank
27 Poultry
London
EC2P 2BX
Tel: 0171 260 8000
Fax: 0171 260 7065

Mother Cares
Tel: 01242 255125
An independent finan-
cial service for mothers
by a mother

National Association
of Pension Funds Ltd
12 Grosvenor Gardens
London SW1W 0EB
Tel: 0171 498 6604

National & Provincial
Provincial House
Bradford BD1 1NL
Tel: 0800 80 80 84
(8am-8pm, seven days
a week)

National Westminster
Bank
41 Lothbury
London
EC2P 2BP
Tel: 0171 726 1000

Norwich Union
PO Box 6
Surrey Street
Norwich NR1 3NS
Tel: 01603 681522

The Occupational
Pensions Advisory
Service (OPAS),
11 Belgrave Road
London SW1V 1RB
Tel: 0171 233 8080

Pearl Assurance
The Pearl Centre
Lynch Wood
Peterborough PE2 6FY
Tel: 01733 470470
Fax: 01733 472300

Pensions Ombudsman
11 Belgrave Road
London SW1V 1RB
Tel: 0171 834 9144

Personal Investment
Authority (PIA)
3 Royal Exchange
Building
London EC3V 3NL
Tel: 0171 929 0072

Private Patients Plan
Tel: 01892 512345

**The Registrar of
Pension Schemes**
Occupational Pensions
Board
PO Box 2EE
Newcastle upon Tyne
NE99 2EE
Tel: 0191 225 6414

**SIB (Securities and
Investment Board)**
2 Bunhill Row
London EC1Y 8SR
Tel: 0171 638 1240

**Towry Law Pension
Services Limited**
Southern Division
Towry Law House
57 High Street
Windsor
Berkshire SL4 1LX
Tel: 01753 868244
Fax: 01753 868257

TSB
25 Milk Street
London EC2V 8LU
Tel: 0171 606 7070

Chapter 6
Networking

**9 to 5 Working
Women in Education**
614 Superior Avenue
NW Cleveland
OH 44113
USA
Tel: 216 566 1699

**Academic Women's
Achievement Group**
Tel: 0181 362 6075

**Andover Women In
Business Club**
Tel: 01264 364422

**Association of Women
Executives**
Tel: 0121 743 3268

**Association of
German
Businesswomen
(Verband Deutscher
Unternehmerinnen)**
PF. 511030
50946 Köln
Germany
Tel: 221 37 50 74 75

**Association of Women
Barristers**
13 Old Square
Lincoln's Inn
London WC2A 3UA
Tel: 0171 242 6105

**Association of Women
Travel Executives**
Tel: 0181 672 8125

**British Association of
Women Entrepreneurs**
33 Caithness Road
London W14 0JA
Tel: 0171 602 4656
Fax: 0171 602 9397

**British Federation of
Women Graduates**
142 Battersea Park Road
London SW11 4NB
Tel: 0171 498 8037

**British Women's
Pilots Association**
Rochester Airport
Chatham
Kent ME5 9SD
Tel: 01604 861340

**Businesswoman's
Breakfast Club**
3 Cricklewood Court
Swindon
Wiltshire SN1 3EY
Tel: 01793 513774
Fax: 01793 496631

**Business &
Professional Women
UK Ltd**
23 Ansdell Street
London W8 5BN
Tel: 0171 938 1729
Fax: 0171 938 2037

**Chinese Association of
Women's Groups**
680 Commercial Road
Sailors Place
London E14 7HA

City Women's Network
925 Uxbridge Road
Hillingdon Heath
Middlesex UB10 0NJ
Tel/Fax: 01895 272178

CIX
Tel: 0181 390 8446

Club 2000
2/60 Hamilton Terrace
London NW8 9UJ
Tel: 0171 266 3368

CompuServe
Tel: 0800 28 93 78

**Co-operative Women's
Guild**
342 Hoe Street
London E17 9PX
Tel: 0181 520 4902

**Council for the Status
of Women**
32 Upper Fitzwilliam
Street
Dublin 2 Eire
*Tel: 353 1 661
5268/1791*
Fax: 353 1676 0860

Demon
Demon Systems
42 Hendon Lane
London N3 1TT
Tel: 0181 349 0063
Fax: 0181 349 0309

**Dutch Women's
Council (Nederlandse
Vrouwen Raad)**
Groot Hertinnelaan 41
2517 EC Den Haag
Tel: 3170 346 93 04

**The East of Scotland
Businesswoman's
Club**
Tel: 0131 662 1626

Emily's List UK
PO Box 708
London SW10 0DH
Tel: 0171 352 7759
Fax: 0171 352 5168
Sponsors Labour
women who want to
stand for Parliament

Engender
c/o Scottish Women's
Aid
12 Torphichen Street
Edinburgh EH3 8JQ
Tel: 0141 357 0180
A research and
campaigning organisa-
tion for women in
Scotland

**European Network of
Women Journalists**
Office of the European
Commission
Tel: 49 228 53009 20
or
Europublic
21 Riesstrasse
D-53113 Bonn
Germany
Tel: 49 228 914230

**European Women's
Lobby**
La Place Quetele
1030 Brussels
Belgium
Tel: 32 2 217 9020

**European Women's
Management
Development Network**
Rue Washington 40
B-1050 Brussels
Belgium
Tel: 32 2 648 03 85
Fax: 32 2 646 07 68

(UK representative)
21 Essex Street
Whitstable
Kent CT5 4HR
Tel: 01277 276899
Fax: 01277 371371

**Executive Women
International**
31 Bedford Square
London
WC1B 3EG
Tel: 0171 323 2722
Fax: 0171 631 4659

**Executive Women in
Travel**
Tel: 01543 275223

Fawcett Society
46 Harleyford Road
London SE11 5AY
Tel: 0171 587 1287
Fax: 0171 793 0451
Campaigns for equal
rights and opportunities
and for shared respon-
sibility between men
and women

**Federation of Business
and Professional
Women's Clubs**
Hon. Sec.,
17 Rockville Crescent
Blackrock
Co. Dublin
Eire
Tel: 353 1 2883113
*(general) 6614810 or
353 21 965328*

**The Federation of
Icelandic Women's
Associations
(Kvenfélagasamband
Islands)**
Túngötu 14
101 Reykavík
Iceland

**The Film, Video &
Television
Organisation For
Women**
Vera Productions
30–38 Dock Street
Leeds LS10 1JF
Tel: 0113 24288646

Forum UK
237 Baring Road
London SE12 0BE
Tel: 0181 851 7412

**International
Federation of
Women's Travel
Organisations**
Tel: 0181 672 8125

**Labour Women's
Network**
PO Box 708
London SW10 0DH
Tel: 0171 352 7759
Fax: 0171 352 5168

**Law Society
(Association of
Women Solicitors)**
113 Chancery Lane
London WC2A 1PL
Tel: 0171 242 1222

**London Business
School Women's
Network**
Tel: 0171 635 9344

**London
Businesswoman's
Network**
Lancaster Terrace
London W2 2TY
Tel: 0171 262 6737

**London Chamber of
Commerce Women in
Business Group**
33 Queen Street
London EC4R 1BX
Tel: 0171 248 4444

**Married Women's
Association**
16 Hollycroft Avenue
London NW3 1QL
Tel: 0171 794 2884

**Medical Women's
Federation**
Tavistock House North
Tavistock Square
London WC1H 9HX
Tel: 0171 387 7765

**National Alliance of
Women's Organisations**
279–281 Whitechapel
Road
London E1 1BU
Tel: 0171 247 7052

**National Assembly of
Women**
104 Dyche Drive
Sheffield S8 8DN
Tel: 01742 376330

**National Association
of Women Business
Owners (NAWBO)**
600 South Federal
Street
Ste. 400
IL 60605
USA
Tel: 312 922 6222

**National Association
of Women's Clubs**
5 Vernon Rise
Kings Cross Road
London WC1X 9EP
*Tel: 0171 837 1434
(9am-4.30pm)*

**National Council of
German Women's
Organisations
(Deutscher Frauenrat)**
Simrockstrasse 5
D-53113 Bonn 1
Germany
Tel: 02 28/22 30 08

**The National Council
of Women in
Denmark (Danske
Kvinders Nationalråd)**
Niels
Hemmingsensgade 10,2
Postboks 1069
1008 København K
Denmark
Tel: 45 33 12 80 87

**The National Council
of Women of Great
Britain**
36 Danbury Street
London N1 8JU
*Tel: 0171 354 2395
Fax: 0171 354 9214*

**National Council of
Women – Scottish
Standing Committee**
49 Kier Street
Bridge of Allan
Stirling FK9 4QJ
Tel: 01786 832064

**National Federation of
Women's Institutes**
104 New Kings Road
London SW6 4LY
*Tel: 0171 371 9300
Fax: 0171 736 3652*

19 Cathedral Road
Cardiff CF1 9LJ
*Tel: 01222 221712
Fax: 01222 287236*

**National Joint
Committee of
Working Women's
Organisations**
150 Walworth Road
London SE17 1JJ
Tel: 0171 701 1234

**National Women's
Register**
9 Bank Plain
Norwich
Norfolk NR2 4SL
Tel: 01603 765392

**Network: The
Association For
Women in the
Professions,
Commerce, Industry
and the Arts**
Tel: 01895 256972

**Northern Ireland
Women's European
Platform**
127 Ormeau Road
Belfast BT7 1SH

**North West Women
Into Management**
26 Windsor Avenue
Flixton
Urmston
Manchester M31 3GP
Tel: 0161 748 6081

**NUCPS: Women's
Advisory Committee**
124-126 Southwark
Street
London SE1 QTU
Tel: 0171 928 9671

Pepperell Network
48 Bryanston Square
London W1A 7LN
Tel: 0171 262 2401
X303
Fax: 0171 706 1096

**Research Institute for
the Development of
the European Cultural
Area**
International Women's
Associations Addresses
50 rue de Roumanie
B-1060 Brussels
Belgium
Tel: 32 2 537 97 60

**Royal Institute of
British Architects –
Women Architects
Group**
66 Portland Place
London W1N 4AD
Tel: 0171 580 5533

**Scottish Convention of
Women**
88 Main Street
Davidson's Mains
Edinburgh EH4 5AB
Tel: 0131 336 3630

**Scottish Trades Union
Council Women's
Conference**
16 Woodlands Terrace
Glasgow G3 6DR
Tel: 0141 332 4946

**Shadow Women's
Ministry**
c/o Mo Mowlam MP
House of Commons
London SW1A 0AA
Tel: 0171 219 3000

**Society of Women
Writers and
Journalists**
110 Whitehall Road
Chingford

London E4 6DW
Tel: 0181 529 0886

**Standing Conference
of Women's
Organisations**
Cap D'Or,
Whidbourne Avenue
Marine Drive
Torquay TQ1 2PQ
Tel: 01803 296564

**State Secretariat for
the General Concerns
of Women**
Ballhausplatz 1
1014 Vienna
Austria
Tel: 43 1 0222/531 15
X2725/2414/2228

The 300 Group
19 Borough High Street
London SE1 9SE
Tel: 0171 357 6660
Fax: 0171 378 6032

Townswomen's Guilds
Chamber of Commerce
House
75 Harborne Road
Edgbaston
Birmingham B15 3DA
Tel: 0121 456 3435
Fax: 0121 452 1890

**Trades Union
Congress (TUC)
Women's Committee**
Congress House
Great Russell Street
London WC1B 3LS
Tel: 0171 636 4030

**Triangle-Association
of Executive
Secretaries (NW)**
Ashbourne House
224 Wellington Road
North
Stockport SK4 5DA
Tel: 0161 442 6060

**Wales Assembly of
Women (Cynulliad
Merched Cymru)**
3 Cefn Esgair
Llanbadarn Fawr
Aberystwyth
Dyfed SY23 3JG
Tel: 01970 615701

**Womankind
Worldwide**
Albion Place
London W6
Tel: 0181 563 8607/563
8608
Charity working with
developing countries

**Women and Manual
Trades**
52–54 Featherstone
Street
London EC1Y 8RT
Tel: 0171 251 9192

**Women In Banking
and Finance**
55 Bourne Vale
Bromley
Kent
BR2 7NW
Tel: 0181 462 3276

**Women in Business
Group**
44 Sydney Road
Haywards Heath
West Sussex
RH16 1QA
Tel/Fax: 01444 414222

Women In Docklands
Kall Kwik
13 Harbour Exchange
Square
Isle of Dogs
London E14 9GE
Tel: 0181 980 8870

Women in Economic and Social History
Oxford Brookes University
Oxford OX3 0DB
Tel: 01865 819570

Women in Film and Television
Garden Studios
11–15 Betterton Street
London WC2H 9BP
Tel: 0171 379 0344
Fax: 0171 379 1625

Women in Management
64 Marryat Road
Wimbledon
London SW19 5BN
Tel: 0181 944 6332
Fax: 0181 944 8406

Women in Medicine
21 Wallingford Avenue
London W10 6QA
Tel: 0181 960 7446

Women in Music
Battersea Arts Centre
Lavender Hill
London SW11 5TF
Tel: 0171 976 4823
Fax: 0171 978 5207

Women in Physics Committee
The Institute of Physics
47 Belgrave Square
London SW1X 8QX
Tel: 0171 235 6111
Fax: 0171 259 6002

Women in Property
39 King Street
London WC2E 8JS
Tel: 0171 497 9707

Women in the Public Sector Network
(Secretary, Fran Stewart)

London Borough of Merton Housing & Social Services Department
Merton Civic Centre
London Road
Morden
Surrey SM4 5DX
Tel: 0181 545 4104
Fax: 0181 545 3926

Women in Publishing
c/o *The Bookseller*
12 Dyott Street
London WC1A 1DA
Tel: 0171 836 8911
Fax: 0171 836 6381

Women Into Information Technology Foundation
The Campaign Office
Concept 2000
250 Farnborough Road
Farnborough
GU14 7LU
Tel: 01252 528329
Fax: 01252 528178

Women into Public Life
110 Riverview Gardens
Barnes
London SW13 9RA
Tel: 0181 748 1427

Women into Science and Engineering
Nottingham Trent University
Burton Street
Nottingham NG1 4BU
Tel: 0115 9418418 X2101

Women Liberal Democrats
4 Cowley Street
London SW1P 3NB
Tel: 0171 222 7999
Fax: 0171 799 2170

Women Into Work
c/o IMS Trust
107 McDonald Road
Edinburgh EH7 4NW

Women Returners Network
8 John Adam Street
London WC2N 6E
Tel: 0171 839 8188

Women Writers Network
23 Prospect Road
London NW2 2JU
Tel: 0171 794 5861

Women's Engineering Society
Imperial College of Science & Technology
Department of Civil Engineering
Imperial College Road
London SW7 2BU
Tel: 0171 589 5111 X4731

The Women's Environmental Network
Aberdeen Studios
22 Highbury Grove
London N5 2EA
Tel: 0171 354 8823

Women's Farm and Garden Association
175 Gloucester Street
Cirencester
Gloucestershire
GL7 2DP
Tel: 01285 658 339

Women's National Commission
Level 4
Caxton House
Tothill Street
London SW1H 9NF
Tel: 0171 273 5486

Chapter 7
Childcare choices

Black and Ethnic Minority Childcare Working Group
Wesley House
4 Wild Court
London WC2 5AU

British Nursing Association Carers
443 Oxford Street
London W1A 2NR
Tel: 0171 629 9030

Business in the Community
227a City Road
London EC1N 1LX
Tel: 0171 253 3761/2309

Carers National Association
29 Chilworth Mews
London WC2 3R
Tel: 0171 724 7700

Childcare Umbrella
c/o 77 Holloway Road
London N7 8JZ
Tel: 0171 500 5771

Childcare Vouchers Limited
50 Vauxhall Bridge Road
London SW1V 2R8
Tel: 0171 834 6666
Fax: 0171 931 0700

Chiltern Nursery Training College
16 Peppard Road
Caversham
Reading RG4 8J2
Tel: 01734 471847

Council for the Disabled
8 Wakley Street

London EC1V 7QE
Tel: 0171 843 6058

Daycare Trust/ National Childcare Campaign
Wesley House
4 Wild Court
London WC2B 4AU
Tel: 0171 405 5617
Fax: 0171 831 6632

Employment Agency Licensing Office
2–16 Church Road
Stanmore
Middlesex HA7 4AW
Tel: 0181 954 7677

Gingerbread
35 Wellington Street
London
Tel: 0171 240 0953
Fax: 0171 836 4500

Kids Clubs Network
Oxford House
Derbyshire Street
London E2 6HG
Tel: 0171 247 3009

Maternity Alliance
15 Britannia Street
London W1C 9JP
Tel: 0171 837 1265

Nannies Need Nannies
28 May Street
South Shields
Tyne and Wear
NE33 3A7
Tel: 0191 454 2617

National Association of Certificated Nursery Nurses (NACNN)
10 Meriden Court
Great Clacton
Essex CO15 4XH
Tel: 01255 476707

National Childcare Campaign/Daycare Trust
Wesley House
4 Wild Court
London WC2B 5AU
Tel: 0171 405 5617
Fax: 0171 831 6632

The National Childminding Association
8 Mason's Hill
Bromley
Kent BR2 9EY
Tel: 0181 464 6164

National Children's Bureau
8 Wakley Street
London EC1V 7QE
Tel: 0171 843 6000

The National Council For One Parent Families (NCOPF)
255 Kentish Town Road
London NW5 2LX
Tel: 0171 267 1361

National Nursery Examination Board
8 Chequer Street
St Albans
Herts AL1 3X2
Tel: 01727 47636/67333

National Stepfamily Association
162 Tenison Road
Cambridge CB1 2DP
Tel: 01233 460312 or 01233 460313 (counselling)

National Stepfamily Association (Scotland)
10 Abbotsford Crescent
Edinburgh EH10 5DY
Tel: 0131 447 4131

279-281 Whitechapel
Road
London E1 1BY
Tel: 0171 247 3009
Fax: 0171 247 4490

**Norland Nursery
Training College**
Denford Park
Hungerford
Berks RG17 0PQ
Tel: 01488 82252

Parents At Work
77 Holloway Road
London N7 8JZ
Tel: 0171 700 5771
Fax: 0171 700 1105

**Pre-School Playgroups
Association**
61-63 Kings Cross
Road
London WC1X 9LL
Tel: 0171 933 0991
Fax: 0171 837 4942

**Princess Christian
Nursery Training
College**
26 Wilbraham Road
Fallowfield
Manchester M14 6JX
Tel: 0161 224 4560

**Professional
Association of
Nursery Nurses
(PANN)**
St James Court
77 Friar Gate
Derby DE1 1BT
Tel: 01332 43029

Special Care Agency
1st Floor
45 Pembridge Road
London W11 3HG
Tel: 0171 221 5894

**The Thomas Coram
Foundation for
Children**
41 Brunswick Square
London WC1N 1AZ
Tel: 0171 278 2424

**Voluntary
Organisations Liaison
Council for Under
Fives (VOLCUF)**
77 Holloway Road
London N7 8JZ
Tel: 0171 607 9573
Fax: 0171 700 1105

**Working for
Childcare**
77 Holloway Road
London N7 8JZ
Tel: 0171 700 0281

**The Workplace
Nurseries Campaign**
77 Holloway Road
London N7 8JZ
*Tel: 0171 7000 281
(campaign) 0171 7000
274 (consulting)*

Chapter 8
Image

Acne Support Group
Tel: 0891 318220

**Clairol Advisory
Service**
Haircare and colour
advice.
Tel: 0800 181184

**CMB Image
Consultants**
49 Greencoat Place
London SW1P 1DS
Tel: 0171 627 5211
Fax: 0171 828 4493

**Dickins and Jones
Personal Shopping
Suite**
224/244 Regent Street
London W1A 1DB
Tel: 0171 734 7070 X322

**The Fashion Advisory
Service**
*Tel: 0115 9812321/
405789*
Fax: 0115 9405559

**Federation of Image
Consultants**
Tel: 01956 701018

**Harrods Executive
Suite**
Knightsbridge
London SW1X 7XL
Tel: 0171 581 4874

**Harvey Nichols
Personal Shopping**
Knightsbridge
London SW1X 7RJ
*Tel: 0171 235 5000
X2229*
Fax: 0171 259 6084

Impact
(personal marketing)
Tel: 0181 424 2630

**The Institute of
Management**
Management House
Cottingham Road
Corby
Northamptonshire
NN17 1TT
Tel: 01536 204222

**The Institute of
Personnel
Development**
IPD House
35 Camp Road
Wimbledon
London SW19 4UX
Tel: 0181 971 9000

Mavala Hotline
Nailcare advice
Tel: 01962 852099

Self-Esteem Company
PO Box 354
London W13 9NV
Tel: 0181 579 0435

Voiceworks
223 Hamlet Gardens
Hammersmith
London W6 0TS
Tel: 0181 748 8318
Fax: 0181 563 7802

Wardrobe
3 Grosvenor Street
London W1X 9FA
Tel: 0171 629 7044

42 Conduit Street
London W1R 9FB
Tel: 0171 494 1131

Chapter 9
Health and safety

Acne Support Group
PO Box 230
Hayes
Middlesex UB4 9HW

**Action On Smoking
And Health**
5–11 Mortimer Street
London W1N 7RH
Tel: 0114 289 2345

**Breastcare and
Mastectomy
Association**
Admin: 0171 867 8275
Helpline: 0171 867 1103

Department of Health
Richmond House
79 Whitehall
London SW1A 2NS
Tel: 0171 210 3000

**Health and Safety
Executive**
Baynards House
1 Chepstow Place
Westbourne Grove
London W2 4TF
Tel: 0171 243 6000

HMSO bookshops
41 High Holborn
London WC1V 6HB

9–21 Princes Street
Manchester M60 8AS

71 Lothian Road
Edinburgh EH3 9AZ

16 Arthur Street
Belfast BT1 4GD

**Institute for
Complementary
Medicine**
Unit 4
Tavern Quay
London SE16 1AA
Tel: 0171 237 5165

Maternity Alliance
15 Britannia Street
London WC1X 9JN
Tel: 0171 837 1265
Fax: 0171 837 1273

**National Aids
Helpline**
Tel: 0800 567 123
(24hr)

Refuge
PO Box 855
London W4 4JF
Tel: 0181 995 4430
(24hr)

RSI Association
Chapel House
152–154 High Street
Yewsley
West Drayton
Middlesex UB7 7BE
Tel: 01895 431134

**Women's Health
Information and
Support Centre**
23 Mill Street
Ashwell
Herts SG7 5LY

Chapter 10
Travel in the UK

**AA (Automobile
Association)**
Tel: 0800 919595
(membership)

**Air Transport Users'
Committee**
129 Kingsway
London WC2B 6NN
Tel: 0171 242 3882

**Association of British
Travel Agents (ABTA)**
55 Newman Street
London W1P 4AH
Tel: 0171 637 2444

British Airways PLC
Tel: 0181 759 5511

British Rail
PO Box 28
York Y01 1FB
Tel: 0181 200 0200
(Timetables)

Ellis Associates
41 Scott's Road
London W12 8HP
Tel: 0181 743 9657
Fax: 0181 743 2855

**The Facilitator
Service**
2 Chantry Place
Harrow
Middlesex HA3 6NY
Tel: 0181 420 1220
Fax: 0181 420 1691/93

Forte Crest
166 High Holborn
London WC1V 6TT
Tel: 0171 836 7744
Tel: 0800 40 40 40
(reservations)
Fax: 0171 240 9993

Hertz Reservations
Tel: 0181 679 1799
(London)
Tel: 0161 499 1313
(Manchester)
Tel: 01345 555888
(all other areas)

Hyatt International Hotels
113 Upper Richmond Road
London SW15 2TL
Tel: 0181 780 2240

InterCity
Tel: 0181 200 0200
(timetables)

London Regional Transport (Underground)
55 Broadway
London SW1H 0BD
Tel: 0171 918 4040
(Customer Services Centre)

London Transport Passengers' Committee
26 Old Queen Street
London W1H 9HP
Tel: 0171 222 8777

Motorail
Tel: 01345 090700

National Breakdown
Tel: 01532 362410

National Bus Company
25 New Street Square

London EC4 3AP
Tel: 0171 583 9177

National Express
Victoria Coach Station
172 Buckingham Palace Road
London SW1W 9TN
Tel: 0171 730 0202

Pavilion
Tel: 0800 515836
Nine motorway stopovers, seven with overnight accommodation

Premier Lodge
Tel: 0800 118833

RAC (Royal Automobile Club)
Tel: 0800 550 550
(membership)

Scottish Citylink Services
Victoria Coach Station
Buckingham Palace Road
London SW1W 9TP
Tel: 0171 636 9373

Scottish Coach Travel Service
298 Regent Street
London W1R 6LE
Tel: 0171 580 4708/636 9373

Travel Centre (Scotland)
Buchanan Bus Station
Glasgow G2 1NQ
Tel: 0141 332 9191

St Andrew's Square
Bus Station
Edinburgh EH1 3DU
Tel: 0131 556 8464

Chapter 11
International travel

Information about individual countries can be obtained from the relevant Embassy or High Commission or from the country's tourist board

Air Transport Users Committee
103 Kingsway
London WC1X 9LP
Tel: 0171 242 3882

American Women's Club of Luxembourg
PO Box 2341
L-1023 Luxembourg Gare
Grand Duchy of Luxembourg

The Arab-British Chamber of Commerce
Business Information Membership Services Department
6 Belgrave Square
London SW1X 8PH
Tel: 0171 235 4363
Fax: 0171 235 1748

Association of British Chambers of Commerce
4 Westwood House
Westwood Business Park
Coventry CV4 8HS
Tel: 01203 694484

Association of British Travel Agents Ltd (ABTA)
55 Newman Street
London W1P 4AH
Tel: 0171 637 2444
Fax: 0171 637 0173

Association of German Businesswomen (Verband Deutscher Unternehmerinnen)
PF. 511030
50946 Köln
Germany
Tel: 221 37 50 74 75

Avis Rent A Car
(Reservations)
Hayes Gate House
Uxbridge Road
Hayes UB3 4DJ
Tel: 0181 848 8733

British Association of Women Entrepreneurs
33 Caithness Road
London W14 0JA
Tel: 0171 602 4656
Fax: 0171 602 9397

Brittany Ferries
Tel: 01705 827701

Euro Info Centre
8 Storey's Gate
London SW1P 3AT
Tel: 0171 973 1992

4 Cathedral Road
Cardiff CF1 9JG
Tel: 01222 371631

Windsor House
9-15 Bedford Road
Belfast BT2 7EG
Tel: 01232 240708

7 Alva Street
Edinburgh EH2 4PH
Tel: 0131 225 2058

Federal Ministry for Women's Affairs (Bundesministerium für Frauenangelegenheiten)
Ballhausplatz 2
1014 Vienna
Austria
Tel: 43 1 53115 2851
Fax: 43 1 535 0338

The Federation of Icelandic Women's Associations (Kvenfélagasamband Islands)
Túngötu 14
101 Reykavík
Iceland

Focus
23 Rue Lebroussart
1050 Brussels
Belgium
Tel: 2 646 65 30

Foreign and Commonwealth Office
Travel Advice Unit
Consular Department
Clive House
Petty France
London SW1H 9HD
Tel: 0171 270 4129
Fax: 0171 270 4228

French Railways (Motorail)
Tel: 0171 409 3518

Hospital for Tropical Diseases, Travel Clinic
4 St Pancras Way
London NW1 0PE
Tel: 0171 387 4411

Hoverspeed
Tel: 01304 240241

Le Shuttle
Tel: 01303 271100

Mauritius Export Development and Investment Authority
Level 2
BAI Building
25 Pope Hennessy Street
Port Louis
Mauritius
Tel: 230 208 7750, 212 8047
Fax: 230 208 5965

Ministry of Community Development, Women and Children
The Principal Secretary
PO Box 3448
Dar Es Salaam
Tanzania

Moroccan General Economic Confederation (CGEM)
23 Bd. Mohamed Abdou
Casablanca
Morocco
Tel: 212 2 25 26 96
Fax: 212 2 25 38 39

National Council of Women in Switzerland (NCWS)
Bund Schweizerscher Frauenorganisationen
Altikofenstrasse 182
3048 Worblaufen
Switzerland
Tel: 031 921 48 48

New Zealand House
Haymarket
London
SW1Y 4TE
Tel: 0171 973 0380
Fax: 0171 973 0104

Overseas Trade Services, Department of Trade and Industry (DTI)
Ashdown House
123 Victoria Street
London SW1E 6RB
Tel: 0171 215 5000
Fax: 0171 828 3258

Passport Office (PO)
Clive House
70 Petty France
London SW1H 9HD
Tel: 0171 279 3434

5th floor
India Buildings
Water Street
Liverpool L2 0QZ
Tel: 0151 237 3010

Olympia House
Upper Dock Street
Newport
Gwent NP9 1XA
*Tel: 01633
244500/244292*

Aragon Court
Northminster Road
Peterborough PE1 1QG
Tel: 01733 895555

3 Northgate
96 Milton Street
Cowcaddens
Glasgow G4 0BT
Tel: 0141 332 0271

Hampton House
47–53 High Street
Belfast BT1 2QS
Tel: 01232 232371

**P&O European
Ferries**
Tel: 0181 575 8555

**Simplification of
International Trade
Procedures Board
(SITPRO)**
Almack House
26–28 King Street
London SW1Y 6QW

**Stichting
VrouwenNetwork
Nederland (SVN)**
PO Box 84106
2508 AC The Hague
Netherlands
Tel: 31 70 3383737
Fax: 31 70 351602

The Swedish Institute
PO Box 7434

S-103 91
Stockholm
Sweden

**Centre for
Management Training
and Development in
the Middle East**
City Campus
Cowcaddens Road
Glasgow G4 0BA
Tel: 0141 353 2168/331
Fax: 0141 331 3005

Travel Advice Unit
Consular Department
Foreign and
Commonwealth Office
Clive House
Petty France
London SW1H 9HD
Tel: 0171 270 4129
Fax: 0171 270 4228

Travel Bookshop
13 Blenheim Crescent
London W11
Tel: 0171 229 5260

**The Traveller's
Bookshop**
25 Cecil Court
London WC2
Tel: 0171 836 9132

**Vrowen in Bedrijf en
Beroep**
(promoting equality of
women in business and
profession)
PO Box 11069
1001 GB Amsterdam
The Netherlands

**The Women's
Association**
PO Box 130
Abu Dhabi
UE
Tel: 9712 477049/475122
Fax: 9712 475202

**Chapter 12
Sexual harassment
at work**

**Asian Women's
Resource Centre**
134 Minet Avenue
London NW10 8AP
Tel: 0181 961 5701

**Belfast Rape Crisis
Centre**
41 Waring Street
Belfast
Tel: 01232 249696

**Campaign Against
Domestic Violence**
PO Box 2371
London E1 5NQ

**Citizens' Advice
Bureaux**
The address of your
nearest bureau can be
found in your local
telephone directory.

**Equal Opportunities
Commission**
Overseas House
Quay Street
Manchester M3 3HN
Tel: 0161 833 9244
Fax: 0161 835 1657

**Equal Opportunities
Commission For
Northern Ireland**
Chamber of Commerce
House
22 Great Victoria
Street
Belfast BT2 2BA
Tel: 01232 242752

**Federation of
Recruitment &
Employment Services**
36 Mortimer Street
London W1N 7RB
Tel: 0171 928 9272

Free Representation Unit
13 Gray's Inn Square
London WC1R 5JP
Tel: 0171 831 0692

Justice for Women
55 Rathcole Gardens
London N8 9NE
Tel: 0181 340 3699

Law Centres Federation
Duchess House
18–19 Warren Street
London W1P 5DB
Tel: 0171 387 8570

Lesbian and Gay Employment Rights (LAGER)
St Margaret's House
21 Old Ford Road
London EC1 9TL
Tel: 0181 983 0694

Malicious calls helplines (BT)
Tel: 0800 666700 (advice)
Tel: 0800 661441 (Specialist Bureau)

National Association of Citizens' Advice Bureaux
115 Pentonville Road
London N1 9LZ
Tel: 0171 833 2181

Rape Crisis Centre
PO Box 69
London WC1X 9NJ
Tel: 0171 837 1600
They can refer you to your local centre, or you can find the address of your nearest centre in your local phone book

Rights of Women
52–54 Featherstone Street
London EC1Y 8RT
Tel: 0171 251 6577

Samaritans
Check your local phone book for your nearest Samaritans

Scottish Women's Aid
1319 North Bank Street
Edinburgh EH1 2LN
Tel: 0131 225 8011

The Suzy Lamplugh Trust
14 East Sheen Avenue
London SW14 8AS
Tel: 0181 392 1839
Fax: 0181 392 1830

TUC (Trades Union Congress)
Congress House
Great Russell Street
London WC1B 3LS
Tel: 0171 636 4030

Welsh Women's Aid
(2nd floor)
12 Cambrian Place
Aberystwyth
Dyfed SY23 1NT
Tel: 01970 612748
38–48 Crwys Road
Cardiff CF2 4NN
Tel: 01222 390874
(1st floor)
26 Wellington Road
Rhyl
Clwyd LL18 1BN
Tel: 01745 334767

Women Against Sexual Harassment (WASH)
312 The Chandlery
50 Westminster Bridge Road
London SE1 7QY

Tel: 0171 721 7592
Fax: 0171 721 7594

Women's Aid Federation England
PO Box 391
Bristol BS99 7WS
Tel: 0117 9633494 or 0117 9633542 (helpline)

Women's National Commission
Caxton House
Tothill Street
London SW1H 9NF
Tel: 0171 273 5486
Fax: 0171 273 4906

Chapter 13
Losing your job

Advisory, Conciliation & Arbitration Service (ACAS)
Clifton House
83 Euston Road
London NW1
Tel: 0171 396 5100

Ageworks
(Erco Employment Agencies)
Tel: 0171 371 5411

Campaign Against Age Discrimination in Employment (CAADE)
395 Barlow Road
Altrincham
Cheshire
WH14 5HW

Careers Continued
High Holborn
London WC1V 7LL
Tel: 0171 680 0033

Department of Social Security
Richmond House
79 Whitehall
London SW1A 2NS
Tel: 0171 210 3000

Forties People
7 Old Bailey
London EC4M 7NB
Tel: 0171 329 4044

Recruit
Tel: 01442 233550

Retired Executives Action Clearing House (REACH)
89 Southwark Street
London SE1 0HX
Tel: 0171 928 0452

Chapter 14
Self-employment

Alliance of Small Firms and Self Employed People
33 The Green
Calne
Wiltshire SN11 8DJ
Tel: 01249 817003

Bank Action Group (BAG)
c/o National
Co-ordinator
Park Gates
Leagram
Chipping
Lancashire PR3 2GS
Tel: 01995 61049

The Banking Ombudsman
70 Gray's Inn Road
London WC1X 8NB
Tel: 0171 404 9944

Board of Inland Revenue

Somerset House
London WC2R 1LB
Tel: 0171 438 6622

British Coal Enterprise Ltd
Tel: 01623 826833
Fax: 01623 826800

British Franchise Association
Thamesview
Newtown Road
Henley-on-Thames
Oxon RG9 1HG
Tel: 01491 578049
Fax: 01491 573517

British Steel Industry Ltd
Tel: 01724 731612

Companies House
Crown Way
Cardiff CF4 3UZ
Tel: 01222 388588

Data Protection Registry
Wycliffe House
Water Lane
Wilmslow
Cheshire SK9 5AX
Tel: 01625 535711
(admin)
01626 535777
(enquiries)

Department of Economic Development (Northern Ireland)
Netherleigh
Massey Avenue
Belfast BT4 2JP
Tel: 01232 763244
Fax: 01232 768857

Department of Social Security
Richmond House
79 Whitehall
London SW1A 2NS
Tel: 0171 210 3000

Department of Trade and Industry (DTI)
Ashdown House
123 Vauxhall Street
London SW1E 6RB
Tel: 0171 215 6468

(NE)
Stanegate House
2 Groat Market
Newcastle-upon-Tyne
NE1 1YN
Tel: 0191 232 4722
Fax: 0191 232 6742

(NW)
Sunley Tower
Piccadilly Plaza
Manchester M1 4BA
Tel: 0161 838 5000
Fax: 0161 228 3740

(Yorkshire & Humberside)
25 Queen Street
Leeds LS1 2TW
Tel: 0113 2443171
Fax: 0113 2338301/2

(Midlands)
20 Middle Pavement
Nottingham NG1 7DW
Tel: 0115 9506181
Fax: 0115 9587074

(West Midlands)
77 Paradise Circus
Queensway
Birmingham B1 2DT
Tel: 0121 212 5000
Fax: 0121 212 1010

(SW)
The Pithay
Bristol BS1 2PB
Tel: 0117 9272666
Fax: 0117 9299494

(SE - London)
Bridge Place
88/89 Eccleston Square
London SW1V 1PT
Tel: 0171 215 5000
Fax: 0171 828 1105

(E)
Building A
Westbrook Centre
Milton Road
Cambridge CB4 1YG
Tel: 01233 461939
Fax: 01223 461941

**Direct Marketing
Association**
1 Oxendon Street
London SW1Y 4EE
Tel: 0171 321 2525

**Direct Selling
Association**
29 Floral Street
London WC2E 9DP
Tel: 0171 497 1234

**DTI Small Firms
Division**
Level 2
St Mary's House
c/o Employment
Department
Moorfoot
Sheffield S1 4PQ
Tel: 0114 2597508

**Federation of Small
Businesses**
140 Lower Marsh
London SE1 7AE
Tel: 0171 928 9272

**Handy Insurance
Services**
22 Lombard Street
Stourport-on-Severn
Worcestershire
DY13 8DT
Tel: 01299 822645
Fax: 01299 827359

Helplines

Assurance, Healthcare
& Pensions
(Philip H. Bradshaw)
Tel: 0500 100 017

Business Communi-
cations (Mercury/
Enterprise Magazine)
Tel: 0500 100 012

Company Accounts/Tax
(Cree Publishing/
Kidsons Impey)
Tel: 0500 100 015

Franchising
(Master Brew/Mundays
Solicitors)
Tel: 0500 100 016

IT/Computers &
Software (IBM/Advice
by Telephone)
Tel: 0500 100 013

Office Automation
(Rank Xerox)
Tel: 0500 100 014

**Industrial Common
Ownership Movement
Ltd (ICOM)**
Vassalli House
20 Central Road
Leeds LS1 6DE
Tel: 0113 2461 737

The Industrial Society
3 Carlton House
Terrace
London SW1Y 5DG
Tel: 0171 839 4300

**Institute of
Management**
Small Firms
Information Service
Management House
Cottingham Road
Corby
Northamptonshire
NN17 1TT
Tel: 01536 204222

**The Institute of Sales
and Marketing
Management**
Tel: 01582 411130

Fax: 01582 45640

**Local Enterprise
Development Unit**
c/o Trevor Nuttall
Arthur Anderson & Co
St Paul's House
Park Square
Leeds LS1 2PJ
Tel: 01532 438222

**London and
Edinburgh Insurance
Group**
The Warren
Worthing
West Sussex BN14 9QD
Tel: 01903 820820
Fax: 01903 20849

**National Association
of Teleworkers**
Island House
Midsomer Norton
Bath
Avon BA3 2HL
Tel: 01761 413869
(membership)

**National Federation of
Enterprise Agencies**
Tel: 01246 207379

**National
Homeworking Unit**
Tel: 01132 454273

New Ways To Work
309 Upper Street
London N1 0PD
Tel: 0171 226 4026

**Office of the Data
Protection Register**
Wycliffe House
Water Lane
Wilmslow
Cheshire SK9 5AX
Tel: 01625 535711
(admin)
01625 535777
(enquiries)

Office of Fair Trading
Field House
Breams Buildings
London EC4A 1PR
Tel: 0171 242 2858

Own Base
68 First Avenue
Bush Hill Park
Enfield EN1 1BN
(for home workers)

**Registrar of
Companies**
Companies House
Crown Way
Maindy
Cardiff CF4 3UZ
Tel: 01222 388588

**Rural Development
Commission**
141 Castle Street
Salisbury
Wiltshire SP1 3TP
Tel: 0722 336255

**Scottish Business
Shop**
Tel: 0141 248 6014

Scottish Enterprise
120 Bothwell Street
Glasgow G2 7JP
Tel: 0141 248 2700

**Scottish Office
Industry Department**
Alhambra House
45 Waterloo Street
Glasgow G2 6AT
Tel: 0141 248 4774
Fax: 0141 242 5404

**Small Business
Bureau**
46 Westminster Palace
Gardens
Artillery Row
London SW1P 1PR

**Small Business
Research Centre**
Kingston University
Kingston Hill
Surrey KT2 7LB
Tel: 0181 547 7247

**The Telecottage
Association**
The Other Cottage
Shortwood
Nailsworth
Gloucestershire
GL6 0SH
Tel: 01453 834874
Fax: 01453 836174

Teleworkers Insurance
Daved Sanders
Associates
The Old Post House
Bewdley
Worcestershire
DY12 2AE
Tel: 01299 401345
Fax: 01299 404491

Tolsen Messenger Ltd
148 King Street
London W6 0QU
Tel: 0181 741 8361
Fax: 0181 741 9395

**Training Enterprise
Councils (TECs)**
Tel: 0800 300787

**Welsh Development
Agency**
Pearl House
Greyfriars Road
Cardiff CF1 3XX

**Welsh Office Industry
Department**
Crown Building
Cathays Park
Cardiff CF1 3NQ
Tel: 01222 825111
Fax: 01222 823088

**Women's Enterprise
Development Agency**
Tel: 0121 525 2558

**Women's Enterprise
Forum**
c/o Warrington
Business Venture
Warrington Business Park
Long Lane
Warrington
Cheshire WA2 8TX
Tel: 01925 633309

Chair: Deborah
Ackerley
c/o 22 Station Road
Wootton Bassett
Swindon
Wiltshire SN4 7EG
Tel: 01793 854646
Fax: 01793 851551

Chapter 15
Taking a break

**BOSS (British
Offshore Sailing
School)**
58 Earls Road
Southampton SO14 6SF
Tel: 01703 227724
Fax: 01703 338133

Canopy Training
Helen Bovey
7 Jackson Tor Road
Matlock
Derbyshire DE4 3JS
Tel: 01629 584600
Fax: 01629 8260535

Fawcett Mill Fields
Gaisgill
Tebay
Penrith CA10 3UB
Tel: 01539 624 408

Island Horizons
Jean Stewart
'Junipers'

Lochcarron
Wester Ross
Scotland
Tel: 01520 722232
Fax: 01520 722238

**Royal Yachting
Association**
Tel: 01703 627400

**Single Parent Travel
Club**
17 Redmond Avenue
Lockstock Hall
Preston
Lancashire PR5 5XN
(*Enclose large 9x6 SAE*)

**Talbontdrain Guest
House**
Hilary Matthews

Uwchygarreg
Machynlleth
Powys SY20 8RR
Tel: 01654 702192

Tiger Travel UK
56 Bowden Hill
Newton Abbot
Devon
TQ12 1BH
Tel/Fax: 01626 62528

Travel Companions
110 High Mount
Station Road
London NW4 3ST
Tel: 0181 202 8478
(please enclose a SAE
when making enquiries
by post)

Wild Rose
Sheila Gwyn
2 Blerrick Cottages
Anthony
Torpoint
Cornwall PL11 3BA
Tel: 01752 822609

**The Women's Travel
Advisory Bureau**
'Lansdowne'
High Street
Blockley
Gloucestershire
GL56 9HF
Tel: 01386 701082

Further Reading

Chapter 1 Equal opportunties

Abercrombie, Nicholas & Ward, Alan, with Soothill, Keith, & Walby, Sylvia, *Contemporary British Society* (Polity Press, 1992)

Clements, Phil & Spinks, Tony, *The Equal Opportunities Guide* (Kogan Page, 1994)

Guide for Women (Scarlett Press, 1993)

Hutt, Jane, *Making Opportunities: A Guide for Women and Employers* (NCVO, 1992)

UK Employer Initiatives (Parents at Work, 1994)

'Women in Europe' Supplements (European Commission)

Chapter 2 The working woman's lifestyle

Bird, Polly, *Tame That Phone* (Pitman, 1994)

Godefroy, Christian H. & Clark, John, *The Complete Time Management System* (Piatkus, 1995)

Josephs, Ray, *How To Gain An Extra Hour Every Day* (Thorsons, 1994)

Livesay, Corinne R., *Getting and Staying Organised* (IRWIN, 1994)

Winston, Stephanie, *The Organised Executive* (Kogan Page, 2nd edition, 1994)

Chapter 3 Pay and promotion

Flanders, Margaret L., *Breakthrough: The Career Woman's Guide To Shattering The Glass Ceiling* (Paul Chapman Publishing, 1994)

Fletcher, Joan, *How To Get That Job* (How To Books, 3rd edition, 1993)

Francis, Dave, *Managing Your Own Career* (HarperCollins, 1994)

Jackson, Tom, *The Perfect CV* (Piatkus, 1991)

Jackson, Tom, *Perfect Job Strategies* (Pitakus, 1994)

Johnstone, Judith, *How To Start A New Career* (How To Books, 1992)

Johnstone, Judith, *How To Apply For A Job* (How To Books, 1993)

Jones, Roger, *How To Manage Your Career* (How To Books, 1994)

Leeds, Dorothy, *Secrets of Successful Interviews* (Piatkus, 1993)

Perkins, Graham, *Snakes or Ladders?* (Pitman, 1991)

Skeats, Judy, *CVs and Written Applications* (Ward Lock, 1994)

Weeks, Willet, *Moving Ahead With Your Career* (Pitman, 1994)

Wright, Bridget, *Which Way Now?* (Piatkus, 1992)

Chapter 4 Training for the top

The Association of MBAs Guide to Business Schools (Pitman)

Bickerstaff, George, *Which MBA?*

(Addison-Wesley, annual)

Cameron, Sheila, *MBA Handbook: essential study skills* (Pitman, 1944)

The Economist, 25 St James's Street, London SW1A 1GH, Tel: 0171 839 7000

Fearns, Peter, *Teach Yourself Business Studies* (Hodder & Stoughton, 1992)

Financial Times, Number 1, Southwark Bridge, London SE1 9HL, Tel: 0171 873 3000

Floodlight, c/o ALA, 36 Old Queen Street, London SW1H 9JF, Tel: 0171 222 0193, *Fax*: 0171 976 7434.

The Guardian, 119 Farringdon Road, London EC1R 3ER, Tel: 0171 278 2332, *Fax*: 0171 837 2114.

Pearson, Barrie & Thomas, Neil, *The Shorter MBA* (Thorsons, 1991)

Teleworker Magazine (Telecottage Association) (See 'Useful Addresses', p.206 for details.)

TOPwoman, 44 Gray's Inn Road, London WC1X 8LR, *Tel: 0171 242 3592, Fax: 0171 242 3598*

Which Business Qualification? (The Edition XII Publishing Co., annual)

Which MBA? The MBA Courses Directory (Addison-Wesley, annual)

Chapter 5   The working woman's finances

Baker, Helen, *Money Matters for Women* (Penguin, 1993)

Burr, Rosemary & Harris, Jenny, *Financial Choice for Women* (Rosters Ltd, 1990)

Chase de Vere Guide to PEP, Tel: 0171 404 5766

Chesworth, Niki, *Daily Express Guide: Your Money and How to Make the Most of It* (Kogan Page, 1994)

Donald, Pamela, *500 Ways To Save Money* (Piatkus, 1992)

Financial Times, Number 1, Southwark Bridge, London SE1 9HL, Tel: 0171 873 3000

Garsia, Marlene, *How To Write A Will and Gain Probate* (Kogan Page, 1993)

Jennings, Marie, *Women and Money: The Midland Bank Guide* (Penguin, 1988)

Lowe, Jonquil, *450 Money Questions Answered* (Consumers Association, 1994)

Mitchel, Alison, *The New Penguin Guide To Personal Finance* (Penguin, 1994)

Nichols, Paul, Korn, Anthony & Cowell, Emma, *Croner's Guide To Pregnancy, SMP and Maternity Rights* (Croner Publications, 2nd edition, 1994)

Part-time Workers – a Negotiators' Guide (Labour Research Department, 78 Blackfriars Road, London SE1 8HF, 1992)

Poynter, Richard and Martin, Clive, *Rights Guide to Non-Means-Tested Benefits* (CPAG, 1992)

Reardon, A, *Allied Dunbar Pensions Guide* (1992)

Sunderland, Ruth, *The Woman's Guide to Finance* (Kogan Page/Daily Express, 1995)

Velmans, Marianne and Litvino, Sarah, *Working Mother* (Pocket Books, 1993)

Walsh, Noelle, *The Good Deal Directory* (Macmillan, 1995)

Chapter 6   Networking

Bryce, Lee, *The Influential Woman* (Piatkus, 1989)

Butler, Mark, *How to Use the Internet* (2D Press)

Conrad Levinson, Jay and Rubin, Charles, *Guerrilla Marketing on the Internet* (Piatkus, 1995)

Gilster, Paul, *The Internet Navigator* (John Wiley & Sons)

Macdonald, Fiona, *The Women's Directory* (Bedford Square Press, 1991)

Sergman-Peck, Dr Lily M, *Networking & Monitoring: A Woman's Guide* (Piatkus, 1991)

Women's Organisations in the UK, (Women's National Commission, Level 4, Caxton House, Tothill Street, London SW1H 9NF, biennial)

Chapter 7   Childcare choices

Beard, Mary, *The Good Working Mother's Guide* (Duckworth, 1989)

The Employer's Guide to Childcare (Parents at Work, 1991)

Gomer, Charlotte & Hilaire, *The Good Nanny Guide* (Vermilion, 1993)

The Lady, 39–40 Bedford Street, London WC2E 9ER, Tel: 0171 379 4717, Fax: 0171 497 2137

Nursing Times & Nursing Mirror, 4 Little Essex Street, London, WC2R 3LF, Tel: 0171 836 6633, Fax: 0171 379 4204

Nursery World, The Schoolhouse Workshop, 51 Calthorpe Street, London WC1X 0HH, Tel: 0171 837 7224, Fax: 0171 278 3896

Steiner, Judith M., *How To Survive As A Working Mother* (Kogan Page, 1989)

Velamans, Marianne & Litvinoff, Sarah, *Working Mother* (Corgi, 1993)

Woodford, S. & De Zoysa, A., *The Good Nursery Guide* (Vermilion 1993)

Working Parents Handbook (Parents at Work, 1994)

Chapter 8   Image

Bird, Polly, *Sell Yourself* (Pitman, 1994)

Cosmopolitan, National Magazine House, 72 Broadwick Street, London W1V 2BP, Tel: 0171 439 5000, Fax: 0171 439 5016

Davies, Philippa, *Your Total Image* (Piatkus, 1991)

Dobson, Ann, *How To Communicate At Work* (How To Books, 1994)

Godefroy, Christian & Barrat, Stephanie, *Confident Speaking* (Piatkus, 1993)

Goldman, Heinz, *How To Communicate and Win People* (Pitman, 1995)

Good Housekeeping, National Magazine House, 72 Broadwick Street, London W1V 2BP, Tel: 0171 439 5000, Fax: 0171 439 5591

Jackson, Carole, *Colour Me Beautiful* (Piatkus, 1983)

Jay, Anthony, *Effective Presentation* (Pitman, 1993)

Leeds, Dorothy, *Marketing Yourself* (Piatkus, 1992)

Pooser, Doris, *Always in Style* (Piatkus, 1987)

Spillane, Mary, *Presenting Yourself for Women* (Piatkus, 1993)

Watson, Linda & Martin, Rosie, *More Dash Than Cash* (Condé, Nast, 1992)

Chapter 9   Health and safety

Balancing Work and Home: A practical guide to managing stress (Parents at Work, 1994)

Chalmers, Wendy, *Repetitive Strain Injury* (Thorsons, 1994)

Dalton, Katharina, *Once a Month* (Fontana, 1991)

Eisenberg, Ronni with Kelly, Kate, *Organise Yourself* (Piatkus 1992)

Essential Facts: Premises, Health & Safety (GEE Publications, 1994)

Essentials of Health and Safety at Work (Health & Safety Executive, 1994)

Inkeles, Gordon, *Super Massage: Simple techniques for instant relaxation* (Piatkus, 1989)

Jackson, Dr Arthur, *Stress Control through Self-Hypnosis* (Piatkus, 1990)

Nichols, Paul & Cowell, Emma, *Croner's Guide To Pregnancy, SMP and Maternity Rights* (Croner Publications, 1993) (for employers)

Saunders, Dr Roger, Wheeler, Timothy, *Handbook of Safety Management* (Pitman, 1990)

Stranks, Jeremy, *Handbook of Health and Safety Practice* (Pitman, 1994)

Stranks, Jeremy, *Health and Safety Law* (Pitman, 1994)

Stranks, Jeremy, *A Manager's Guide to Health and Safety at Work* (Kogan Page, 3rd edition, 1994)

Stranks, Jeremy, *Occupational Health and Hygiene* (Pitman, 1994)

Thomas, Colin, *Teach Yourself Employment Law* (Hodder & Stoughton, 1993)

Williams, Stephen, *Managing Pressure for Peak Performance* (Kogan Page, 1994)

The Health and Safety Executive publishes many useful books on different aspects of Health and Safety (see 'Useful Addresses', p.215)

Chapter 10   Travel in the UK

Benjamin, Julie, *Essential Safety Awareness for Women* (Boatswain Press, 1993)

Gostelow, Mary, *The Complete Woman's Reference Book* (Viking, 1985)

Chapter 11   International travel

For information about individual countries contact their Embassy, High Commission or tourist board in the UK. Tourist brochures contain lots of useful information and maps.

Breenan, Lynne & Block, David, *The Complete Book of Business Etiquette*, (Piatkus Books, 1993)

de Rouffignac, Paul Danton, *How To Sell To Europe* (Pitman, 1990)

Drew, John, *Doing Business in the European Community* (Whurr Publications, 1992)

Dudley, James W., *1992 Strategies for the Single Market* (Kogan Page, 1990)

Gibbs, Paul, *Doing Business in the European Union* (Kogan Page, 3rd edition, 1994)

Golzen, Godfrey, *The Daily Telegraph Guide to Working Abroad* (Kogan Page, 17th edition, 1994)

Hogan, James, *The European Marketplace* (Macmillan Press, 1991)

Ingham, Bruce, *Simple Etiquette in Arabia and The Gulf States* (Simple Books, 1993)

Mole, John, *Mind Your Manners* (Nicholas Brealey Publishing, 1995)

Mort, David, *European Market Information* (Pitman, 1992)

Moss, Maggie and Gemma, *Handbook for Women Travellers* (Piatkus Books, 1995)

Newcomer (Ackroyd Publications S.A.,

329 Avenue Molière, 1060 Brussels, Belgium, Tel: 00 2 343 99 09)

Nicholson, Louise, *Louise Nicholson's India Companion* (Random Century, 1991)

Reuvid, Jonathan (consulting editor), *Doing Business with China* (Kogan Page, 1994)

Six Language Business Directory (Colt Books with The Association of British Chambers of Commerce, 1989)

Spillane, Mary, *The Complete Style Guide* (Piatkus, 1994)

Turing, Penelope, *Visiting Arab Countries of the Middle East: A Personal Guide for Women* (Centre for Management Training and Development in the Middle East, Glasgow Caledonian University, 1993)

Vandome, Nick, *How To Find Temporary Work Abroad* (How To Books, 1994)

Chapter 12   Sexual harassment at work

Brant, Clare & Too, Yun Lee, *Rethinking Sexual Harassment* (Pluto Press, 1994)

Collier, Rohan, *Combatting Sexual Harassment in the Workplace* (Open University Press, 1995)

Curtis, L, *Making Advances, What You Can Do About Sexual Harassment At Work* (BBC Books, 1993)

Davies, Jessica, *Protect Yourself* (Piatkus, 1990)

Dealing With Sexual Harassment. Guidelines for Members and Representatives (Transport & General Workers Union, 1993)

Independent on Sunday, 40 City Road, London EC1Y 2DB, Tel: 0171 253 1222, Fax: 0171 956 1469

Kremer, J & Marks, J, *Sexual Harassment at work in Northern Ireland* (Belfast Equal Opportunities Commission for Northern Ireland, 1992)

Lamplugh, Diana, *Without Fear: The Key to Staying Safe* (Old Bakehouse Publications, 1994)

Lamplugh, Diana, Whitehead, Jackie,

Woods, Mike, *Working Alone* (Pitman, 1993)

Minson, J, *Questions of Conduct, Sexual Harassment. Citizenship. Government* (MacMillan, 1993)

No Offence? Sexual Harassment, How It Happens And How To Beat It (The Industrial Society, 1993)

NUPE Union Stewards Handbook

Painter, R.W. & Puttick, K., *Employment Rights* (Pluto Press, 1993)

Pattison, T. foreword by Proops, M: *Sexual Harassment* (Futura, 1991)

Rae, M, *Women and the Law* (Longman, 1986)

Stop Sexual Harassment in the Workplace. Guidelines for NALGO Branches (NALGO National Women's Committee, 1992)

Sexual Harassment of Women in the Workplace: A Guide to Legal Action (WASH, 1990)

Sexual Harassment at Work (Transport & General Workers Union, TGWU)

UCATT Code of Practice on Dealing with Cases of Sexual Harassment at Work

UCATT Employment of Women Working Party: *Blueprint for Equality*

Chapter 13   Losing your job

Cane, Sheila & Lowman, Peter, *Putting Redundancy Behind You* (Kogan Page, 1993)

Croner's Guide To Managing Fair Dismissal (Croner Publications, 5th edition, 1995)

Du-Feu, Vivian, *Croner's Guide to Contracts of Employment* (Croner Publications, 1994)

Henderson, Joan, *A Guide To The Employment Acts* (Nicholas Brealey, 1994)

Marlow, Joyce, *Industrial Tribunals and Appeals* (Bedford Square Press, 1991)

Painter, Richard W. & Puttick, Keith, *Employment Rights* (Pluto Press, 1993)

Pritchard, John, *The New Penguin Guide to the Law* (Penguin, 1993)

Spicer, Robert, *How To Know Your Rights At Work* (How to Books, 1991)

Surviving your Partner's Redundancy (Coutts Career Consultants Ltd, 1990)

Thomas, Colin, *Teach Yourself Employment Law* (Hodder & Stoughton, 1993)

Chapter 14   Self-employment

Barrow, C. & Golzen, G., *Taking up a Franchise: The Daily Telegraph Guide* (Kogan Page, 1992)

Beckman, Malcolm, *Running Your Own Mail Order Business* (Kogan Page, 1992)

Bird, Drayton, *Commonsense Direct Marketing* (Kogan Page, 3rd edition, 1993)

Bird, Polly, *How To Make Money from your Personal Computer* (Piatkus, 1994)

Business Franchise, (Monthly) Newspaper House Tannery Lane, Penketh, Warrington, Cheshire WA5 2UD, Tel: 01925 724326, Fax: 01925 791924

Business Opportunity World (Merlin Publications Ltd, 14 Hove Business Centre, Fonthill Road, Hove BN3 6HA Tel: 01273 888992, Fax: 01273 888994)

Clarke, Greg, *Readymade Business Opportunities* (Kogan Page, 1994)

Clayton, Patricia, *Law for the Small Business: The Daily Telegraph Guide* (Kogan Page, 7th edition, 1991)

Clayton, Patricia, *Forming A Limited Company* (Kogan Page, 4th edition, 1995)

Dewhurst, Jim & Burns, Paul, *Small Business Management* (Macmillan Press, 3rd edition, 1993)

Enterprise Haland House, 66 York Road, Weybridge, Surrey KT13 9DY

Evans, Hazel, *Making Money From Home* (Piatkus, 1994)

Executive Woman (Quarterly) 2 Chantry Place, Harrow, Middlesex HA3 6NY, Tel: 0181 420 1210, Fax: 0181 420 1693

Golzen, Godfrey, *Going Freelance* (Kogan Page, 3rd edition, 1991)

Golzen, Godfrey, *Working for Yourself*

(Kogan Page, 14th edition, 1993)

Gouch, Brian, *The Computer Guide for Small Businesses* (The Computer Guide Ltd, 1991)

Hawkins, Barries, *How To Run A Part-time Business* (Piatkus, 1994)

Home Run (Active Information, 75 Black Lion Lane, London W6 9BG) (on subscription)

Ingham, Christine, *101 Ways to Start Your Own Business* (Kogan Page, 1992)

Jenks, Philip, Fisk, Jim, Barron, Robert, *The Official High Fliers Handbook* (Harriman House, 1994)

Jones, Graham, *How To Start A Business from Home* (How To Books, 1991)

Lewis, Mel, *50 Businesses to Start from Home* (Piatkus, 1994)

McMullan, David, *Be Your Own Boss!* (Kogan Page, 1994)

Marshall, Peter, *How To Master Book-Keeping* (How To Books, 1992)

Mendelshohn, Martin, *A Guide To Franchising* (Cassell, 1993)

Morris, Michael J., *Starting a Successful Small Business* (Kogan Page, 1993)

Morris, Roz, *Working for Yourself* (Piatkus, 1995)

Phillipson, Ian, *How To Work From Home* (How To Books, 1992)

Phipps, Rosemary, *Start A Successful Business* (BBC Books, 1994)

Taylor, Peter, *How To Keep Business Accounts* (How To Books, 2nd edition, 1990)

TOPwoman (44 Gray's Inn Road, London WC1X 8LR, Tel: 0171 242 3595, Fax: 0171 242 3598)

Wells, Gordon, *Make Money at Home* (Foulsham, 1991)

Williams, David, *Don't Pay Too Much Tax if You're Self-Employed* (Nicholas Brealey, 1994)

Williams, David, *Running Your Own Business* (Nicholas Brealey, 1994)

Williams, Sarah, *Lloyds Bank Small Business Guide* (Penguin, 1995)

Chapter 15   Taking a break

Adventure Holidays (Vacation Work, annual)

Hotel Guide (RAC, annual)

The Hotel Guide (AA, annual)

Lumsden, Les, *Cycle UK!* (Sigma Press, 1994)

Moss, Maggie & Gemma, *Handbook for Women Travellers* (Piatkus, 1994)

Museums & Art Galleries in Great Britain & Ireland (Reed Information Services, 1995)

The Women's Travel Information Pack (The Women's Travel Advisory Bureau, 1993)

Index

Abbey Life, 61, 62
Abbey National, 51, 93
Access cards, 139
accessories, 23
accident insurance, 136
accidents, 113–15
accountancy, training, 42–3
accounts, self-employment, 190–2
Action for Cities programme, 192
adult education classes, 47
adult training, 36–9
advertisements, for paid help, 20
Advisory, Conciliation and Arbitration
    Service (ACAS), 176
aeroplanes, 128–9, 136
after-school care, 82–3
agencies: head-hunting, 33, 178
    nannies, 85–6
    for older workers, 178
    travel agents, 129, 136, 139, 141
Ageworks, 178
AIDS, 137
Air Miles, 129
air travel, 128–9, 136
alarms: car, 123
    personal, 182
annual reports, 75
annuities, retirement, 57
ante-natal care, 108
Arab countries, 151–2
articles, writing, 75, 98
assault, sexual, 157–9
assertiveness, 32, 36, 157
Association of Accounting Technicians
    (AAT), 42
Association of British Travel Agents
    (ABTA), 129
Association of MBAs (AMBA), 41
au pairs, 20, 86–8
audiences, presentations, 102

Automobile Association (AA), 78, 123,
    140
AVCs (additional voluntary
    contributions), 58, 59

babies see childcare; pregnancy
babysitters, 20, 89–90
babysitting circles, 90
Bank of Scotland, 52
banks: financial advisers, 51–2
    loans to self-employed, 181
    savings accounts, 64–5
Barclays Bank, 51, 139, 181, 189
barristers, training, 43
behaviour: image and, 96–7
    international travel, 143
Belgium, 144
Birkbeck College, London, 39
Body Shop, 184
book-keeping, 190–1
BOSS (British Offshore Sailing School),
    199–200
breakfast, 116
breast examinations, 109–10
briefcases, 17, 138–9
Bristol University, 41
British Airways, 128
British Coal Enterprise Ltd, 193
British Franchise Association, 185
British Gas, 189
British Rail (BR), 127, 128, 189
British Steel Industry Ltd, 194
British Telecom (BT), 156, 189
Brussels, 140, 144
building societies, 63, 64–5
BUPA, 111
business cards, 74, 98, 142
Business in the Community, 189
Business Expansion Scheme, 193
Business Franchise, 185

Piatkus Business Books

Piatkus Business Books have been created for people who need expert knowledge readily available in a clear and easy-to-follow format. All the books are written by specialists in their field. They will help you improve your skills quickly and effortlessly in the workplace and on a personal level.

Titles include:

General Management and Business Skills

Be Your Own PR Expert: the complete guide to publicity and public relations Bill Penn
Complete Conference Organiser's Handbook, The Robin O'Connor
Complete Time Management System, The Christian H Godefroy and John Clark
Confident Decision Making J Edward Russo and Paul J H Schoemaker
Corporate Culture Charles Hampden-Turner
Energy Factor, The: how to motivate your workforce Art McNeil
Firing On All Cylinders: the quality management system for high-powered corporate performance Jim Clemmer with Barry Sheehy
How to Implement Change in Your Company John Spencer and Adrian Pruss
Influential Manager, The: How to develop a powerful management style Lee Bryce
Influential Woman, The: How to achieve success in your career – and still enjoy your personal life Lee Bryce
Lure the Tiger Out of the Mountains: timeless tactics from the East for today's successful manager Gao Yuan
Managing For Performance Alasdair White
Managing Your Team John Spencer and Adrian Pruss
Problem Solving Techniques That Really Work Malcolm Bird
Right Brain Time Manager, The Dr Harry Alder
Seven Cultures of Capitalism, The: value systems for creating wealth in Britain, the United States, Germany, France, Japan, Sweden and the Netherlands Charles Hampden-Turner and Fons Trompenaars
Smart Questions for Successful Managers Dorothy Leeds
Think Like A Leader Dr Harry Alder

Personnel and People Skills

Best Person for the Job, The Malcolm Bird
Dealing with Difficult People Roberta Cava
Problem Employees: how to improve their behaviour and their performance Peter Wylie and Mardy Grothe

240

Psychological Testing for Managers   Dr Stephanie Jones
Tao of Negotiation: How to resolve conflict in all areas of your life   Joel
   Edelman and Mary Beth Crain

Financial Planning

Better Money Management   Marie Jennings
Great Boom Ahead, The   Harry Dent
How to Choose Stockmarket Winners   Raymond Caley
Perfect Legal Tax Loopholes   Stephen Courtney
Practical Fundraising For Individuals And Small Groups   David Wragg

Small Business

How to Earn Money from Your Personal Computer   Polly Bird
How to Run a Part-Time Business   Barrie Hawkins
Making Money From Your Home   Hazel Evans
Marketing On A Tight Budget   Patrick Forsyth
**Profit Through the Post: How to set up and run a successful mail order
   business**   Alison Cork

Motivational

Play to Your Strengths   Donald O Clifton and Paula Nelson
Super Success   Philip Holden
Winning Edge, The   Charles Templeton

Self-Improvement

Brain Power: the 12-week mental training programme   Marilyn vos Savant
   and Leonore Fleisher
Creative Thinking Michael LeBoeuf
Napoleon Hill's Keys to Success   Matthew Sartwell (ed.)
Napoleon Hill's Unlimited Success   Matthew Sartwell (ed.)
NLP: The New Art and Science of Getting What You Want   Dr Harry Alder
Personal Growth Handbook, The   Liz Hodgkinson
Personal Power   Philippa Davies
Quantum Learning: unleash the genius within you   Bobbi DePorter with
   Mike Hernacki
**Right Brain Manager, The: how to use the power of your mind to achieve
   personal and professional success**   Dr Harry Alder
10-Minute Time and Stress Management   Dr David Lewis
Three Minute Meditator, The   David Harp with Nina Feldman
Total Confidence   Philippa Davies

Sales and Customer Services

Art of the Hard Sell, The   Robert L Shook

Commonsense Marketing For Non-Marketers   Alison Baverstock
Creating Customers   David H Bangs
Guerrilla Marketing Excellence   Jay Conrad Levinson
Guerrilla Marketing   Jay Conrad Levinson
Guerrilla Marketing On The Internet   Jay Conrad Levinson and Charles Rubin
How to Succeed in Network Marketing   Leonard Hawkins
How to Win a Lot More Business in a Lot Less Time   Michael LeBoeuf
How to Win Customers and Keep Them for Life   Michael LeBoeuf
How to Write Letters that Sell   Christian Godefroy and Dominique Glocheux
Life's A Pitch: How to outwit your competitors and make a winning presentation   Don Peppers
One-to-One Future, The   Don Peppers and Martha Rogers
Professional Network Marketing   John Bremner
Sales Power: the Silva mind method for sales professionals   José Silva and Ed Bernd Jr
Telephone Selling Techniques That Really Work   Bill Good
Winning New Business: a practical guide to successful sales presentations   Dr David Lewis

Presentation and Communication

Better Business Writing   Maryann V Piotrowski
Confident Conversation   Dr Lillian Glass
Confident Speaking: how to communicate effectively using the Power Talk System   Christian H Godefroy and Stephanie Barrat
He Says, She Says: closing the communication gap between the sexes   Dr Lillian Glass
Personal Power   Philippa Davies
Powerspeak: the complete guide to public speaking and presentation   Dorothy Leeds
Presenting Yourself: a personal image guide for men   Mary Spillane
Presenting Yourself: a personal image guide for women   Mary Spillane
Say What You Mean and Get What You Want   George R. Walther
Your Total Image   Philippa Davies

Careers and Training

How to Find the Perfect Job   Tom Jackson
Jobs for The Over 50s   Linda Greenbury
Making It As A Radio Or TV Presenter   Peter Baker
Marketing Yourself: how to sell yourself and get the jobs you've always wanted   Dorothy Leeds
Networking and Mentoring: a woman's guide   Dr Lily M Segerman-Peck
Perfect CV, The   Tom Jackson
Perfect Job Search Strategies   Tom Jackson

Secrets of Successful Interviews   Dorothy Leeds
Sharkproof: get the job you want, keep the job you love in today's tough job market   Harvey Mackay
10-Day MBA, The   Steven Silbiger
Ten Steps To The Top   Marie Jennings
Which Way Now? – how to plan and develop a successful career   Bridget Wright

For a free brochure with further information on our complete range of business titles, please write to:

Piatkus Books
Freepost 7 (WD 4505)
London W1E 4EZ

PIATKUS